Monographs

of the Rutgers Center of Alcohol Studies

No. 6

Monographs of the

Rutgers Center of Alcohol Studies

Under the editorship of Mark Keller

This monograph series was begun as "Monographs of the Yale Center of Alcohol Studies" and Numbers 1, 2 and 3 in the series were published at Yale. Beginning with Number 4 the series has been continued as Monographs of the Rutgers Center of Alcohol Studies. The change conforms with the transfer of the Center from Yale to Rutgers University. The works published in this series report the results of original research in any of the scientific disciplines, whether performed at Rutgers or elsewhere.

No. 1. Alcohol and the Jews. A Cultural Study of Drinking and Sobriety. By CHARLES R. SNYDER.

No. 2. Revolving Door. A Study of the Chronic Police Case Inebriate. By DAVID J. PITTMAN and C. WAYNE GORDON.

No. 3. Alcohol in Italian Culture. Food and Wine in Relation to Sobriety among Italians and Italian Americans. By GIORGIO LOLLI, EMIDIO SERIANNI, GRACE M. GOLDER and PIERPAOLO LUZZATTO-FEGIZ.

No. 4. Drinking among Teen-Agers. A Sociological Interpretation of Alcohol Use by High-School Students. By GEORGE L. MADDOX and BEVODE C. McCALL.

No. 5. Drinking in French Culture. By ROLAND SADOUN, GIORGIO LOLLI and MILTON SILVERMAN.

No. 6. American Drinking Practices. A National Study of Drinking Behavior and Attitudes. By DON CAHALAN, IRA H. CISIN and HELEN M. CROSSLEY.

American Drinking Practices

Distributed by

COLLEGE & UNIVERSITY PRESS · *Publishers*

263 CHAPEL STREET   NEW HAVEN, CONN.

American Drinking Practices

A National Study of Drinking Behavior and Attitudes

BY

DON CAHALAN, IRA H. CISIN AND HELEN M. CROSSLEY

PUBLICATIONS DIVISION

RUTGERS CENTER OF ALCOHOL STUDIES

NEW BRUNSWICK   NEW JERSEY

Library of Congress catalog card number: 70-626701
SBN: 911290-37-0

MANUFACTURED IN THE UNITED STATES OF AMERICA BY
UNITED PRINTING SERVICES, INC.
NEW HAVEN, CONN.

This monograph is dedicated to the memory of

JIM FOX

without whose inspiration the whole job
would have been impossible

D. C.
I. H. C.
H. M. C.

Acknowledgments

This study was made possible through a special grant from the National Institute of Mental Health. It is one of a series of studies in the general field of drinking behavior being conducted at the Social Research Group under the general direction of Ira H. Cisin. This monograph is based on a preliminary report (9), which is now out of print.

Heartfelt thanks are due to the many persons on the staff of the Social Research Group and to the many others who helped in the planning and carrying out of this study. Among those who contributed, the following are owed a special note of appreciation:

GENEVIEVE KNUPFER, former Director of the Drinking Practices Study, Mental Research Institute, Berkeley, California, for helpful counsel at several stages;

ARTHUR D. KIRSCH and CAROL H. NEWCOMB for assistance in planning of the content and the analysis, as well as the carrying out of many administrative responsibilities;

HUGH J. PARRY, RAYMOND FINK, ELAINE K. HAYDEN, MARGARET L. MAGNUSSON and ROBIN ROOM for their suggestions on the draft of the manuscript;

BEN L. OWEN, for direction of the data collection;

EVANGELINE WELLS COOPER, NANCY GATZKE JACOBY, NANCY GOTTLIEB, JACK NEWTON and MARGARET SCHAFER for supervision of the data-processing and preparation of tables;

EDITTA MANNIX, KAAREN MAHONEY and SANDRA ROEDER for assistance in the production of the manuscript.

Contents

Index of Tables

Each table reports the percentage of respondents, or of drinkers, or of the five drinking groups (abstainers, infrequent, light, moderate and heavy drinkers), by the following variables:

A. DEMOGRAPHIC AND SOCIAL CORRELATES

B. Wine, Beer and Distilled Spirits

C. Social Activities

D. Family

E. Drinking Circumstances

F. Changes in Drinking

List of Figures

List of Charts

Introduction

ADDING an introduction to a book, especially by someone unrelated to its production, might be considered something of a reproach to the authors: Didn't they know enough to indicate the purposes and general orientation of what they were doing? Were they so unknown to the probable readers that some pontifical blessing was felt to be a necessary salesmanship ploy? Was their communication so esoteric or so confused that an interpretation was needed? Or was their position so extreme that a plea for tolerance to the reader from a member of "the establishment" (or the "opposition") would make the volume more palatable?

1. Why an Introduction?

In the present instance none of these possible explanations can be entertained: Cahalan, Cisin and Crossley know quite well what they are doing and they do it in a highly sophisticated fashion; not only are they known in the field, but this very project was widely discussed during the past several years in professional circles, preliminary reports have been published, and its final appearance has been awaited with interest; which "establishment" this introducer is felt to represent poses at least one interesting question: Is there an "establishment" or an established dominant view about alcohol, about its use, about so-called problems, or about programs to meet those problems?

This query suggests an answer to the question, "Why an introduction," a question not to be resolved either in terms of authors or of the book. In part the answer is to be found in the scope and complexity of the phenomena; but above all, it is located specifically in the character of reactions and responses in the United States to alcohol, to drinking, to related problems and to consequent programs. It is the current state of such attitudes and actions which may justify such preliminary remarks.

The same rationale could be postulated for, among many possible examples, a book on alcohol and the body by a physiologist, a book on alcohol legislation by a lawyer, or a book on alcohol taxation or beverage pricing by an economist. The setting or atmosphere into which such books are projected in the 1970s as in the 1960s is not "established" or settled, but rather is in a state of turmoil, in fact, a state of several quite different turmoils. As a result, the findings and ideas of the authors may well be viewed in strikingly different fashion by various groups, may be used for purposes of not only different but even inimical nature, and as a result may with equal intensity be heralded as essential or condemned as unimportant. The authors of *American Drinking Practices* are not describing this world of attitudes and policies about problems related to alcohol and its use, even though reflections of the differences, confusion and uncertainty on this level frequently appear. It is the purpose of this introduction to suggest some of the salient characteristics of this changing, turbulent arena of responses to alcohol use and to its related problems and, I hope, even stimulate more extensive and appreciative comprehension of the significant contribution which the authors have made to the field. Because this field has so many audiences, is equipped with so many often conflicting languages, opinions and emotions, the very freedom to recognize and appreciate is often shackled or left unused.

Seventy, fifty and, with only a handful of exceptions, even thirty years ago, the need for an introduction of this sort would have been slight, perhaps nonexistent. During those years there was a settled, one might even say "established," situation in the United States in the responses to the fact of alcohol use and to the perceptions of related problems. There were three significant segments to this pattern. Two of them are quite familiar in terms of grand old stereotypes, the Wets and the Drys. The latter had a simple, sweeping and radical interpretation of use and problems (use itself being the chief problem). The Wets had an even simpler position: they were against the Drys. One hardly had to be literate to determine whether a statement or program was the one or the other. In fact, if there was room for doubt, affiliates of both groups would join in condemning such an "irrelevant" or "weasel worded" position. The third type of response by 1920 or so had become the major American reaction in almost all leadership groups—in education, in health, in the sciences, in industry, in most churches and most political groups, in the arts, and among the large majority of the better educated, more affluent and more powerful segments of the society. That mode of response can be summed up in one word —avoidance. That many people voted on the matter in 1919 and in 1932 in no way contradicts, in fact even strengthens, this interpretation. In neither case did anything like the majority of these people vote *for* either group or either group's position. Very clearly they voted against; first against one group and then against the other. As the President of the United States explicitly and with the greatest publicity announced, "A plague on both your houses." The overwhelming majority, whether in state governments or other leadership positions, could be seen as expressing the position—"Let's get it over with and let's forget it."

So why any introductions? Either a book or a speech or a program on this subject (*a*) was "Wet" or was "Dry" and (*b*) for the majority the apparent reaction in either case was, "I'm not interested; further, I find the whole matter distasteful."

That situation clearly persisted until the period 1940–45. And then with equal clarity it showed signs of weakening. By 1965–70 it was broken wide open. The long period of intellectual sterility and stereotyped avoidance was over. The reasons for the change are neither esoteric nor complex: (*1*) The directly related and increasingly obvious problem manifestations such as uncontrolled drinking behaviors, drunkenness and alcoholism were becoming so obtrusive that they just couldn't be hidden or avoided any longer. (*2*) Since 1900 knowledge in arts and sciences of all sorts had made such advances, and ever more extensive education and public communication over the same period had so disseminated these advances, that the by now archaic and stereotyped explanations in this field, whether for action or nonaction, were blatantly anachronistic and ridiculous—were, in fact, societally intolerable. (*3*) Striking developments in both understanding and action had occurred in the first half of the 20th century in attacking societal problems, e.g., poverty, old age, crime, mental illness, many physical diseases, all sorts of "accidents," illiteracy, and many others; as a result both the *total* failure to do anything with this problem and also the increasingly extensive and persistent occurrence of this problem as a large contributor to many of those *other* problems (which otherwise were being rather successfully attacked) made further avoidance or further repetition of rigidly structured and obviously ineffective procedures not only professionally disgraceful but popularly intolerable.

And so the dam broke. And the area, so long avoided by all but the two camps of 19th-century warriors, was suddenly flooded by reform groups, by scientists, lawyers, engineers, doctors, faith healers, politicians, writers, by those who had suffered the problems, public-relations artists, educators, etc., and the old warriors were there too. Where there had been two musty old tents, a great tower was emerging—in some ways reminiscent of the tower of Babel. And it is this Babel-like situation which may explain why a sort of translation or introduction is felt useful for any potentially helpful message or book which is to be published in the alcohol and alcohol-problems field.

2. The Many Problems; the Many Answers

The so-called problems related to alcohol include such phenomena as unacceptable or frightening behaviors by youth using alcohol, "excessive availability," disapproved alcohol-affected behavior, public drunkenness, the very specific matter of highway crashes affected by alcohol, the alcoholisms; for at least a century the very use of alcohol was held to be *the* problem by a large minority. Frequently these problems were expressed in terms of a compound phrase: alcohol (or drunkenness or drinking or alcoholism) and something else, e.g., alcohol and poverty, alcohol and divorce, or alcohol and disease or disgrace or crime or immorality; the listing included almost every known social "ill." But even this list includes only what may be termed the "initiating" problems.

These initiating problems elicited various reactions or responses intended to alleviate, control or prevent. There were many types of such response—law and law enforcement to control or prohibit, educational programs, religious policy and regulation, penal systems, taxation schemes, therapeutic programs, campaigns of public information and public indoctrination, and so on. And during the period 1789 to 1939 it can be stated without question that all of these patterns of response were (1) widely felt to be ineffective in reducing or controlling the initiating problems, (2) widely felt to be *in and of themselves* destructive of major societal values (creating hypocrisy, lawlessness, immorality), and (3) manifestly creative of conflict on almost every level of social organization—e.g., between religion and other social institutions and between and within religious groups, between (and within) families. Many of the intended "answers" or systems of response had themselves become "problems." To many persons these response problems were more societally damaging than the so-called initiating problems.

Yet another type of "alcohol problems," one entirely in the response area, concerns the language, logic and methodology of explanation and of policy determination. That the phenomena of alcohol use as well as of so-called alcohol problems involve physiological, psychological, pharmacological, sociological, legal, ethical, medical, economic, religious, political, educational and other aspects is hardly deniable. However, there is widespread disagreement about which of these aspects is "more" (or "most") important, relevant and demanding of immediate action—disagreements which are intensified by the different languages employed by the conflicting parties.

Not only does it appear that there are "too many" problems, but it is equally clear that there are "too many" answers. Cahalan, Cisin and Crossley have made a major and comprehensive contribution toward, if not a resolution, at least a significant diminution of this confusion and disagreement. They have presented the most representative and reliable body of data about users of alcoholic beverages that has yet appeared, information which will allow more mature and more discriminating utilization of existing knowledge and available policy than has hitherto been possible. They have done this primarily by describing the phenomenon of "users" as a whole rather than by adopting the more usual (for this field) procedure of indiscriminately mixing problem with nonproblem or labeling some segment of the whole as the phenomenon in its entirety.

3. Ologies and Pathologies

It is typical of the historical development of systems of knowledge and policy that, in their first appearance, they are concerned with the wondrous, with the most desirable or the most painful. There is need to avoid or control earthquakes or volcanoes, or to discover gold or a lodestone. There is need to avoid or control this or that disease or to gain the fountain of youth. There is need to eliminate or alleviate poverty or to control great wealth. And explorations, experiments and analyses point toward such specifics; volcanology, feverology and Utopias become the order of the day. With increasing knowledge and continuing need, however, it is learned that such extremes (whether avoidance of the painful or achievement of the desirable) cannot be effectively understood and cannot be controlled without positioning such phenomena in at least the first larger order of phenomena to which they at least manifestly belong. Volcanoes and earthquakes are found to be rather special manifestations of earth structures and processes; fevers and damaged organs are found to be special manifestations of bodily process and structure; wealth and poverty are special cases of the production, use and distribution of things and services. As these special cases are oriented within their larger phenomenal classes, understanding and purposeful control become enormously more effective. Geology, physiology and economics come to replace volcanology, feverology and Utopian theories.

In the case of drunkenness, the alcoholisms, as well as the many response-type problems related to that set of societal ills, the same "special extremism" has long characterized attempts at increasing knowledge and developing control. Many of the researches and many of the programs of the last 100 or 200 years have not been illogical or ill-intentioned or unuseful *in and of themselves,* but have proven ineffective (even productive of more conflict) largely because they were not positioned in the obviously *next larger* phenomenal field. That manifestly next-larger field comprises the phenomenon of use of beverage alcohol.

Cahalan, Cisin and Crossley have provided us with a means of "cutting these problems down to manageable size," of placing the problems in realistic context, of allowing a more discriminating view of the nature and location of different types of users so that we can focus (for research or for policy) upon those segments of the whole which will manifest this or that specific alcohol problem without confusing our vision with masses of irrelevant observation or without myopically omitting large segments of the relevant by thoughtless use of predetermined systems of labeling. This means could be called a demographic analysis of beverage alcohol users.

The authors do not require others to adopt any particular definition of problem-users. If, for example, one wished to define all "users" as a "problem," the authors might or might not approve on various grounds, but their approach and their description would still stand and would be quite useful for that initial definition, allowing a useful classification of various classes of *that* problem both for understanding and for policy. The same would be true for those at the other extreme who might wish to limit the "problem" label to alcohol addicts.

For all the rest concerned with use and problems, this particular demographic approach has even more obvious utility. For example, what are called "chronic drunkenness offenders" or another category popularly called "alcoholics" are now clearly to be seen as small and readily distinguishable segments of that far larger class which might be called beverage-users. It becomes clear that it is unnecessary (and necessarily confusing) to lump all these people together under one label. For instance, it should become clear to those concerned with increasing knowledge that to develop a "drinker personality" or "the economics of drinking" or "the physiological effects of drinking" for such a different assortment of users is, for most purposes, a silly and self-defeating task. For those concerned with educating youth or with establishing legislative controls or with promoting rehabilitation, it should become clear that they are facing strikingly different categories of behaving people and that certain modes of action, perhaps quite relevant for some categories, can be ridiculous for other categories.

As Cahalan, Cisin and Crossley make amply clear, the differences between amounts of alcohol usually consumed on a drinking occasion and the differences between frequencies of such occasions are (in terms of possible effects on behavior) of extreme magnitude. And they point out with a wealth of data that these differences are regularly patterned, are not just a matter of choice or chance. The patterning is largely sociological. It is predictable.

Merely one or two illustrations of the use of such knowledge will be presented: If a pharmacologist or physiologist states, in his professional capacity, that X amount of alcohol taken with Y frequency will have Z effect on this or that human function or organ, it becomes possible for the nonphysiologists and nonpharmacologists to estimate the relevance of that finding to what are popularly called alcohol problems: if X amount and Y frequency occur among 1% of the population of users (and they can be readily located), then the problem is of one degree of importance and we know where it is located. If X amount plus Y frequency occurs only among one-hundredth of 1% of the population of users, then the degree of importance as well as the location of the problem is necessarily very different. And anyone claiming that the physiological effect described will occur to all users (or to no users) will no longer take up our time, will less and less be able to create further confusions and distractions.

Conversely, it may be hoped that those proposing either research or policy purported to have direct social application will sharpen their sense of relevance.

In a very different field of endeavor, this demographic knowledge could be useful to those in policy fields concerned with education or legislation. Just as in the previous illustration, those proposing programs of teaching or of regulation have all too frequently failed to notice the extraordinary differences in the populations of users as well as in the populations of nonusers who are to be controlled or informed. Programs quite possibly of great utility for one class of users can quite manifestly be absurd or have even opposite to the desired results for other classes of users. For example, systems of control or of education based upon the behaviors, needs and capacities of what are called alcoholics may be not only irrelevant to but can elicit hostile responses from most classes of other users, the latter outnumbering the former perhaps 20 to 1. And the opposite can be equally true: methods of control and education useful for infrequent users of light and medium quantities (by far the majority) can be absurd when applied to alcoholics. But with knowledge of the size, location and characteristics of the different groups, more mature and discriminating action becomes possible.

4. Limitations and Difficulties

A demographic approach to any human societal problem can be enormously useful, but it cannot answer all our questions or provide neatly packaged solutions to all societal ills. The United States Census is of great value for understanding, for stimulating new questions and for evaluation of theories and policies, but in itself it provides no answers to problems. It is a tool, not a completed project. And this is the potentiality of the Cahalan–Cisin–Crossley book: it is a tool. And like most tools of any significance it will undoubtedly be misused as such, it will undoubtedly be applied to questions or problems for which it was not intended, and it is open to refinements and to alterations. Some of the limitations should be noted.

The first has been stated and is of such importance that it should be repeated and illustrated. Demographic data are *not* theoretical or policy statements; they are potentially useful statements of fact expressed in sophisticated and verifiable fashion. Just, for example, because 5%, 45% or 90% of youth or of women or of the total population in New England are known to be "users of such and such a type" does *not* prove that any particular legislation, type of community organization or educational program is good, bad or indifferent. Demography is not philosophy and is not policy. It can be a useful tool for both.

A second limitation will be most obvious to sociologists. Just as the U.S. Census may indicate that, for example, 20 million persons are farmers with bigger or smaller farms and with wheat or cotton or fruit trees as crops, but does *not* describe the styles, procedures and qualities of such farming, so the present book describes the number of, for example, light and infrequent users of alcohol with brewed, fermented or distilled liquid as their usual beverage, but does *not* describe the styles, procedures and qualities of the drinking activity, does not describe the learning of the particular behavior, the sanctions pro or con for unusual performance, the material apparatus, etc., and only considers the sociocultural settings in broad, almost abstract categories. Although some of these attributes of a custom are mentioned or implied, the description is basically in terms of users or nonusers and, if users, these are classified in terms of how much, what type of beverage, and with what frequency.

A major exception concerns one type of use which primarily involves drinkers' apparent attitude about drinking in general and their own purpose in drinking. When the apparently dominant purpose of alcohol ingestion is of an individualistic psychocentric nature, usually expressed in terms of escape from sociopsychic conditions or functioning, the category of "escape" drinker is proposed. To continue the analogy to the U.S. Census, this might be likened to that demographic authority noting in its description and then in its measured categories that some farmers, although manifesting many of the formal practices of the entire category, did these things for reasons and with attitudes which are at least alien to and perhaps incompatible with traditional or common views of farmers in general or of other people when they described farmers; perhaps they were "gentleman farmers," or merely used this life pattern as a tax haven, or had some unusual psychic craving for trees or turnips, a craving unrelated to the economics or to the "usual" attitudes or daily routines of farmers. In their description of attitudes, the present authors—by adding this dimension of description to the usual demography—have given greater justification to their title "drinking practices."

One might consider the following matter to be a difficulty rather than a limitation. If a difficulty, however, it is related to the concept of demography rather than to the particular subject matter or to the mode of communication. Categorizing people into subclasses of age, marital status, wealth, job, residence and the like is enormously useful for many purposes, but it almost unavoidably carries the notion of permanence, of lasting, static position. And this notion can be very misleading. Just as rural people can become urban and vice versa, just as marital status, job status and health status can change, so can position in one or another category of "drinker" change (and nondrinker is one of these categories). Not only do Cahalan, Cisin and Crossley describe this career variability in drinking-class membership, they also indicate the more usual patterns of this process of change (change in amounts consumed, in frequencies and in spacing of consumption occasions) resulting in patterned movement from one category to another. Just as 100 years ago many people wanted only *two* categories, with an individual *having* to be either a drinker or a nondrinker, so perhaps many readers today would like to feel that once a person was in a specified drinking category he would always stay put.

For those concerned with problem drinkers it may well prove, however, that "staying put" in a given category according to amounts consumed and spacing and frequency of occasions may be not only a variation from the usual and accepted custom but also a sign of the status "problem drinker." For example, the *failure* between ages 40 to 50 of a "medium heavy, 3-times-a-week drinker" to "move" into a category of less quantity or less-frequent intake may prove to be a significant variation from the norm. As the authors indicate, the need for longitudinal studies of drinkers is one of the striking gaps in information in this field. The recognition of types of drinkers has perhaps been a difficult step for the concerned public to recognize and accept. It may be even more difficult to recognize and accept the fact that these types are not static, are not absolute, and that movement from one category to another is also patterned and largely predictable.

The most apparent difficulty in reading this book rests in the general readability of demographies. There are those, I understand, who can curl up on the couch on a long, rainy afternoon and become passionately absorbed in the U.S. Census Abstract. On the other hand, I have personal experience with many who feel threatened when asked to read a two-column table with a maximum of four entries; a percent sign or a statement in terms of rates versus number of occurrences can shatter the composure of many otherwise fairly literate and intellectually curious people.

The reading of demographic presentations is rendered even more difficult when the demographers are sufficiently mature and sufficiently honest to recognize and openly state that the translation of social human data into numbers, fantastically useful as this has proven, is also open to error and certainly subject to gross misinterpretation. It is *not* a simple process in construction or in communication. Nor are *any* of the problems of alcohol "simple," as is evidenced by 150 years of obviously unsatisfactory attempts at resolution. The major reason for finding reading difficult often lies in the unjustified expectancy that it will be easy. Anyone feeling that alcoholic-beverage use is easy to understand or easy to change probably shouldn't attempt to read this or, for that matter, any serious publication in the field.

Granted that one has an interest beyond the simple fairy-tale level, however, the authors have tempered the technical approach in a fashion for which those in the alcohol-problems field as a whole will be sincerely grateful. Recognizing that much of their tabulated data is primarily for specialists, they have omitted the bulk from this volume, stating what it is and where and how it is available. They have organized the material so that the salient relevance of both method and data is presented in a logical order for those generally concerned with alcohol problems. The text is composed so that those rendered anxious by tables can proceed with ordinary prose, and the authors have utilized the jargon of demographers with admirable restraint. Very probably the editorial staff at the Rutgers Center of Alcohol Studies should also receive thanks for their role in facilitating this necessarily "difficult" communication.

5. Contribution to Research and Action

A major contribution of *American Drinking Practices* may well be its presentation of a central theme to all those in the many fields of interest and in the many disciplines or modes of approach which characterize each of those fields. In the area of alcohol phenomena and alcohol-related problems there are studies and books and pamphlets, there are conferences and national organizations and films, there are newspaper reports and laws and handbooks on procedures, but they are often so disparate in language and purpose and target of attack that confusion, evasion and even outright hostility are all too frequent. One is concerned with disease, another with accidents, a third with sales control, a fourth with criminal justice. One is based on biochemistry, another on personality, a third on political art or science and a fourth on community organization and public health. Cahalan, Cisin and Crossley have centered attention on the phenomenon central to all these approaches and central to all the problems no matter what their form, no matter what discipline or language is employed: namely, man using alcoholic beverages. Only as this phenomenon occurs do any of the questions, any of the problems and any of the controversies about cause or about policy for action even have existence. Knowledge about this phenomenon is at the base. The other knowledges, e.g., law, psychiatry, metabolism, ethics, may have much to offer this field, but they are not this field itself and they developed their unique theories, methods and assumptions in other settings. Man in society using alcoholic beverages and having attitudes about that use is the basis of this field. All too frequently this core, this essential and crucial precondition to all questions and answers, has been forgotten.

Nor is it merely recognition and description of this central phenomenon which the authors have contributed. They have also presented a sophisticated and open methodology expressing what they have measured and how they have made the measurement. This is not just assertion about the central phenomenon. This is observation, analysis and classification with all the steps described so that other relevantly trained professionals can not only utilize, but also criticize, replicate and improve both methods and analyses. In addition, the authors themselves point out certain weaknesses and certain gaps in this effort and themselves plan to improve upon this work. It is a major national demography of users of alcohol in this country, a most valuable contribution to the field of studies on alcohol and man.

SELDEN D. BACON

Rutgers Center of Alcohol Studies

Chapter 1

Background, Scope and Method

TWENTY-FIVE YEARS AGO, Bacon (2) proposed a long-term program of research as essential to an understanding of drinking behavior at a time of rapid social change. The national survey of drinking behavior, which provides the principal data for the present monograph, was undertaken to help to meet that challenge, with the following principal objectives:

1. To study the range of drinking practices (including related behavior and attitudes) as they exist in the whole society. Thus the planners of the survey tried not to emphasize the negative aspects of alcohol, although many of the findings have a bearing on them. The basic mission of the study is to describe the use of alcohol, rather than to prescribe solutions for reducing alcoholism.

2. To analyze many correlates of drinking behavior—e.g., demographic variables, personality characteristics and attitudes—some of which have been analyzed singly in individual smaller-scale studies, but whose interactions have not been studied before on a national probability sample of this size (2746).

3. To lay the groundwork and to serve as a baseline for future studies of a longitudinal nature, in which the same individuals are being followed up over a period of years in order to measure changes in their drinking over time. Single descriptive studies such as this national survey are an essential first stage in understanding the broad range of phenomena associated with various types of drinking. Parallel samples at a later date can suggest over-all group changes. However, only true longitudinal studies of individuals can establish conclusively which attributes of the individual—such as sex, age, personality traits, reference group memberships—are actually associated with later changes in drinking habits.[1]

Use of alcohol has continued to be a controversial topic through-

---

[1] Two programs of studies of change in drinking behavior are now in progress. One is the Drinking Practices Study in the San Francisco area, formerly under the direction of Dr. Genevieve Knupfer (14, 43, 72) and now directed by Don Cahalan. The other is the program of national surveys being conducted by the Social Research Group at the George Washington University. These programs, both of which are being carried out through NIMH grants, are discussed in Chapter 7.

out American history, as evident in songs, social movements and statistics. Attempts at social controls over drinking have had dramatic ups and downs throughout the last 300 years, as documented by Gusfield (26). The fact that actual drinking practices within the population have not hitherto been well charted may be a reflection of the controversial and ambivalent status of alcohol in America. For example, much of the controversy over alcohol continues to be moral in tone: the conflict of "Protestant ethic" versus hedonism, laissez-faire or liberalism. In the medical and public-health field, this controversy is paralleled by the conflict between those who maintain that any drinking is likely to increase the risk of alcoholism, and those who argue that alcohol for most people serves as a socially useful relaxant or catalyst which is less harmful than likely substitutes (e.g., drugs) and provides an essential safety valve for the pressures of modern society.

The ambivalence of those who write about moral and public health matters is matched by a marked ambivalence on the part of the general public. For example, as will be shown later, while two-thirds (68%) of adults reported that they drank at least once a year, almost half (47%) did not find alcohol sufficiently useful in their lives to warrant drinking as often as once a month. Of the total national sample, 35% said "nothing good" could be said for drinking; and substantial numbers of even those classified as "heavy drinkers"[2] said that drinking does more harm than good and that alcoholism is a serious problem. Yet at the same time, almost one-third (29%) said that having a drink was helpful to them when they were depressed or nervous; and one-third of those who drank once a year or more often said that they would miss drinking if they had to give it up.

There is continuing controversy concerning the definition of "alcoholism" and whether it constitutes a true disease entity, and also concerning the prevalence of alcoholism and whether it is increasing or decreasing. Most authorities at the present time, however, are in fair agreement on the characteristics of alcoholism in its broad definition as "a psychogenic dependence on or a physi-

---

[2] "Heavy drinking" is defined later in this chapter. As used in this study it covers a range from those who drink higher amounts (e.g., five or more drinks per occasion) at least two or three times a month to those drinking any amount on three or more occasions per day. Because of its specific definition in this work, it will not be set off in quotation marks hereinafter.

ological addiction to ethanol, manifested by the inability of the alcoholic consistently to control either the start of drinking or its termination . . ." (35, *p. 312*). Many authorities agree on the plausibility of Keller's carefully qualified estimate of about 4 to 5 million alcoholics in the United States[3] (or about 4% of the total adult population), even though Keller himself offered the estimate with grave reservations to serve only in the absence of better-established facts. But the issue regarding a change in the rate of so-called alcoholism is another point of controversy, with some claiming that the increase in the rate of admissions of alcoholics to state mental hospitals implies an increase in alcoholism, while others (in a National Institute of Mental Health publication) say that "the data are so incomplete, the methods of diagnosing and reporting in different communities and professional groups so different, and the interpretations so controversial, that it is impossible to determine today if the rate of alcoholism is increasing, decreasing or remaining steady" (57, *p. 11*).

There is also disagreement over the interpretation of statistics on consumption of alcoholic beverages. Recent data indicate that aggregate per capita consumption in the United States has increased somewhat in recent years.[4] However, it may well be that this apparent increase in per capita consumption (ratio of total consumption to population) is a reflection of an increase in the proportion of users of alcohol rather than an increase of the amount consumed by those who drink. This was suggested by Jellinek in 1947 concerning an apparent increase in drinking since 1940 (32). (This inference is plausible, in the light of the findings of the present study regarding the drinking behavior of various subgroups.)

Jellinek also inferred from the change in the relative amount of spirits, wine and beer consumed in 1850 and 100 years later that there is now a larger proportion of moderate as opposed to heavy drinkers. Yet it also could be argued that if the proportion of per-

[3] Keller (35, *p. 318*). This estimate was based upon Jellinek's formula for the presumed ratio between liver cirrhosis deaths and alcoholism, a formula which both Keller and Jellinek himself seriously challenged.

[4] The Annual Statistical Report of the Distilled Spirits Industry for 1966 shows a gain in the per capita consumption of distilled spirits between the late 1950s and the late 1960s, the consumption averaging 1.28 gallons in 1959 and 1.51 gallons in 1965. Data are based on the states in which the sale of distilled spirits was legal. However, they are for total, not adult, population and do not take account of the changing age distribution in the country.

sons who drink at all is increasing, there is therefore a greater proportion of persons who are at risk of alcoholism, especially in view of such factors as the stresses of modern-day living, or the increase in urbanization of the population with consequent lessening of social controls from the family and the community.

The prevailing values of the American middle-class culture have given a decidedly antialcohol slant to much of the sociopsychological research on drinking practices. Other than Chafetz (12), few American writers have given much emphasis to the general social usefulness of drinking. The prevailing assumptions and interests of readers and users of research have tended to focus the attention of research upon the negative aspects of alcohol. As Maddox and McCall have said,

"A primary reason why research attention has typically been directed to the pathological aspects of alcohol use is that all drinking has frequently been conceived as abnormal, as maladaptive, or as only a prelude to alcoholism. From this point of view the distinction between drinking, drunkenness and alcoholism has often been reduced to one of degree and duration. This focus on the most visible and dramatic aspects of alcohol use has placed a decisive stamp on orientations to the study of drinking, on the formulation of research questions, and on the types of explanations of drinking behavior which have been proposed. The personal and social dysfunctions of drinking have been emphasized almost to the exclusion of any broader consideration of drinking as an acceptable form of social behavior" (47, pp. 10–11).

Part of the general tendency toward equating the study of drinking with the study of "alcoholism" or drinking problems undoubtedly stems from the concern of medically oriented researchers with alcoholism as a disease. Much can be traced, however, to the middle-class "Protestant ethic" alluded to by Maddox and McCall (47, p. 10) and the legacies of middle-class moral standards from an earlier era (26). These morally tinged values seem to continue to be endemic in the American culture. This cultural heritage, as well as the health aspects, may help to explain why it is that even though the Public Health Service emphasizes that the vast majority of drinkers do not appear to have any problems which demonstrably spring directly from drinking (57, p. 5), and cites research which shows that no substantial correlation exists between the per capita consumption of alcohol and the rate of alcoholism (p. 25), many researchers remain interested in studying only the negative implications of alcohol.

SCOPE AND METHOD OF SURVEY

In 1962, the National Institute of Mental Health awarded a special grant to the Social Research Group of The George Washington University to carry out a full-scale national survey to describe in detail the drinking practices of Americans as objectively as possible. The survey was one phase in a longer-term program of longitudinal studies to measure levels and changes in drinking behavior.

This study has drawn heavily upon a series of community and pilot surveys which were conducted from 1959 to 1964 as part of the same NIMH-sponsored program of research into drinking practices. Begun by Cisin and continued by Knupfer, these included two community surveys on the West Coast, under the aegis of the California Department of Public Health, and a community survey and a methodological experiment on the East Coast, conducted through The George Washington University. The Western studies were carried out in Berkeley (20, 21, 22, 38, 39) and San Francisco (41); the Eastern studies were done in Hartford, Conn. (8), and Richmond, Va. (37). The preliminary studies tested alternative techniques of questioning, interviewer training and data collection, while obtaining detailed information for comparison of drinking practices in several distinct communities. We have also drawn upon the experience of Mulford and Miller (51–55) and Maxwell (48) in earlier state and local surveys, and upon the pioneering work of Riley and Marden (61) in their national quota sample in 1946.

The full-scale survey utilized a national probability sample drawn so that the findings would be representative of the total population of persons aged 21 years or older living in households within the contiguous United States (exclusive of Alaska and Hawaii). It entailed a multi-staged sampling operation calling for personal interviews with randomly predesignated adults in an average of 30 randomly selected households in each of 100 Primary Sampling Unit areas, each about the size of a census enumeration district. Every household was given an equal chance to be selected; then an adult was randomly selected from each chosen household. To compensate for differential individual probabilities caused by variation in household size, each person's responses were weighted according to the number of adults in his household.

The 2746 interviews represented a rate of completion of more than 90% from eligible households.[5] This high completion rate was set up as a standard because of the possibility that the most hard-to-find people would include a disproportionate number of heavier drinkers. It was achieved through repeated visits and telephone calls to track down those respondents who were seldom at home. (Further details on the sampling operation are provided in Appendix II.)

All interviews were conducted in respondents' own households. More than 100 trained interviewers participated. Most of the interviewers

---

[5] Households occupied by one or more persons 21 years or older, excluding only those too ill or senile to be interviewed.

were men,[6] since earlier studies (37) had indicated that men interviewers were likely to get answers indicating a somewhat higher level of drinking than women interviewers, and it is assumed that the likelihood of underestimation of drinking is more to be guarded against than overestimation. Only nonabstaining interviewers were used since nonabstainers were found by Mulford and Miller (51, 55) to get reports of higher rates of drinking than did abstainers. The interviewers were closely supervised, and respondents were revisited or telephoned to retrieve any missing information of any importance. The data gathering was carried out between October 1964 and March 1965.

The questionnaire is shown in Appendix IV. The topics covered fall into eight major categories:

1. Estimates of the amount of drinking within various subgroups (e.g., sex, age, socioeconomic status, region, size of town, race, national origin, religion);

2. Drinking of specific beverages: wine, beer, or spirits;

3. Circumstances related to drinking: usual recreational activities, places where people drink, and weekend as against weekday drinking;

4. Retrospective reports of changes in amount of drinking: when respondent started to drink; whether he ever drank more or less than at present, and for what presumed reasons;

5. Drinking effects and problems: self-perception of one's own drinking; effects of drinking experienced during the previous year; whether others had tried to get respondent to drink more or less during the previous year;

6. Opinions about drinking: good and bad things that can be said about drinking; acquaintance with drinkers believed to have problems;

7. Correlation of personality attributes with drinking behavior, including analysis of such attributes as the respondent's general outlook on his own fortunes and values, activities he may have engaged in to relieve depression or nervousness, scores on seven brief personality scales (e.g., neuroticism, alienation, religious fundamentalism);

8. Characteristics of persons who drink to escape from personal problems, in comparison to others who drink only for presumably social reasons.

The emphasis in this analysis is upon the description of relationships between the dependent variables of drinking and of heavy drinking and a number of independent variables, both demographic (sex, age, etc.) and sociopsychological (values, attitudes, perceptions), taking into account such moderator variables as may be especially useful in accounting for variations in drinking (or nondrinking) behavior.[7] Since knowledge about drinking behavior among various subgroups in the American

---

[6] Except that a few interviews, primarily with women, were conducted by women supervisors after first attempts at interviews by men interviewers resulted in refusals.

[7] For simplicity in presentation the term "drinking behavior" used in the context of this study may also include nondrinking behavior, i.e., not only the "when, what, how often, etc." aspects of drinking, but also the "whether."

population is sparse, such a descriptive approach is seen as more appropriate at this stage than would be the isolation and intensive investigation of presumed causal relationships between a very restricted number of variables and drinking. Consequently, the study has been planned and presented in terms of description and estimation rather than the statement and testing of hypotheses.

Multivariate analysis of the data has been carried out through successive cross tabulations which divide the sample into successive subgroupings as finely as seems warranted by the prospects of finding differences in drinking behavior. Thus, for example, drinking behavior of men and women has been analyzed separately by sex, separately by age within the two sex groups, and separately by social-position groups within six sex–age groupings, with even more detailed subdivisions where appropriate.

Multivariate subgroup analyses of a descriptive variety, rather than any formal multiple regression analyses, have been adopted for the following reasons: (a) Many of the variables with which we are concerned are nonmetric and so do not lend themselves readily to interval, or even ordinal, scaled values required for regression methods; (b) many of the relationships are not linear in nature; and (c) we are more interested in discovering and describing some of the subtleties of interaction among several variables and drinking behavior than we are in forcing the data into a multiple regression mold in order to account for as much as possible of the variance statistically. The importance of exploring the direction and extent of the interactions among the principal variables is believed to outweigh any advantages which might have ensued from routine application of standardization or regression techniques to isolate the effects of single variables.

The purpose of the present work, in sum, is to provide a volume of descriptive information which will be useful to professional social scientists working in the field of drinking behavior and allied phenomena. It is hoped that the many tables (including the lengthier ones deposited with the National Auxiliary Publications Service) will serve as a "data bank" which will stimulate further research. The principal findings are contained in briefer compass in the Summary, Conclusions and Research Implications (Chapter 7).

Some Theoretical Perspectives

One general shortcoming of past studies of drinking has been the limited, piecemeal and particularistic character of hypotheses and measurements of drinking behavior.[8] Such a state of poverty in the art of

---

[8] One exception to the generally untheoretical approach to alcohol research is that of Bacon (2, 3), who more than 20 years ago delineated a broad sociological framework for the study of alcohol. In commenting upon the implications of alcohol in modern society, Bacon discussed the presumed effects of social stratification and the growth of individualism and lessening of social controls upon drinking behavior in complex urban societies.

theory building is inevitable until a sound enough foundation of empirical facts has been laid down upon which to build theories to be tested. There already does exist, however, a body of middle-range theory regarding drinking behavior which can contribute to better understanding and prediction of at least the less socially approved types of behavior described in this monograph. The theory comes from a combined set of sociological and psychological concepts relating to the correlates of deviance which have been set forth recently by Jessor and his associates (34).[9] Their theoretical framework may be summarized as follows:

Their sociological concepts draw upon Merton's theory of social structure and anomie (49) and the theories of Cloward and Ohlin regarding delinquent gangs (15). These theories postulate that persons will behave in a deviant manner if this is more likely to lead to the attainment of goals than is nondeviant behavior. Drawing upon these theories, Jessor and his associates have focused on three sociocultural substructures which should correlate with deviance: the opportunity structure (or the channels of access to the achievement of goals valued in the American culture), the normative structure (the values and goals toward which striving is to be directed), and the social control structure (the socially patterned opportunities for learning and performing deviant and other behaviors).

In their psychological concepts, Jessor and his colleagues draw upon the social-learning theories of Rotter (64), as follows: "The likelihood of occurrence of deviant behavior will vary directly with the degree of personal disjunction, alienation, belief in external control, tolerance of deviance, and tendencies toward short-time perspective and immediate gratification characterizing an individual at a given moment in time" (34, *p. 111*).

In analyzing their data on drinking problems and other deviance in their triethnic community, Jessor and his associates combined these sociocultural and social-psychological concepts by scoring a large number of individual survey items into a number of indices which, when merged together, helped to explain much more of the variance in drunkenness and other delinquent behavior than would have been accomplished by using any one of the indices singly. Their sociocultural indices included a multiitem measure of socioeconomic status, a measure of exposure to "deviant role models" within the family, and a measure of social-control influences of a primary-group variety. The social-psychological variables included indices of personal disjunctions (e.g., misfortunes), attitudes toward deviance, and feelings of individual alienation vis-à-vis society. All these variables were combined into a "field theoretical pattern analysis" in which, within each of three sociocultural groupings, each group was subdivided further on social-psychological

[9] In the Tri-Ethnic Project, supported by NIMH, Spanish speaking, Ute Indian, and Anglo-American members of a relatively isolated Colorado community were contrasted in a study of the correlates of deviance, including problem drinking.

variables. Their analysis examined the correlates of social-psychological measures at each of three different levels of sociocultural status; and at each level it was found that variation in personality patterns made a consistent difference in the prevalence of deviance (34, *Ch. 11*).

The concepts of Jessor and his associates are more appropriate to studies which focus primarily upon heavy or problem drinking than they are to the present national survey, which touched upon a wide range of various aspects of drinking practices rather than concentrating upon drinking problems. Even so, the theories set forth by Jessor and his colleagues will be seen to be highly relevant in most respects to the findings of this national survey as regards the correlates of what we have called heavy drinking.

In the triethnic study (34) and the recent Hartford follow-up study by one of the present authors (10), many survey items were consolidated into sets of single scores or indices constituting independent variables, and sets of these indices were then combined to predict the dependent variable (drunkenness and problem drinking, respectively). Some of the practical applications of the theories of deviant behavior discussed above were illustrated in the Hartford follow-up study, in which the association between problem drinking and the following independent variables was shown: *Sociological variables:* (*1*) Sociocultural status (e.g., Index of Social Position); (*2*) Exposure to heavy or frequent drinking; permissiveness of significant others regarding one's drinking; (*3*) Social control status (e.g., whether close friends are from church or neighborhood or family connections; whether reared by both parents); (*4*) Social activities in the evening (e.g., how often one visits significant others). *Psychological variables:* (*1*) Personal disjunctions and alienation (e.g., bad luck; unhappy childhood; alienation vis-à-vis society); (*2*) Attitudes related to conformity and delayed gratification (e.g., impulsivity score, "Protestant ethic" values); (*3*) Attitudes about drinking (e.g., whether drinking does more good or harm).

Again, the caution should be borne in mind that concepts useful in discussing heavy or "problem" drinking are not necessarily appropriate for predicting the mere fact of whether the individual drinks or not: as will be shown at the end of this monograph, most of the explained variance on whether the individual drinks can be accounted for by such primarily sociocultural variables as sex, age, socioeconomic status, urbanization and ethnic origin, without invoking any personality variables (9, 39).

Where heavy or "problem" drinking is involved and personality variables are most relevant, it is to be expected that the sociological and psychological variables sometimes will have interactional rather than additive effects. For example, in the Hartford follow-up study it was found that those with low social scores (such as lower social status and social activity) and higher psychological scores (higher alienation and other attributes likely to be correlated with problem drinking) had a higher rate of problem drinking than the obverse group with higher social and lower psychological scores (10). Further replications,[10] utilizing a broader range and better balance of items, are needed to amplify this finding. But the point remains that the study of the peculiar nonmonotonic interactions among variables related to drinking appears to represent a more rewarding path toward understanding the causal relationships in drinking behavior than would a multiple correlation analysis of individual contributing factors—at least at the present state of the art.

In order to explore relevant nonlinear relationships, we analyzed the data from this national study largely on a descriptive item-by-item basis, leaving it to later studies to consolidate descriptive information of this kind in arriving at new syntheses which will be useful in forecasting future drinking behavior.

Measurement of Levels of Drinking

The Issue of Validity

In dealing with such a presumably sensitive issue as measuring the amount of alcoholic beverages people consume, the basic question of validity is "How do you know they are telling the truth?" The case for the relative validity of respondent self-reports on their own drinking practices was presented by Cisin as follows:

"In pursuit of the validity question, it seems appropriate to point out that what is of interest here is not the detailed accuracy of any subject's report; the uniqueness of any individual and the reproducibility of his behavior should be the problem of clinical studies, not of gross, large-scale surveys. Rather, what is of interest here is the classification of individuals into rather broad categories. Thus, the question of validity ought not to be asked about the *truthfulness* of any individual statements, but about the resultant *summary* classification of each individual. One should ask whether the subject's responses will be so distorted that he will end up in the wrong one of a small number of categories. This argument is sometimes pushed further; since the ultimate interest of the study is in relationships between drinking behavior on the one hand and psychological, social, and demographic characteristics on the other, the validity question ought to be asked thus: 'To what extent will misclassification of drinking behavior result in serious distortion of reported relationships?'" (13, *pp. 608–609*).

The validity of the questions on quantity and frequency of consumption of alcoholic beverages in the national survey was subjected to test in a small-scale study conducted in Richmond, Va. (37). In this study, the interview was administered to 81 persons who were presumed to include a higher-than-average proportion of heavy drinkers, on the grounds that they had been registered at an alcoholism clinic (although they had not undergone treatment). The respondents did not know they had been selected as a criterion group; and the purpose of the study

---

[10] Such an analysis is currently being carried out on the data of the national follow-up study conducted by the Social Research Group in 1967.

was also concealed from both the control group (81 persons matched on sex, race, age and neighborhood) and the interviewers, who believed this was a sample survey of the general population.

The findings of the pilot study were that most of the alcoholism-clinic registrants freely specified a present or past level of consumption which would clearly qualify them as heavy drinkers by any criteria. Moreover, while the criterion group of clinic registrants did not register significantly higher than the matched-sample control group on "social" reasons for drinking, they did exhibit a much higher rate of "escape" reasons for drinking.

It is possible that clinic registrants might be more likely to report a high level of drinking than would an equally heavy-drinking group who have not yet attained the "social reality" implied in being referred to an alcoholism clinic (by one's spouse, a judge, other significant persons, or by themselves). However, this preliminary study showed such a large difference between the criterion and comparison groups, both in levels of past drinking and in "escape" reasons for drinking, that the findings are regarded as providing a sufficient validation of the interview method for the purpose of comparing drinking behavior among subgroups within the general population.

Measurement of Amount and Variability of Drinking

The problem of measuring alcoholic beverage consumption and classifying people according to amount of drinking has many facets. While a number of research workers have devoted considerable attention to the problem, there has been no consensus as to what constitutes "light," "moderate" or "heavy" drinking. Several factors such as the quantity consumed, the type (or strength) of beverage drunk, and the frequency, regularity and consistency of drinking habits all need to be considered. Since various researchers have had different goals, no single criterion has proved adequate.

Many workers in the field have used some kind of quantity–frequency (Q–F) index of the amount of alcoholic beverages consumed over a period of time. Straus and Bacon (68) initially developed the Q–F index which was later adapted by Mulford and Miller (52) in their Iowa studies and by Maxwell (48) in a study of drinking in Washington State. The Q–F index estimates the approximate amount a person drinks over a period of time by multiplying the amount he reports he usually drinks (on an average occasion) by the reported frequency over a stated period (such as a month).

The statistical reliability of any method of measurement which depends on respondents' judgments of their "usual" behavior is limited by several human factors (including the natural tendency to respond in terms of modal rather than mean behavior). Hence the reliability and validity of reports of "usual" drinking may not be high enough for precise placement of individuals on a scale or for reliable projected estimates of total national consumption. For purposes of total consumption estimates a more useful tool might be exact reports of the quantity drunk in a specific, brief, recent period, such as the preceding 24 hours or 7 days. But this procedure would catch certain respondents at atypical times and lead to incorrect groupings for average, usual behavior. As Mulford and Miller say (52), the Q–F index is most useful as a convenient tool for the purpose of group comparisons. Since the goal of the present survey is to describe usual behavior in terms of group differences rather than to make measurements for national projections, the analysis is based upon a variant of this type of index.

The national survey built upon the earlier types of quantity–frequency analysis and upon an expanded system, first used in the California study of Knupfer (42), based on 12 questions that took into account the quantity of alcohol per occasion, the frequency or number of occasions, and the variability or fluctuations in time and amount, as follows: The *quantity* of a beverage consumed at a sitting (this was measured separately for wine, beer and spirits by asking how often the person had as many as five or six, or three or four, or one or two drinks); The *frequency* with which each of the three types of beverage was usually drunk; The *variability* of drinking, as shown by a combination of the modal (most usual) amount consumed and the highest amount drunk at least occasionally. Thus, the drinking index used in the national survey might be called, instead of a Q–F index, a Q–F–V index (for quantity, frequency and variability).

The method used in making these three types of measurement was as follows:

Respondents were first handed a small, four-page, multicolored booklet as the interviewer made the statement, "The next few questions ask you about your own use of various types of drinks. Will you please take this booklet and on the first page put a check mark next to the answer that tells how often you *usually* have wine. . . . Now please turn to the green page and do the same for *beer*. . . . Now please turn to the pink page and do the same for drinks containing *whisky* or *liquor*, including scotch, bourbon, gin, vodka, rum, etc. . . . And now turn to the yellow page and please check how often you have *any* kind of drink containing alcohol, whether it is wine, beer, whisky or any other drink."

On the booklet, wine was further defined as "(or a punch containing wine)"; and drinks containing whisky or liquor were further defined as "(such as martinis, manhattans, highballs, or straight drinks)."

The *frequency scale* for each beverage, printed in the booklet to be checked by respondents, was as follows: "Three or more times a day; Two times a day; Once a day; Nearly every day; Three or four times a week; Once or twice a week; Two or three times a month; About once a month; Less than once a month but at least once a year; Less than once a year; I have never had wine (beer, drinks containing whisky or liquor, any kind of beverage containing alcohol)."

The rationale for a scale so heavily loaded with responses indicating very frequent drinking was to give the respondent the impression that no matter how frequently he drank, there must be many others who drank even more frequently than he—thus possibly reducing any reluctance to check a category indicating frequent drinking.

For each of the three types of beverages, three questions measuring quantity and variability were then asked in series:

"Think of all the times you have had . . . recently. When you drink . . ., how often do you have as many as five or six?"
"When you drink . . ., how often do you have three or four?"
"When you drink . . ., how often do you have one or two?"

Quantity was expressed in terms of "glasses" of wine, "glasses" or "cans" of beer, and "drinks" of beverages containing spirits. The response categories were: "Nearly every time"; "More than half the time"; "Less than half the time"; "Once in a while"; and "Never."

These questions on quantity consumed and relative frequency were asked for each beverage which the respondent reported drinking about once a month or more often. The replies permitted classification of each respondent by modal quantity for each beverage (i.e., the quantity he drank "nearly every time" or "more than half the time") and by the maximum quantity he drank at least "once in a while." Thus a person who said that when he had beer he had one or two glasses or cans more than half the time, but once in a while drank five or more, would be classified as having a *modal* quantity of one or two and a *maximum* of five or more.

This two-way approach permitted the quantity–variability classification for each beverage shown in Chart 1.

In order to classify each drinker into one of five over-all Q–F–V groups, a cross-tabulation was made of the frequency of over-all drinking of any beverage containing alcohol (from "three or more times a day" down to "never had") against the above quantity–variability classification for the particular beverage respondent used most frequently (or, if two beverages were tied in frequency, the beverage which he drank in

CHART 1.—*Quantity–Variability Classifications*

Quantity–Variability Class	Modal Quantity (amount drunk "nearly every time" or "more than half the time")	Maximum Quantity (highest quantity drunk)
1	5–6	5–6
2	3–4	5–6 "less than ½ time"
3	3–4	5–6 "once in a while"
4	no mode specified	5–6 "less than ½ time"
5	3–4	3–4
6	1–2	5–6 "less than ½ time"
7	no mode specified	5–6 "once in a while"
8	1–2	5–6 "once in a while"
9	1–2	3–4 "less than ½ time"
10	1–2	3–4 "once in a while"
11	1–2	1–2

greatest quantity). These groupings were then combined into five over-all Q–F–V classes used in much of this analysis (Heavy, Moderate, Light, or Infrequent drinkers, and Abstainers). These consist of the types shown in Chart 2 (they are shown graphically in Figure 1).

The Q–F–V classifications used in this analysis, although arbitrary, are based on the general principle that those who drink larger amounts of alcoholic beverages per occasion should get a heavier-drinking classi-

CHART 2.—Q–F–V Classifications

Q–F–V Group	Frequency (of any alcoholic beverage)	Quantity–Variability Class (beverage drunk most often)[a]
1. Heavy Drinkers (324 persons, 12% of weighted[b] total)		
	a. Three or more times a day	1–11
	b. Twice a day	1–9
	c. Every day or nearly every day	1–8
	d. Three or four times a week	1–5
	e. Once or twice a week	1–4
	f. Two or three times a month	1
2. Moderate Drinkers (354 persons, 13%)		
	a. Twice a day	10–11
	b. Every day or nearly every day	9–10
	c. Three or four times a week	6–9
	d. Once or twice a week	5–9
	e. Two or three times a month	2–8
	f. About once a month	1–6
3. Light Drinkers (766 persons, 28%)		
	a. Every day or nearly every day	11
	b. One to four times a week	10–11
	c. Two or three times a month	9–11
	d. About once a month	7–11

4. Infrequent Drinkers

(404 persons, 15%): Drank less than once a month but at least once a year (quantity questions not asked).

5. Abstainers

(898 persons, 32%): Drank none of the three beverages as often as once a year (quantity questions not asked).

[a] Modified when necessary (because two beverages were tied in frequency or because a lower quantity for the most frequently consumed beverage than for another would have resulted in a lower Q–F–V classification). No person was classified in any over-all Q–F–V group lower than his drinking of any one beverage would place him.

[b] All responses in this survey have been weighted in proportion to the number of adults in the respondent's household, in order to give appropriate representation to all persons within the total household population. Weighted percentage base is 5321.

QUANTITY - VARIABILITY CLASS FOR BEVERAGE DRUNK MOST OFTEN

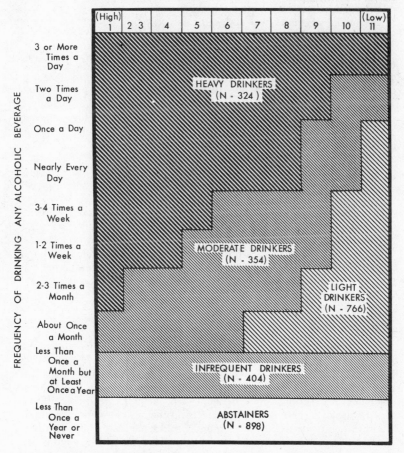

FIGURE 1.—*Quantity–Frequency–Variability Classifications*

fication than those who consume about the same volume through drinking small quantities over a period of time. The reasoning behind this assumption is that very few of those who never drink as many as five drinks on any occasion would be likely to become intoxicated or to have serious present problems related to drinking (although it is certainly possible that they might develop problems in the future if the regularity of habit leads to an increase in quantity).

In about 2% of the total cases, the final classification was raised so that the over-all group assignment would be no lower than that for any one of the three types of beverages. This classification conflict could arise if the beverage drunk most frequently was drunk in much smaller amounts than some other beverage. For example, an individual might drink a moderate amount of beer once or twice a week, and a large amount of spirits two or three times a month, giving his over-all frequency (including small amounts of wine) as three or four times a week. On the basis of his over-all frequency and the amount of the beverage most frequently drunk (beer) the respondent would have been classified as a moderate drinker. But since he drank enough of a beverage (spirits) to put him into the heavy class for that one beverage alone, he would be classified as a heavy drinker.[11]

To minimize respondent fatigue, those who did not usually drink any of the three specific beverages as often as once a month were not asked the questions on the amounts they drank per occasion. However, a small group of less than 1% who did not drink any one of the three beverages as often as once a month did drink enough of different beverages to qualify as drinking once or twice a month on an over-all basis; these have been arbitrarily classified as light drinkers.

Since persons who said they drank less than once a month were not asked the quantity they had per occasion, the survey failed to single out those who may drink less than once a month but go on extended "benders" one or more times per year. While the less-than-once-a-month "spree" drinker is believed to be relatively rare, some measurement of the number and characteristics of such drinkers should be carried out in future surveys of this type.

Need for a Better Index of Relative Drinking Behavior

As mentioned previously, no one index of drinking behavior has yet been developed to serve all analytic purposes. Knupfer has made the point (42) that a Q–F index which classifies people primarily in terms of their approximate aggregate consumption of drinks over a given period mixes together various types of people who actually are quite different in their use of alcohol and in its effects on them. For example, a person who has one or two (but never more) drinks per day is likely to have a quite different life style than the person who seldom drinks more than once a week but often has five or more drinks when he does. Thus a group of "daily light" drinkers in the San Francisco survey contained a higher proportion of wine drinkers, Catholics and those who said they "did not enjoy getting drunk" than was true of "weekly heavy" drinkers of about the same total weekly consumption. In order to reflect such differences in groups with similar aggregate consumption but dissimilar

[11] Special classification decisions were made for very rare types of drinkers: 8 persons who drank only about once a month but had at least 5 drinks once in a while were classified as light drinkers, although they may have deserved a higher classification; 3 persons who had a mode of 5 or more drinks per occasion but drank only about once a month were classified as moderate drinkers, although they might perhaps belong among the heavy drinkers. The 11 persons in these two possibly underclassified groups constitute only 4/10 of 1% of the sample.

spacing of their drinking, the Berkeley and San Francisco studies therefore were reported in terms of five rather than four drinker groups (excluding abstainers), the light drinkers being divided into "frequent light" and "infrequent light" and the moderate drinkers into "frequent moderate" and "infrequent moderate" (39, 41).

We have developed another variability-of-drinking index (for use in a later study but applicable to the data of this national survey) based on the principle that the spacing or bunching of drinks is more important than aggregate volume alone in characterizing an individual's drinking patterns. This index involves computing each person's estimated monthly consumption of all three types of alcoholic beverages and also classifying him as to whether he ever has as many as five drinks per occasion. In the resultant Volume–Variability Index (also sometimes called a "Volume–Maximum Index"), eight groups were isolated for analysis: abstainers and infrequent drinkers (as in the Q–F–V index), and those in three volume-per-month groups (defined as low, medium and high volume), each of which was divided into those who did and those who did not sometimes drink as many as five drinks per occasion.

Analyses of subgroup differences among the respondents in the national survey according to this newer v–v index are presented in Appendix I. As can be noted in Table 105 of Appendix I, the heavy drinkers under the Q–F–V system include most of the same persons who were classified as "High Volume, High Maximum" under the v–v system. Since the Q–F–V index already had been utilized in preparing the bulk of the analyses of subgroups regarding the proportions of drinkers and heavy drinkers before the v–v index was developed, the Q–F–V index is used generally throughout this monograph; the v–v index is given only where it is important to show the difference between massed and spaced drinking when volume is held constant. We would recommend the use of some type of Volume–Variability (or Volume–Maximum) index for most purposes in the future, because it has all of the useful characteristics of the Q–F–V index and also preserves the distinction between those who consume a given volume by bunching or massing their drinks and those who space them out.

Chapter 2

Demographic and Sociological Correlates of Levels of Drinking

ONE of the primary objectives of this study is to analyze the interrelationships among many correlates of drinking behavior which have been examined on a piecemeal basis in earlier studies but not yet studied in combination. As a preliminary to multivariate analysis of the correlates of drinking, the general levels of drinking within the total adult population and within various subgroups will be discussed.

Levels in the Total Population

The primary emphasis in this analysis is upon exploring the relative differences in levels of drinking from group to group, rather than upon arriving at absolute measurements of either drinking or "heavy" or "excessive" drinking in the population as a whole. The reason for this emphasis is that it is essential to know the relative group-to-group differences in order to understand how drinking is related to other behavior. As pointed out earlier, the Q–F–V classifications of drinking level are not exact enough to permit drawing literal interpretations of an absolute variety. However, it will be of interest to compare the general and subgroup findings with past national surveys which were conducted with different sampling methods[1] and questions.[2]

This national survey yielded the distribution of levels of drinking, in terms of the five Q–F–V groupings already described, shown in Figure 2.

---

[1] The national survey reported in this monograph was conducted through application of probability sampling principles at all stages down to the individual within the household, with no substitutions permitted. The Gallup (1) and Mulford (56) surveys utilized probability principles in sampling down to the selection of neighborhoods or households, with controls for sex and other factors. The 1946 survey reported by Riley and Marden (61) used quotas for age, sex and socioeconomic status and permitted substitutions.

[2] The usual Gallup wording, also used by Mulford and by Riley and Marden, was: "Do you ever have occasion to use alcoholic beverages such as liquor, wine, or beer, or are you a total abstainer?"

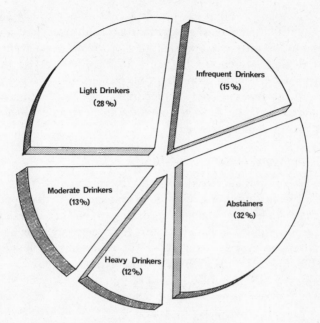

FIGURE 2.—*Distribution of Q–F–V Groups in the United States (N=2746).*
Abstainers—drink less than once a year or not at all; *Infrequent drinkers*—drink
at least once a year, but less than once a month; *Light drinkers*—drink at least
once a month, but typically only one or two drinks on a single occasion;
Moderate drinkers—drink at least once a month, typically several times, but
usually with no more than three or four drinks per occasion; *Heavy drinkers*—
drink nearly every day with five or more per occasion at least once in while,
or about once weekly with usually five or more per occasion.

Two-thirds (68%) of the total said they drink at least once a
year. It should not be concluded, however, that this majority of
American adults are regular drinkers. When the infrequent drinkers
and abstainers are added together, the total adult population is
seen to be fairly evenly divided between the 47% who do not drink
as often as once a month and the 53% who drink once a month
or more.

The proportion of drinkers and nondrinkers shown in this study
is similar to that reported by Gallup (1) and by Mulford (56).
The February 1966 Gallup Poll release reported that 65% of American adults "ever" drink alcoholic beverages, which is very close to
the 68% nonabstainers found in the present survey. Mulford, using
the Gallup question in a national sample in the summer of 1963,

found 71% who qualified as drinkers. Thus these various surveys yield about the same aggregate proportion of drinkers and abstainers despite the differences in sampling procedures and techniques of questioning. Moreover, the Mulford 1963 survey also yielded about the same relative proportions of drinkers and heavy drinkers as the present survey wherever comparisons can be made upon such subgroups as sex, age, socioeconomic status, degree of urbanization and region of country.

Trends in Aggregate Levels of Drinking

The Gallup poll has asked virtually the same question on drinking at intervals during a span of 20 years, and its findings indicate that the percentage of drinkers (according to the Gallup definition) in the adult population has risen in recent years, after declining in the post-World War II period (1). The reported percentages are: 1945, 67; 1946, 67; 1947, 63; 1949, 58; 1950, 60; 1951, 59; 1952, 60; 1956, 60; 1957, 58; 1958, 55; 1960, 62; 1964, 63; 1966, 65. The apparent increase is not constant across the board, but seems to differ by group, particularly by sex.

As established by earlier surveys (1, 56, 61), the present study showed that higher proportions of men than women were drinkers and also drink more. Considerably more men (77%) than women (60%) reported drinking at least once a year; 21% compared to 5% were heavy drinkers.

There is some evidence from other studies, however, that the gap between the sexes in drinking habits is narrowing, with the proportion of drinkers among the women appearing to be on the increase. Mulford, in comparing his 1963 findings with those of Riley's 1946 national quota sample, drew the conclusion that the proportion of drinkers among women (particularly those aged 21 to 25 years) had increased more than the proportion among men (56). Published Gallup data show little change in the percentage of drinkers among men since 1958, but an apparent fairly steady increase among women.[3]

While women are becoming more like men in the proportions

---

[3] In March 1958, 55% of the total, 67% of the men and 45% of the women, were drinkers; in May 1960, the total was 62%, men 69%, women 54%; in February 1964, total 63%, men 70%, women 56%; in February 1966, total 65%, men 70%, women 61%. Data courtesy of the American Institute of Public Opinion (Gallup Poll).

who drink at least occasionally, men and women still differ markedly in most aspects of the drinking practices studied in this survey. Accordingly, sex is held constant in most of the analyses in the following sections of this monograph, with most results by other variables (e.g., age, socioeconomic status, urbanization) being presented separately for men and women.

Sex and Age (Table 1)

In general, the percentage of abstainers was higher in the older age groups. Among men, the largest proportion of abstainers (38%) was in the oldest age group. When infrequent drinkers are added to abstainers, more than half (54%) of all men 65 years and over were not regular drinkers. Not only did the incidence of drinking decline with age, but also the extent of heavy drinking among drinkers: The lowest percentage of heavy drinkers among men was also observed in the oldest age group. Of particular interest is the fact that 40% of men drinkers aged 45 to 49 qualified as heavy drinkers, compared to only 11% of men drinkers aged 65 or over.

Among women, close to a majority in each age group up to age 50 either did not drink at all or drank infrequently (less than once a month); among women aged 50 to 64 about two-thirds fell in one of these two categories, while of those 65 and over about three-quarters drank infrequently or not at all. Among the women as among the men drinkers there was a peak of heavy drinking at ages 45 through 49, but also another peak at ages 21 to 24. It is noteworthy too that while the proportion of women heavy drinkers was inconsequential after the age of 50, the proportion of heavy drinkers among men continued to be higher than 20% up to the age of 65.

There are undoubtedly many factors behind the particularly high incidence of heavy drinking among both men and women at the ages of 45 to 49 and the somewhat uneven fluctuations at other ages (which tend to level out if ages are grouped in 10-year instead of 5-year intervals). For example, one may speculate that differences in drinking habits may result from metabolic or psychological factors: older people may have more unpleasant physical reactions to alcohol or feel less desire or need for it to relieve tension, either because they are under less strain or have turned

TABLE 1.—*Percentage of Respondents in Q–F–V Groups, by Sex and Age*

	N^a	Abst.	D R I N K E R S Infreq.	Light + Mod.	Heavy	% Heavy of All Drinkers
Total sample	2746	32	15	41	12	18
Men	1177	23	10	46	21	28
Women	1569	40	18	37	5	8
Age 21–29	472	24	15	47	14	18
30–39	588	22	17	46	15	19
40–49	597	29	12	44	15	21
50–59	462	40	14	36	10	25
60+	624	47	15	32	6	11
Age not given	3^b					
Men						
Age 21–24	100	16	8	54	22	26
25–29	116	17	8	51	24	29
30–34	109	12	7	51	30	34
35–39	134	16	12	50	22	26
40–44	150	18	8	54	20	24
45–49	114	25	7	38	30	40
50–54	116	25	13	41	21	28
55–59	81	30	14	34	22	31
60–64	82	30	5	41	24	35
65+	175	38	16	39	7	11
Women						
Age 21–24	112	32	20	39	9	13
25–29	144	29	21	45	5	7
30–34	156	29	23	42	6	8
35–39	189	27	22	44	7	10
40–44	189	35	16	43	6	9
45–49	144	36	14	40	10	15
50–54	147	51	16	32	1	3
55–59	118	50	14	35	1	3
60–64	110	47	20	31	2	3
65+	257	60	15	24	1	2

[a] In this and later tables N = the number of actual cases in each base group (unweighted). Percentages are calculated on weighted numbers; the weighted base for the total sample is 5321 which represents the total number of adults in the 2746 households.

[b] The three respondents (all women) who did not give their ages are omitted from all subsequent age tables.

to tranquilizers or other coping mechanisms rather than to drink. Some differences in drinking habits by age groups may also result from life-cycle phenomena specific to our culture; thus, younger women may drink more while working or dating than in the earlier stages of married life when they are at home with small children; middle-aged couples may have more money and time to enjoy drinking at leisure. Still other factors may be social, such as differences between generations in types of leisure activities or changes in social mores over time, as well as differences in the description of the types of drinking behavior which are appropriate at certain life cycles. These generational differences can be illustrated by the finding (Appendix I) that younger people tend to drink larger quantities less often and older people tend to drink more frequently but in lesser quantities. Later sections of this monograph will bring out additional findings relating to many of these factors; but their specific interrelationships with increases in age can only be determined through intensive study of a substantial number of persons over an extended period of time.

A crucial question is whether the differences in the amount of drinking at various age levels are primarily attributable to changes in individuals' drinking as they get older, or to changes in drinking levels between generations. In other words, whether the sharp decrease in proportions of men aged over 64 or women over 49 who drink (or drink heavily) reflects an actual decrease or quitting of drinking by many persons near these ages, or a longer-term intergenerational increase in the general level of drinking (with today's younger people still drinking more when they reach the age of 50 or 60 than their elders did at that age).

Comparing the findings in his 1963 study of drinking with the 1946 Riley–Marden survey (utilizing somewhat different questions and samples), Mulford (56) found higher drinking rates within the age group 38–42, compared to those who were aged 21–25 17 years earlier, and lower rates within the oldest comparable groups. He considered these results "consistent with findings of previous studies showing a rather sharp drop in rates of drinkers at about the age of 40 to 50." Finding present prevalence rates generally higher than those of earlier studies, he concluded that "while trend indications were not strong, the evidence suggested that the rate of drinkers is increasing. Each new generation has a larger proportion of drinkers and most of them remain drinkers throughout life. Some drinkers, however, do abandon the practice. Those who quit are most likely to do so about age 40 and again past the age of 60 years."

A summary of Gallup Poll findings is consistent with Mulford's comments: it shows an increase in the percentage of drinkers in all three age levels in recent years, but a distinctly lower level of drinking after age 50, a very consistent picture over almost a 20-year span covering nearly a whole generation. Since those in their 50s now were in their 30s in 1947, it is evident that fewer of them drink now than formerly. Thus the results clearly suggest that the observed decrease in the proportion of drinkers aged over 50 is at least partially attributable to the cessation of drinking on the part of individuals who did drink when they were younger (even allowing for the possibility of higher mortality rates among drinkers than among nondrinkers).[4]

The findings of Mulford and Gallup regarding the decline in the incidence of drinking among older age groups can be extended on the basis of the results in Table 1 to indicate a reduction in the amount of drinking by people aged over 60 who do not give it up entirely. The percentages of heavy drinkers declined significantly in men at age 65 or over and in women at age 50 and over; and there was also a decline in light and moderate drinkers among the older age groups, while the proportion of infrequent drinkers remained fairly constant. Here higher mortality may be more weighty in explaining the findings.

Index of Social Position (Tables 2, 3, 4)

A variant of the Hollingshead Index of Social Position (28) was used in this survey as the principal index of socioeconomic status, in what is believed to be the first time in a published national survey. The index (ISP) takes into account the respondent's education, the occupation of the family breadwinner, and the status or power position associated with the occupation.[5]

Table 2 shows the percentages in the various Q–F–V groups of each of 10 ISP groupings (divided into approximate deciles) for the

[4] This is, of course, a comparison of percentages based on the age distribution of the living population—the same result would have been produced if a substantial proportion of drinkers aged 30 died before they reached the age of 50, leaving relatively more nondrinkers in the percentage base. Having no follow-up statistics available on this point, we are not prepared to conclude that so many drinkers die young; we prefer the more conventional interpretation that people just tend to cut down on their drinking when they get older.

[5] The ISP index (which is more fully described in Appendix II) achieves much the same results as the index based on a combination score of income, occupation and education which was developed by Knupfer and Room for use in the San Francisco survey of drinking practices (41). Its main advantage over individual or family income as a measure of socioeconomic status is that it is not unduly af-

TABLE 2.—*Percentage of Respondents in Q–F–V Groups, by Index of Social Position and Sex*

	N	Abst.	Infreq.	Light + Mod.	Heavy	% Heavy of All Drinkers
Total sample	2746	32	15	41	12	18
ISP						
11–19 (high)	265	17	10	61	12	14
20–30	274	18	16	52	14	17
31–39	249	25	16	45	14	18
40–44	365	29	15	44	12	17
45–50	212	33	12	43	12	18
51–54	280	31	17	39	13	19
55–58	305	39	18	32	11	18
59–62	266	36	16	35	13	21
63–69	264	45	15	29	11	19
70–77	266	49	10	31	10	20
Men						
11–19	123	18	6	56	20	24
20–30	127	14	6	57	23	27
31–39	103	19	8	46	27	33
40–44	142	22	10	47	21	27
45–50	101	23	7	49	21	27
51–54	131	24	12	41	23	30
55–58	131	26	16	38	20	28
59–62	121	24	12	42	22	29
63–69	98	32	13	37	18	27
70–77	100	28	9	42	21	29
Women						
11–19	142	17	13	65	5	6
20–30	147	22	26	48	4	6
31–39	146	30	22	44	4	6
40–44	223	33	18	43	6	9
45–50	111	42	17	37	4	7
51–54	149	38	21	37	4	7
55–58	174	49	19	28	4	8
59–62	145	48	18	28	6	11
63–69	166	53	17	24	6	13
70–77	166	63	11	23	3	8

fected by artifacts which influence income level (e.g., multiple incomes within the household, differences in regional wage levels and in earnings of those of different ages). The ISP is also superior for most purposes to educational level alone since it is less affected by age and sex variations, and also because, by taking occupation into account, it reflects more closely the daily life situation, which is likely to affect social behavior. For these reasons, the analysis in this report emphasizes the ISP results rather than the separate variables of income, occupation or education, although special tabulations of the latter are provided in certain instances.

total and for men and women separately. It is clear from this table that those of highest status are much more likely to be drinkers (i.e., nonabstainers) and, if drinkers, somewhat less likely to be heavy drinkers than are those of lower status. It also can be seen that drinking varies by ISP group much more among women than among men.

In determining drinking habits Knupfer and Room (41) found in San Francisco that the three variables of sex, age and socioeconomic status had a cumulative effect. Table 3 bears out their main finding: the proportion of drinkers was consistently higher in the higher ISP groups than in the lower when sex and age were held constant. There was a steady decrease in the proportion of light or moderate drinkers going down the social scale in almost every sex–age group.

There was very little difference by ISP, however, in the distribution of heavy drinkers among the various sex–age groups. This finding should modify the legend of the "abstemious middle classes" referred to by Dollard (17) who implied that those in the upper and lower classes drink more than those of the middle class.[6]

The relative differences in drinking patterns by men and women of different ages and ISP are shown more distinctly in Table 4, in which the data on drinking and heavy drinking are restated in terms of differences in the percentages of men and women drinkers. The following findings stand out clearly: (1) The differences in the proportions of men and women drinkers were generally smaller in the upper ISP groups than in the lower; but (2) the differences in the proportions of men and women who were heavy drinkers formed no consistent pattern among the various socioeconomic levels.

The first finding tends to confirm the hypothesis stated by Knupfer and Room (41) that "There is more sexual equality and less social differentiation of the sexes in the upper classes than in the lower ones." The interrelationships of these results with other factors will be explored later in this work.

[6] The findings of this national study indicate that in interpreting this legend a distinction should be made between drinking per se and heavy drinking: more of the well-to-do than of the poor drink at least occasionally, but no more of the well-to-do who do drink, drink heavily. This finding suggests that alcohol may serve somewhat different purposes for the well-to-do and for the lowest-status groups. Further analysis of differences in reasons for drinking, presented later in this monograph, will shed more light on this issue.

TABLE 3.—*Percentage of Respondents in Q–F–V Groups, by Sex, Age and Index of Social Position*

	N	Abst.	Infreq.	Light + Mod.	Heavy	% Heavy of All Drinkers
Total sample	2746	32	15	41	12	18
Men						
Age 21–39						
Highest ISP[a]	132	12	5	59	24	27
Upper middle	119	14	12	50	24	28
Lower middle	127	13	12	49	26	30
Lowest	81	25	6	44	25	33
Age 40–59						
Highest ISP	137	20	7	50	23	28
Upper middle	110	21	8	45	26	33
Lower middle	121	27	14	38	21	29
Lowest	93	27	12	38	23	31
Age 60+						
Highest ISP	39	21	14	52	13	16
Upper middle	53	36	4	52	8	12
Lower middle	74	42	16	28	14	25
Lowest	91	36	14	36	14	22
Women						
Age 21–39						
Highest ISP	171	14	23	58	5	6
Upper middle	147	25	23	44	8	11
Lower middle	151	38	22	35	5	7
Lowest	132	41	18	32	9	16
Age 40–59						
Highest ISP	128	23	12	61	4	6
Upper middle	153	32	17	45	6	9
Lower middle	150	50	18	28	4	8
Lowest	167	59	14	22	5	12
Age 60+						
Highest ISP	62	41	23	35	1	2
Upper middle	98	58	18	24	0	0
Lower middle	89	52	16	29	3	7
Lowest	118	66	13	21	0	0

[a] The ISP group = Highest, 11–36; Upper middle, 37–48; Lower middle 49–59; Lowest, 60–77. These groupings differ somewhat from Hollingshead's social class groupings; they were based on over-all frequencies so as to divide the total sample into approximate quartiles. The same dividing points are used in all subsequent tables showing four ISP groups.

TABLE 4.—*Sex Differences in the Percentage of Drinkers and Heavy Drinkers, by Age and Index of Social Position*

	DRINKERS			HEAVY DRINKERS		
	Men	Women	% Dif- ference	Men	Women	% Dif- ference
Total sample	77	60	17	21	5	16
Age 21–39						
Highest ISP	88	86	2	24	5	19
Upper middle	86	75	11	24	8	16
Lower middle	87	62	25	26	5	21
Lowest	75	59	16	25	9	16
Age 40–59						
Highest ISP	80	77	3	23	4	19
Upper middle	79	68	11	26	6	20
Lower middle	73	50	23	21	4	17
Lowest	73	41	32	23	5	18
Age 60+						
Highest ISP	79	59	20	13	1	12
Upper middle	64	42	22	8	0	8
Lower middle	58	48	10	14	3	11
Lowest	64	34	30	14	0	14

In view of the complex relationships of the sex, age and ISP factors illustrated above, subsequent ISP analyses generally will be given in multivariate form, holding sex and age constant.

Income (Table 5)

For reasons discussed earlier, the ISP rather than income alone is emphasized as a socioeconomic variable in this report. However, since several past studies have analyzed drinking behavior by income groups, an analysis by income is presented in Table 5, both to permit direct comparison with other studies and to check whether income as a separate variable yields any findings that are significantly different from the ISP analysis. Drinking practices by income level are given separately for men and women in Table 5 to show differences by sex, and also to control for the fact that the lower-income households contained relatively more women.

There was a marked difference by income level in the proportions who drank at least once a year, the percentage of drinkers ranging from a low of 44% of persons with family incomes of less than $2000 to a high of 84% in families with $15,000 or more. Among women the contrast was even greater—37 to 83%.

TABLE 5.—*Percentage of Respondents in Q–F–V Groups, by Family Income and Sex*

	N	Abst.	Infreq.	Light + Mod.	Heavy	% Heavy of All Drinkers
Total sample	2746	32	15	41	12	18
Family Income						
Under $2000	349	56	13	26	5	11
$2000–3999	450	49	14	29	8	16
$4000–5999	547	36	14	39	11	18
$6000–7999	521	25	17	43	15	20
$8000–9999	387	24	14	48	14	18
$10,000–14,999	315	16	16	51	17	20
$15,000+	174	16	11	58	15	18
No information	3					
Men						
Under $2000	111	44	13	35	8	14
$2000–3999	173	34	14	39	13	20
$4000–5999	223	21	11	46	22	28
$6000–7999	253	21	11	44	24	31
$8000–9999	168	18	7	51	24	29
$10,000–14,999	158	13	8	50	29	34
$15,000+	89	15	4	57	24	28
Women						
Under $2000	238	63	13	21	3	8
$2000–3999	277	60	14	21	5	11
$4000–5999	324	47	16	34	3	7
$6000–7999	268	29	23	42	6	8
$8000–9999	219	28	19	47	6	8
$10,000–14,999	157	18	25	52	5	6
$15,000+	85	17	17	60	6	7

The proportion of heavy drinkers was lowest in the two income groups under $4000. Men and women differed in that the proportion of heavy drinkers among drinkers was lowest among men with family incomes of less than $4000, but no lower than average among women from households of this low income level. This difference by sex is consistent with the findings of the ISP analysis (Table 3).

Occupation (Table 6)

The findings by occupational distribution show a number of patterns which are probably not attributable merely to the fact that the various occupational groups reflect differences in income:

1. The largest proportion of abstainers was found, among both

TABLE 6.—*Percentage of Respondents in Q–F–V Groups, by Occupation of Chief Breadwinner and Sex*

	N	Abst.	In- freq.	Light + Mod.	Heavy	% Heavy of All Drinkers
Total sample	2746	32	15	41	12	18
Professional	288	19	13	59	9	11
Manager, proprietor, official	512	25	13	47	15	20
Semiprofessional, technical	81	22	9	53	16	21
Farm owner	134	58	15	21	6	14
Clerical	217	30	16	43	11	16
Sales	141	21	13	55	11	14
Craftsman, foreman	558	34	16	39	11	17
Operative	471	38	17	30	15	24
Service worker	179	39	12	35	14	23
Laborer (incl. farm labor)	149	43	13	34	10	18
No family breadwinner	16					
Men						
Professional	122	18	6	61	15	18
Manager, proprietor, official	245	19	8	49	24	30
Semiprofessional, technical	39	24	4	43	29	38
Farm owner	61	40	11	37	12	20
Clerical	64	21	5	50	24	30
Sales	68	21	7	51	21	27
Craftsman, foreman	256	23	14	44	19	25
Operative	203	27	12	35	26	36
Service worker	54	14	8	54	24	28
Laborer (incl. farm labor)	65	25	16	39	20	27
Women						
Professional	166	19	19	57	5	6
Manager, proprietor, official	267	30	19	45	6	9
Semiprofessional, technical	42	20	14	61	5	6
Farm owner	73	74	19	7	0	0
Clerical	153	34	21	40	5	8
Sales	73	21	19	59	1	1
Craftsman, foreman	302	44	18	34	4	7
Operative	268	46	21	27	6	11
Service worker	125	52	15	25	8	17
Laborer (incl. farm labor)	84	58	10	29	3	7

men and women, in the farm-owner group—40% of men and 74% of women.

2. The largest proportions of drinkers (nonabstainers) were in the professional, semiprofessional, and technical, sales and managerial groups. Here there were some notable differences by sex, however. While men from families in which the chief breadwinner was a manager or official had about the same proportion of drinkers

as those in the professional group, the men from primarily business families had almost twice as many heavy drinkers among the drinkers. On the other hand, materially more women from such families were abstainers (30%) than were women in professional families (19%), although the proportion of heavy drinkers among those who drank at all was as high or higher among women in managerial as among those in professional families.

3. One category that showed sharp differences between men and women was families in which a service worker was the chief breadwinner. In such families, very few men were abstainers (14%) but relatively many women (52%) were. But women drinkers from service worker families had the highest proportion of heavy drinkers of any occupational group; this was not true of men. Here is another illustration of the tendency for heavy drinking among women to be found relatively more often at the lower-status levels.

4. Among men semiprofessional and technical workers and operatives, the proportion of heavy drinkers was relatively high.

It should be pointed out here that these tabulations on occupation are in terms of the job held by the chief breadwinner of the family, on the ground that the main earner's occupation generally will be a better index of the family's life style and social status than will the occupations of respondents with other positions in the household (e.g., housewives or adult sons or daughters).

Education (Table 7)

Education is one of the variables entering into the ISP findings reported above. Table 7, however, reveals some sharper contrasts than the ISP tabulations. One important finding is that the highest proportions of abstainers in both men and women are found among those with only grammar-school education. This difference is specially noticeable among women. Women college graduates were much more likely than other women to be drinkers, but they were much less likely to be heavy drinkers if they drank. Women who had gone to college but who had not graduated had a higher proportion of heavy drinkers among drinkers than those who graduated.

Marital Status (Tables 8, 9)

The single and the divorced or separated had a higher proportion of heavy drinkers on the average than the married or widowed, both

TABLE 7.—*Percentage of Respondents in Q–F–V Groups, by Educational Level and Sex*

	N	Abst.	Infreq.	Light + Mod.	Heavy	% Heavy of All Drinkers
Total sample	2746	32	15	41	12	18
Grammar school or less	710	47	13	29	11	20
Some high school	554	34	16	40	10	15
Completed high school	723	26	18	42	14	19
Some college	444	26	13	46	15	20
College graduate	315	18	11	59	12	15
Men						
Grammar school or less	306	33	11	37	19	28
Some high school	230	25	12	46	17	22
Completed high school	266	16	10	46	28	33
Some college	194	17	9	49	25	31
College graduate	181	17	7	57	19	23
Women						
Grammar school or less	404	60	15	22	3	8
Some high school	324	41	19	36	4	8
Completed high school	457	31	22	41	6	9
Some college	250	33	17	44	6	10
College graduate	134	19	16	63	2	3

among men and women (Table 8). Widows and widowers tended to have the lowest percentages of both drinkers and heavy drinkers, doubtless because of their usually higher age and lower socioeconomic status.

The results are consistent with an interpretation of marital status as a factor in life adjustment, in which it would be expected that the divorced or separated would be less well adjusted and would have a higher proportion of heavy drinkers than those who were currently married and living with their spouses. As in all surveys conducted at one point of time, however, it cannot be established from the correlational data which came first, the separation or the heavy drinking.

When drinking is analyzed by marital status after holding constant sex, age and social position (to control for the fact that an above-average share of the abstainers are women, older persons and those of low socioeconomic status), the connection between heavy drinking and being single or divorced or separated holds true to a marked degree only in men and women of lower socioeconomic status under age 45 (Table 9).

TABLE 8.—*Percentage of Respondents in Q–F–V Groups, by Marital Status and Sex*

	N	Abst.	Infreq.	Light + Mod.	Heavy	% Heavy of All Drinkers
Total sample	2746	32	15	41	12	18
Married	2027	31	15	42	12	17
Single	213	26	10	45	19	26
Divorced or separated	175	28	14	43	15	21
Widowed	331	55	16	26	3	7
Men						
Married	971	23	10	46	21	27
Single	110	17	8	47	28	34
Divorced or separated	45	31	7	37	25	36
Widowed	51	40	14	37	9	15
Women						
Married	1056	38	19	39	4	6
Single	103	38	13	42	7	11
Divorced or separated	130	27	17	45	11	15
Widowed	280	57	17	24	2	5

Children in Household (Table 10)

The presence of children in the home might affect drinking patterns in either of two ways: (*a*) they might be expected to contribute toward moderation in drinking because of the social control inherent in parents' being expected to set a good example; or, on the other hand, (*b*) it is possible that their presence might add sufficient stress to result in an increase in drinking. While the differences found in this connection were not material, a slightly higher proportion of the women with children at home proved to be heavy drinkers than of women who were married but had no children at home.

Parental vs Nonparental Rearing (Table 11)

The drinking behavior of adults might be expected to vary from the norm in persons who were not reared by both their parents, on the assumption that resultant disadvantages in the form of relative deprivations and inconsistency in behavior norms would be associated with a higher rate of heavy drinking. Table 11 provides a partial test of these assumptions. In the aggregate, there was not much difference in general level of drinking between persons who did and did not live with both parents up to the age of 16, except

TABLE 9.—*Percentage of Respondents in Q–F–V Groups, by Marital Status, Age, Index of Social Position and Sex*

	MEN				WOMEN			
	N	Abst. + Infreq.	Light + Mod.	Heavy	N	Abst. + Infreq.	Light + Mod.	Heavy
Total sample	1177	33	46	21	1569	58	37	5
Age 21-44								
Higher ISP[a]								
Married	279	22	55	23	322	40	54	6
Single, divorced, separated[b]	53	19	58	23	74	37	58	5
Lower ISP								
Married	232	30	49	21	313	65	31	4
Single, divorced, separated	43	20	42	38	62	47	36	17
Age 45+								
Higher ISP								
Married	224	31	48	21	187	54	43	3
Single, divorced, separated	20	c	c	c	56	49	45	6
Lower ISP								
Married	236	49	32	19	232	70	27	3
Single, divorced, separated	39	41	34	25	41	67	27	6

[a] Higher ISP = Hollingshead scores of 11–48; Lower = 49–77. The same dividing points are used in all subsequent tables which show two ISP groups.

[b] There were too few widowed persons in the sample to permit a detailed breakdown by sex, age and ISP. Because their drinking patterns were likely to be quite different from those of other nonmarried people, they were not combined with this group. See Table 10 for an analysis by sex and age.

[c] Too few cases for analysis.

TABLE 10.—*Percentage of Respondents in Q-F-V Groups, by Children in Household, Marital Status, Sex and Age*

	MEN				WOMEN			
	N	Abst. + Infreq.	Light + Mod.	Heavy	N	Abst. + Infreq.	Light + Mod.	Heavy
Total sample	1177	33	46	21	1569	58	37	5
Age 21–44								
Single	78	18	52	30	56	43	48	9
Married	511	25	53	22	635	52	42	6
No children at home	70	23	54	23	62	57	40	3
Children at home	441	26	52	22	572	51	43	6
Divorced, separated	18	a	a	a	80	41	46	13
Widowed	2	a	a	a	19	a	a	a
Age 45+								
Single	32	44	35	21	47	63	32	5
Married	460	40	40	20	419	63	34	3
No children at home	264	44	38	18	258	64	35	1
Children at home	196	36	42	22	160	62	32	6
Divorced, separated	27	50	29	21	50	49	44	7
Widowed	49	54	37	9	260	76	23	1

ᵃ Too few cases for analysis.

TABLE 11.—*Percentage of Respondents in Q–F–V Groups, by Parental vs Nonparental Rearing, Sex, Age and Index of Social Position*

	MEN				WOMEN			
	N	Abst. + Infreq.	Light + Mod.	Heavy	N	Abst. + Infreq.	Light + Mod.	Heavy
Total sample	1177	33	46	21	1569	58	37	5
Lived with both parents most of time before age 16	991	33	47	20	1314	58	37	5
Did not live with both parents	186	32	39	29	252	55	40	5
Age 21–44								
Higher ISP								
Lived with both parents	287	20	57	23	348	40	54	6
Not with both	47	29	50	21	57	41	53	6
Lower ISP								
Lived with both parents	227	28	48	24	315	62	31	7
Not with both	48	26	48	26	70	59	34	7
Age 45+								
Higher ISP								
Lived with both parents	222	32	49	19	305	57	40	3
Not with both	34	36	29	35	49	52	44	4
Lower ISP								
Lived with both parents	255	51	33	16	346	75	23	2
Not with both	57	39	30	31	76	65	32	3

that the proportion of heavy drinkers was slightly higher in men brought up by only one parent or by others than in men who lived with both parents until age 16.

Analysis of the results by sex, age and ISP shows that there was little difference in the drinking of younger men or women of either upper or lower ISP who were raised by both parents, compared to those who were not. There was a tendency, however, for more older women (45 years and over) who as children had not lived with both parents, especially those of lower ISP, to be drinkers, although more in moderate than in heavy terms.

There was also a noticeable difference in drinking between the two groups of older men at both upper and lower ISP levels. Among older men of above average status who were raised by both their parents, only 19% were heavy drinkers, while among the comparable group not raised by both parents, 35% were heavy drinkers. Similarly, among older men in lower ISP groups who were raised by both parents, 16% were heavy drinkers, compared with 31% of those not raised by both parents.

The above findings lead to the inference that there is a tendency on the part of men who are not raised by both parents to develop into heavy drinkers relatively late in life (after the age of 45). The causes are obscure.

Region of the Country (Table 12)

There were considerable regional differences in drinking. The highest proportions of both drinkers and heavy drinkers were in the Middle Atlantic, New England, Pacific and East North Central areas, all of which are relatively urban in character. Lowest proportions of drinkers occurred in the East South Central states, followed by other southern areas and the Mountain States.[7]

The southern sections of the country, in general, showed a lower-than-average proportion of persons drinking. These findings are consistent with the other results in this survey regarding the connection between drinking practices and both degree of urbanization and socioeconomic level: the South is relatively less urban and less well-to-do than the other areas which show higher levels of drinking.

---

[7] Findings in the Mountain States are not as conclusive as in the other areas, since they are based on fewer than 100 interviews from only 3 areas, including 1 in predominantly Mormon Utah.

TABLE 12.—*Percentage of Respondents in Q–F–V Groups, by Region and Sex*

	N	Abst.	Infreq.	Light + Mod.	Heavy	% Heavy of All Drinkers
Total sample	2746	32	15	41	12	18
New England	155	21	16	47	16	20
Middle Atlantic	493	17	14	50	19	23
South Atlantic	350	42	15	34	9	16
East South Central	245	65	9	21	5	15
East North Central	599	25	17	45	13	17
West South Central	246	38	15	38	9	15
West North Central	238	34	18	40	8	12
Mountain	87	42	17	32	9	16
Pacific	333	27	11	47	15	21
Men						
New England	61	7	9	55	29	31
Middle Atlantic	219	11	7	48	34	38
South Atlantic	151	32	14	42	12	18
East South Central	95	49	11	30	10	20
East North Central	266	19	8	49	24	30
West South Central	99	25	14	47	14	19
West North Central	93	31	14	44	11	16
Mountain	45	36	13	37	14	22
Pacific	148	17	7	50	26	31
Women						
New England	94	31	21	41	7	10
Middle Atlantic	274	23	20	52	5	6
South Atlantic	199	50	16	27	7	14
East South Central	150	75	7	15	3	12
East North Central	333	31	24	41	4	6
West South Central	147	48	15	33	4	8
West North Central	145	36	21	37	6	9
Mountain	42	50	23	24	3	6
Pacific	185	35	15	44	6	9

Another factor is religion: the more conservative Protestant denominations (which frown upon alcohol) are more prevalent in the South than elsewhere.

"Wet" and *"Dry"* Areas (Table 13)

Another geographic variable is the matter of local control laws. Table 13 presents the findings on the rates of drinking in three types of areas, classified according to the legal availability of alcoholic beverages.

One type of dry area (local communities), which contained 49% abstainers, was found in the East North Central area; another

TABLE 13.—*Percentage of Respondents in Q–F–V Groups, by Legal Availability of Alcoholic Beverages*

	N	Abst.	In-freq.	Light + Mod.	Heavy	% Heavy of All Drinkers
Total sample	2746	32	15	41	12	18
Legal Availability						
Local community permits sale of both beer and spirits	2442	28	15	44	13	18
Local community prohibits sale of spirits (beer also in some instances); both available in other areas of the county	100	49	8	35	8	16
Local community and county prohibit sale of spirits (beer also in some instances); both available in adjacent counties or states	204	65	11	18	6	17

type (counties), where 65% were abstainers, were all southern areas which generally have relatively high proportions of abstainers. These findings contrast with 28% abstainers in areas permitting the sale of all types of alcoholic beverages.

The findings show that while a materially lower than average number of drinkers was reported in both types of areas where distilled spirits cannot be sold legally, a substantial proportion of respondents in legally "dry" areas reported they did drink more than once a year. And, among those in these areas who said they did drink, the proportions of heavy drinkers were about average.

Degree of Urbanization (Tables 14–18)

There are proportionately more drinkers in large cities than in smaller communities, a finding also noted by Riley and Marden (61) and Mulford (56). In order to study this phenomenon a little more closely, our results relating to urbanization were examined in several ways.

1. *Community Size and Type* (Tables 14–16). Sharp differences can be noted in proportions of drinkers according to the degree of urbanization (Table 14). Those drinking at least once a month

TABLE 14.—*Percentage of Respondents in Q–F–V Groups, by Degree of Urbanization and Sex*

	N	Abst.	In-freq.	Light + Mod.	Heavy	% Heavy of All Drinkers
Total sample	2746	32	15	41	12	18
SMSA[a]						
CC[a] over 1 million	260	21	16	45	18	23
CC 50,000–1 million	554	26	14	44	16	22
Outside CC, 50,000– 1 million	189	13	15	60	12	14
Cities 2500–49,999	422	17	16	50	17	20
Nonfarm under 2500	297	31	18	44	7	10
Non-SMSA						
Cities 2500–49,999	372	37	12	40	11	17
Nonfarm under 2500	466	52	12	28	8	17
Farm	186	57	15	23	5	12
Men						
SMSA						
CC over 1 million	109	12	8	46	34	39
CC 50,000–1 million	226	22	8	43	27	35
Outside CC, 50,000– 1 million	87	11	7	59	23	26
Cities 2500–49,999	185	13	6	52	29	33
Nonfarm under 2500	135	24	17	46	13	17
Non-SMSA						
Cities 2500–49,999	140	22	9	49	20	26
Nonfarm under 2500	207	35	12	39	14	22
Farm	88	37	15	39	9	14
Women						
SMSA						
CC over 1 million	151	29	22	44	5	7
CC 50,000–1 million	328	29	19	44	8	11
Outside CC, 50,000– 1 million	102	14	22	61	3	3
Cities 2500–49,999	237	20	24	49	7	9
Nonfarm under 2500	162	37	19	41	3	5
Non-SMSA						
Cities 2500–49,999	232	46	15	34	5	9
Nonfarm under 2500	259	67	12	19	2	6
Farm	98	75	15	9	1	4

[a] SMSA = Standard Metropolitan Statistical Area; CC = central city.

(classified as light drinkers or higher) ranged from only 28% among farm people to 72% among those living in communities of 50,000 to 1 million population which are within metropolitan areas but are not the central cities of such areas (they were chiefly large suburbs).

Heavy drinker rates among those who drank once a year or more did not exactly parallel the rates of drinking in general. The suburban group just mentioned as having the highest rate of total drinkers was among the lowest in rate of heavy drinkers among drinkers. The highest rate of heavy drinkers among drinkers was found among residents of the largest cities, even though these showed a lower proportion of drinkers than did suburban areas. Nonfarm and farm rural areas in general showed relatively low rates of both drinking and heavy drinking.

The same general pattern of differences in the incidence of drinking by degree of urbanization holds for both men and women. There are some contrasts, however, between men and women in the various types of urban areas with respect to drinking versus heavy drinking. A comparison of these differences is given in Table 15.

The difference in percentage of men and women drinkers was lowest in the suburbs of large cities, where the proportions were almost equal. The difference in drinkers was relatively high in the nonmetropolitan and rural areas. On the other hand, the difference in the proportion of men and women heavy drinkers was relatively

TABLE 15.—*Sex Differences in the Percentage of Drinkers and Heavy Drinkers, by Urbanization*

	DRINKERS			HEAVY DRINKERS		
	Men	Women	% Difference	Men	Women	% Difference
Total sample	77	60	17	21	5	16
SMSA						
CC over 1 million	88	71	17	34	5	29
CC 50,000–1 million	78	71	7	27	8	19
Outside CC, 50,000– 1 million	89	86	3	23	3	20
Cities 2500–49,999	87	80	7	29	7	22
Nonfarm under 2500	76	63	13	13	3	10
Non-SMSA						
Cities 2500–49,999	78	54	24	20	5	15
Nonfarm under 2500	65	33	32	14	2	12
Farm	63	25	38	9	1	8

low in the nonmetropolitan and rural areas (where there are fewer heavy drinkers in general), but greater in the more urbanized areas —i.e., a substantially higher proportion of men than women in the larger central cities were heavy drinkers.

Among the primary correlates of high suburban rates of drinking (usually accompanied by relatively modest rates of heavy drinkers) is a higher income level in such suburbs.[8] For this reason it is important to examine the relationship of urbanization to drinking behavior when sex, age and ISP are controlled. The results of this subgroup analysis are presented in Table 16:

(1) Among both men and women in both ISP groups, the more highly urbanized groups contained fewer abstainers or infrequent drinkers and more heavy drinkers than the less urbanized. The same contrast is evident where age is also held constant. (2) The highest proportion of abstainers and infrequent drinkers was found in the 45-years-and-over–lower-ISP–lower-urbanization group among both men and women (65 and 81% respectively); while the highest proportions of heavy drinkers were found in the 21-to-44-years–lower-ISP–higher-urbanization group (34 and 11%).

The data can also be looked at in terms of the interactions of urbanization and ISP with drinking habits. Among the more highly urbanized men, for example, those of lower ISP had approximately the same proportion of abstainers and infrequent drinkers (24%) as those of higher ISP (23%), but more heavy drinkers (32 to 25%); while, among the less urbanized, in contrast, those of lower ISP had a lower proportion of heavy drinkers.

Thus degree of urbanization appears to be related in various ways to drinking by people of different social status. It may be that these variations reflect different social pressures regarding drinking on the part of those of lower status, with greater social control in the smaller cities and urban areas. Another possibility might be independent or interacting psychological pressures (such as alienation or the pace of work or of living) among those of lower ISP in large cities compared to residents of smaller cities. An additional factor, selective immigration of potential heavy drinkers into the larger cities, is examined below.

[8] For examples, 68% of those living in suburbs outside cities of 50,000 to 1 million had family incomes of $8000 or more, in contrast to only 30% among respondents in the very largest class of city.

TABLE 16.—*Percentage of Respondents in Q–F–V Groups, by Urbanization, Index of Social Position, Sex and Age*

	MEN				WOMEN			
	N	Abst. + Infreq.	Light + Mod.	Heavy	N	Abst. + Infreq.	Light + Mod.	Heavy
Total sample	1177	33	46	21	1569	58	37	5
Higher ISP								
Higher urbanization[a]	327	23	52	25	424	36	58	6
Lower urbanization	269	31	51	18	344	61	35	4
Lower ISP								
Higher urbanization	280	24	44	32	394	56	37	7
Lower urbanization	301	53	36	11	407	78	20	2
Age 21–44								
Higher ISP								
Higher urbanization	175	18	57	25	200	28	64	8
Lower urbanization	159	25	55	20	207	51	45	4
Lower ISP								
Higher urbanization	134	16	50	34	192	47	42	11
Lower urbanization	141	40	45	15	191	76	22	2
Age 45+								
Higher ISP								
Higher urbanization	152	28	47	25	221	44	53	3
Lower urbanization	110	39	46	15	137	76	20	4
Lower ISP								
Higher urbanization	146	31	38	31	202	65	32	3
Lower urbanization	160	65	28	7	216	81	17	2

[a] Higher urbanization = SMSA areas of 2500 or more; Lower = SMSA areas under 2500 and all non-SMSA areas.

2. *Size of Town Where Lived When Young* (Tables 17, 18). Consistent with the findings concerning degree of urbanization of respondents' present residence, those who grew up on farms included substantially higher proportions of abstainers and lower proportions of heavy drinkers. The lowest rate of abstainers (14%) was found among those raised in large cities; the proportion rises markedly as size of childhood home town decreases (Table 17).

The correlation of drinking behavior with movement from one size of town to another can be explored to a limited extent by tabulating the size of town in which the respondent lived when he was young (under 16) against the size of city in which he now lives. The only dividing point available for this analysis of movement is at the rather small city size of 25,000. Table 18 (in which sex and age are controlled) compares those who moved from larger to smaller cities (or the converse) to those who stayed in larger or smaller areas most or all of their lives:

(*1*) Men now aged 21 to 44 years who lived in smaller places before the age of 16 did not show any difference in rates of heavy drinkers regardless of whether they were now still living in smaller cities or had moved to larger cities. Also, men now 45 years or older who had lived in larger cities before the age of 16 showed little difference in rates of heavy drinkers regardless of whether they continued to live in larger cities or moved to smaller places. However, young men who moved from larger to smaller cities had a lower proportion of heavy drinkers than the young men who re-

TABLE 17.—*Percentage of Respondents in Q–F–V Groups, by Size of Community Lived in Before Age 16*

	N	Abst.	In-freq.	Light + Mod.	Heavy	% Heavy of All Drinkers
Total sample	2746	32	15	41	12	18
City of more than 500,000	406	14	16	51	19	22
100,000 to 500,000	259	18	14	51	17	21
25,000 to 100,000	256	22	17	51	10	13
5000 to 25,000	384	25	12	44	19	25
Town of less than 5000	434	37	14	38	11	17
In the country but not on a farm	163	32	18	40	10	15
In the country on a farm	843	49	14	31	6	12

TABLE 18.—Percentage of Respondents in Q-F-V Groups, by Movement from Original Community, Sex and Age

	MEN				WOMEN			
	N	Abst. + Infreq.	Light + Mod.	Heavy	N	Abst. + Infreq.	Light + Mod.	Heavy
Total sample	1177	33	46	21	1569	58	37	5
Age 21–44								
Lived in larger cities[a] before age 16, now live in:								
Larger cities	129	14	53	33	191	38	54	8
Smaller places	94	16	65	19	122	41	48	11
Lived in smaller cities[a] before age 16, now live in:								
Larger cities	100	22	57	21	125	37	51	12
Smaller places	286	33	46	21	352	66	32	2
Age 45+								
Lived in larger cities before age 16, now live in:								
Larger cities	115	30	42	28	171	51	45	4
Smaller places	49	24	42	34	47	37	60	3
Lived in smaller cities before age 16, now live in:								
Larger cities	136	36	38	26	186	61	37	2
Smaller places	267	53	37	10	372	78	20	2

[a] Larger cities = 25,000 population or more.

mained in larger cities; and the older men who moved from smaller to larger cities showed a higher proportion of heavy drinkers than the older men who remained in smaller cities. (2) Younger women who lived in larger cities before age 16 did not show much difference in their present level of drinking, whether they still lived in large cities or had moved to smaller ones (perhaps some of the movement to smaller cities was to the suburbs, where a relatively high proportion of women drink). On the other hand, women under 45 years who moved from smaller to larger cities were distinctly more likely to be heavy drinkers than those who stayed in smaller cities. And similarly, women aged 45 and older who had moved from smaller to larger cities were less likely than nonmovers to be abstainers or infrequent drinkers.

The results clearly indicate a tendency to conform to the prevailing drinking customs when one moves to a different-sized locality from that in which one was brought up. The hypothesis can be extended to cover moves made in adult life, as many of these undoubtedly were; but more data on changes in drinking associated with new life situations would be useful. The national follow-up study now being conducted will attempt to determine to what extent people who move continue their old drinking habits or adopt new ones.

Range of Drinking in Interviewing Localities (Table 19)

It has been demonstrated that there are large differences in drinking levels within the various regions and by degree of urbanization. There is evidence also that there may be great variability in drinking practices among individual communities or neighborhoods. Table 19 has been prepared to illustrate how great this range of drinking practices may be in the various neighborhoods across the United States. In preparing this table, the levels of

TABLE 19.—*Percentage of Respondents in Q–F–V Groups, by Proportion of Abstainers and Infrequent Drinkers in Community*

	N	Abst. + Infreq.	Light + Mod.	Heavy
Communities highest in percentage of abstainers and infrequent drinkers	266	85	13	2
Communities lowest in percentage of abstainers and infrequent drinkers	284	13	68	19

drinking were tabulated separately for all 100 interviewing localities. Then the average was computed for the 10 areas highest in
percentage of abstainers and infrequent drinkers, and for the 10
areas lowest in these classifications.

The results in Table 19 illustrate that a substantial number of
neighborhoods (or sampling clusters equivalent to a few city blocks
in population) exist which have an average of under 15% of adults
reporting they drink as often as once a month, as well as a substantial number of neighborhoods in which an average of about 85%
drink at least once a month and in which about one-fifth could be
classified as heavy drinkers. These differences would be watered
down somewhat—but only somewhat—if one were to take into account the proportions of men in each of these two combinations of
sampling clusters, since the proportion of men (more of whom
drink) was somewhat higher (50%) in the set of clusters containing
the highest percentage of drinkers, compared to the clusters with
the lowest proportion of drinkers (which were only 40% male).

In noting the very large differences between these two groups
of areas, it must be borne in mind that each interviewing assignment normally was drawn from a single census enumeration district,
and that the results for any one assignment reflect results for that
small area only, not the whole city or county from which the district
was chosen. The results do show clearly, however, that individual
neighborhoods can vary tremendously in the drinking habits of
their residents. Future research may well show that much of the
variability from neighborhood to neighborhood can be explained
in terms of the distribution of such familiar correlates of drinking
as the sex, age, socioeconomic status, size and type of city, region,
and ethnocultural status of its residents; but perhaps there may
remain a substantial proportion of intercluster variability in drinking which remains to be explained by other factors such as historical
evolution of local drinking practices.

In any case, the high variability of drinking from neighborhood
to neighborhood underscores the need for great care in sampling
in studies of drinking behavior in order to give appropriate representation to the various types of communities. It also suggests that
more intensive study of the characteristics of communities with
high and low drinking rates should be fruitful in explaining the
origins of drinking norms.

Race (Table 20)

White and Negro men varied little in their rates of drinking. However, Negro women differed from White women both in their much higher proportions of abstainers and in their higher rate of heavy drinkers. These results are consistent with the findings of a New York City study reported in 1965 by Bailey, Haberman and Alksne (4) and with an analysis of alcoholism death rates in 1941 reported by Jellinek (31).

These differences may stem from many possible causes such as differences in economic status and in social patterns or controls. The higher rate of abstinence among Negro women may be attributable to lack of money to buy alcoholic beverages or to differences in life styles and general standards of living. The higher proportion of heavy drinkers among Negro women may stem from either greater alienation or unhappiness among the economically deprived, or from the more frequent filling of the (more "manlike") role of head of the household among Negro women (50), which might entail more stress or less of certain kinds of familial constraints against heavy drinking.

Ethnic Background (Tables 21–25)

Most (91%) of the respondents themselves were born in the United States, and 74% said their fathers were also born in this country. These findings underscore the fairly rapid passing of the status of the United States as a melting pot of recent immigrants.

TABLE 20.—*Percentage of Respondents in Q–F–V Groups, by Race and Sex*

	N	Abst.	Infreq.	Light + Mod.	Heavy	% Heavy of All Drinkers
Total sample	2746	32	15	41	12	18
White	2511[a]	31	15	42	12	17
Negro	200	38	12	36	14	23
Men						
White	1082	23	10	45	22	29
Negro	82	21	13	47	19	24
Women						
White	1429	39	19	38	4	7
Negro	118	51	11	27	11	22

[a] Excluded are 35 persons of other races.

Nevertheless, ethnic background still plays an important part in determining patterns of American life, including drinking habits (5, 20, 25, 67, 69, 70).

Several studies have shown the differences in drinking habits of various ethnic and nationality groups. Lolli and his associates (46) found that Italians in Italy and first-generation Italians in the United States drink very frequently but have extremely low rates of alcoholism or problem drinking, but that subsequent-generation American Italians have higher rates of heavier drinking. Sadoun, Lolli and Silverman (65) have presented a good deal of evidence which indicates that the rate of alcoholism is substantially lower among Italians than among the French, even though superficially both countries would appear to have primarily the same type of wine-drinking culture. Snyder has discussed the ritual drinking of Jews in relationship to their low level of alcoholism and delinquency related to alcohol (66, 67); and Glad (24) and Bales (5) have presented comparative research findings and anecdotal evidence bearing upon the relatively high rate of alcoholism among the Irish in comparison to other ethnic and nationality groups. An inference to be drawn from these studies is that there is no necessary correlation between widespread drinking and a high incidence of alcoholism: in most instances, in the ethnic groups in which alcoholic beverages in low concentration (wine or beer) are available on an everyday basis to all members of the family (including the children) and are drunk with meals or at ceremonies within the family circle, the rate of alcoholism appears to be lower than when alcohol (specially in stronger drinks) is drunk less routinely and more as a means of escape from problems or social controls. The following findings bear out the principal conclusions of the studies mentioned above.

1. *Native vs Foreign Born* (Table 21). Because of the small numbers of foreign born in the sample (9%), it is not possible to

TABLE 21.—*Percentage of Respondents in Q–F–V Groups, by Place of Birth*

	N	Abst.	In-freq.	Light + Mod.	Heavy	% Heavy of All Drinkers
Total sample	2746	32	15	41	12	18
White, born in U. S. A.	2273	32	15	41	12	18
All others born in U. S. A.	221	39	12	35	14	23
All foreign born	252	23	16	51	10	13

compare foreign-born respondents by specific country of origin. However, the aggregate of those born outside the United States can be compared with native-born Americans, as shown in Table 21. To control for the factor of race, the native born have been divided into two groups, Whites and others (Negroes or Asiatics in ethnic origin). The results show that the foreign born were less likely than either of the native-born groups to be abstainers, and more likely to be light or moderate drinkers. On the other hand, foreign-born drinkers were also less likely to be heavy drinkers than were members of either of the two groups born in the U. S. A.

2. *Father's Country of Origin* (Tables 22, 23). More of those with foreign-born fathers tended to drink (80%) than did those whose fathers were born in the United States (64%). The two groups were about equal, however, in the proportions of heavy drinkers among drinkers (Table 22). Table 22 also shows that those whose fathers came from Italy tended to lead most groups in the proportion of heavy drinkers, both when computed on the total persons interviewed and when computed on the total drinkers.

TABLE 22.—*Percentage of Respondents in Q–F–V Groups, by Father's Country of Origin*

	N	Abst.	In-freq.	Light + Mod.	Heavy	% Heavy of All Drinkers
Total sample	2746	32	15	41	12	18
Father born in U. S. A.	2038	36	13	40	11	18
Father foreign born	708	20	18	47	15	19
Father's Country of Origin						
United Kingdom	65	16	25	41	18	21
Ireland	41	16	15	55	14	17
Canada	43	21	19	45	15	19
Italy	101	8	14	58	20	22
Latin America or Caribbean	51	36	10	35	19	30
Eastern Europe (Russia, Poland, Baltics)	115	16	22	47	15	18
Germany	91	20	16	55	9	11
Other European	173	26	17	44	13	18
Others[a] (not tabulated)	28					

[a] Includes 12 whose fathers were born in Asia, 10 from miscellaneous countries, and 6 who were uncertain about their father's country of origin.

Because of differences in the tides of immigration of the various nationality groups, the comparisons need refinement to take into account the differences in the age levels of respondents whose fathers were born in the different countries. For example, those whose fathers came from Latin America or from the Caribbean or from Italy were younger than those whose fathers were born in Ireland or Germany; and, as we have seen earlier, drinking varies markedly by age. Accordingly, Table 23 presents a revised analysis in which age is held constant by applying the method of standardization used by Rosenberg (63). With this adjustment, those whose fathers were born in Ireland are seen to have the highest proportion of drinkers (93%) and heavy drinkers (31%) followed at some distance by those whose fathers came from the United Kingdom, Italy and Latin America or the Caribbean.

As has been seen, both the foreign born and their children were more likely than others to drink. Hence there appears to be a carry-over of previous drinking customs to America. When the "old country" tradition calls for drinking wine or beer with meals as is often

TABLE 23.—*Percentage of Respondents in Q–F–V Groups, by Father's Country of Origin, Standardized for Age Level*[a]

	N	Abst.	In-freq.	Light + Mod.	Heavy	% Heavy of All Drinkers
Total sample	2746	28	15	44	13	18
Father born in U. S. A.	2038	38	13	38	11	18
Father foreign born	708	18	17	50	15	18
Father's Country of Origin						
United Kingdom	65	11	23	42	24	27
Ireland	41	7	8	54	31	33
Canada	43	18	15	55	12	15
Italy	101	9	15	57	19	21
Latin America or Caribbean	51	39	15	29	17	28
Eastern Europe (Russia, Poland, Baltics)	115	15	23	48	14	16
Germany	91	15	15	57	13	15
Other European countries	173	23	14	48	15	19
Others (not tabulated)	28					

[a] The original data from Table 22 are standardized by five 10-year age groups to equalize the effect of differences in age distribution.

the case in Continental Europe, whence the bulk of our immigrants to date have come, the net effect might well be to make the children of immigrants heavier drinkers than their contemporaries. (For example, Italians brought up on wine may continue to drink it with meals and add beer and spirits, American-style, in the evenings, ending up in the moderate or heavy categories, although their parents may have been only light drinkers.)

The small size of the samples of persons whose fathers were born in the various countries do not warrant firm comparisons. But the results certainly throw open to question some often-accepted ideas about the drinking practices of various nationality groupings insofar as they are applicable to the habits of the second generation. For example, second-generation Germans show up as more moderate drinkers, as a group, than do those whose fathers were Italian. The results in the second-generation Italians suggest that assimilation into the drinking customs of the New World may be a relatively rapid process.

3. *National Identity* (Table 24). To fill the need for some measure of cultural ties which would go beyond the limited divisions into foreign born versus native born or father's country of birth, an index of national identity was developed for classifying all respondents. The index was based on the country of birth of the 26% of respondents who themselves or whose fathers were born outside the United States and, for others, upon responses to the question, "Which one nationality did most of your family come from?" This national-identity self-classification in many instances was more a matter of psychological identification than of close ethnic ties, since only one-fourth had fathers born outside the country and many families had been in the United States for many generations. Still, the index is useful in analyzing the relationships between ethnic origins and drinking practices in more detail than is possible through analyzing father's country of origin.

The findings on drinking practices by national identity are presented in Table 24. It can be seen that those identifying themselves as primarily Italian in origin had the highest proportion of drinkers, being followed fairly closely by those identifying themselves as Russian, Polish or Baltic. The Scotch-Irish had the highest proportion of abstainers among those identifying themselves with any nationality group. The proportion of heavy drinkers among drinkers

TABLE 24.—*Percentage of Respondents in Q–F–V Groups, by National Identity*

	N	Abst.	Infreq.	Light + Mod.	Heavy	% Heavy of All Drinkers
Total sample	2746	32	15	41	12	18
U.S. White[a]	139	54	15	26	5	11
U.S. others	216	39	11	36	14	23
English, Scotch	585	40	15	35	10	17
Irish	421	36	11	40	13	20
Scotch-Irish	72	50	11	31	8	16
Canadian	43	21	19	45	15	19
Italian	118	9	15	56	20	22
Latin-American, Caribbean	58	37	12	32	19	30
Russian, Polish, Baltic	148	14	23	46	17	20
German	491	26	15	48	11	15
Other European	429	27	15	46	12	16
Miscellaneous	26					

[a] Those who could not name any one nationality from which most of their family came were classified as "U.S.," divided into Whites and others.

was highest among those of Latin-American and Caribbean extraction, the U.S. Nonwhite, and the Italians, with little difference among the other groups.

4. *National Identity by Religion* (Table 25). The relationship of ethnic origins and drinking practices may be explored further by subdividing, where possible, the national identity subgroups by religion. The number of interviews with those identifying themselves as Canadian in extraction was too small to do this; and the Latin-American–Caribbean group did not lend themselves to this type of analysis because all were Roman Catholics. It was possible, however, to subdivide five of the largest groups by religion; the findings within these subgroups are presented in Table 25.

In the four subgroups where there were sufficient interviews to compare the drinking habits of the three major religious groupings, the Catholics were usually highest in proportion of drinkers, being closely followed by the "liberal" Protestants, with the "conservative" Protestants trailing far behind. The proportion of drinkers was highest among Italian and German Catholics and Russian–Polish–Baltic Jews. Catholics were also generally above average in the proportions of heavy drinkers; however, the highest percentage of

TABLE 25.—*Percentage of Respondents in Q–F–V Groups, by National Identity and Religion*[a]

	N	Abst.	In- freq.	Light + Mod.	Heavy	% Heavy of All Drinkers
Total sample	2746	32	15	41	12	18
English, Scotch, Welsh, Scotch-Irish						
Conservative Protestants[b]	417	50	13	30	7	14
Liberal Protestants	136	25	17	48	10	13
Catholics	64	16	23	40	21	25
Irish						
Conservative Protestants	217	53	13	30	4	9
Liberal Protestants	42	19	5	46	30	37
Catholics	145	16	9	53	22	26
German						
Conservative Protestants	216	40	16	35	9	15
Liberal Protestants	158	17	16	55	12	14
Catholics	96	12	13	60	15	17
Russian, Polish, Baltic						
Catholics	85	16	19	48	17	20
Jews	42	10	33	42	15	17
Italian						
Catholics	111	9	15	58	18	20
Other European						
Conservative Protestants	137	43	17	33	7	12
Liberal Protestants	86	20	9	59	12	15
Catholics	159	19	16	46	19	23

[a] Omits groups with insufficient cases to permit tabulation by separate national identity religious groups (e.g., Canadians, Latin American–Caribbean groups, and Italian Protestants).

[b] Denominations are classified as "conservative" or "liberal" only with respect to what is believed to be the general consensus of church leaders within the denomination with regard to alcohol.

heavy drinkers was found among the liberal Protestants of Irish national identity.[9]

The relationship of religion to drinking practices will be discussed in further detail in the next section. The findings thus far make it

[9] It must be noted, however, that liberal Irish Protestants are a relatively small group compared to those of Irish national identity who are Catholics or conservative Protestants. The relatively large number of Irish Protestants, compared to Catholics, probably stems in part from a failure on the part of respondents to distinguish between Northern and Southern Ireland when asked their national background; thus many of them may actually have come from essentially Protestant northern Irish or Scotch-Irish families. In other cases, depending on the time and area of immigration, their forebears are likely to have assimilated much of the religious culture and drinking patterns of the region to which they have moved.

clear that there is a definite association between religion and both drinking and heavy drinking, even when national identity group is held constant. The relationship can be inferred to be a functional one insofar as the role of conservative Protestantism is concerned, for the denominations within this group (by definition) disapprove of drinking. However, it cannot be inferred that Catholic or liberal Protestant status alone is responsible for a higher proportion of drinkers in these groups. As will be seen in the next section, differences in socioeconomic status among the religious groups account for some of it. Yet a contributing factor is undoubtedly the more permissive attitude toward drinking within Catholic and liberal Protestant milieus, stemming not necessarily from religious factors but from differences in general cultural heritage.

Religion (Tables 26–31)

Alcohol has played a part in religious ritual throughout history. With both religion and alcohol being involved in people's lives on a primary-group (family, clan or tribal) basis from time immemorial, correlations would be expected between religious and drinking behavior. Particularly because of the official stands against alcohol taken by conservative Protestant denominations, differences in drinking practices by religious groups in the United States would be expected. According to Pittman and Snyder (59, *p. 154*):

"It is now firmly established that different ethnic groups within the United States exhibit strikingly different rates of drinking. . . . There is evidence also that, despite a common core of opposition to drunkenness, the varieties of religious groups and traditions with which ethnicity is so often intertwined [exhibit] differences [which] persist with surprising tenacity over the generations. Collectively, these facts lend a special significance to the study of ethnic- and religious-group drinking patterns in the context of a concern to understand alcoholism . . . analogous to the challenge offered by Durkheim in connection with varying group rates of suicide."

1. Religious Affiliation (Tables 26, 27). That a relationship exists between nationality group, religion and drinking practices was shown in the previous section. The relationship of religion to drinking practices will now be analyzed in more detail.

As shown in Table 26, Jews and Episcopalians had the lowest rates of abstainers. Jews also had a relatively low rate of heavy drinkers. This is consistent with other studies (67). However, the

TABLE 26.—*Percentage of Respondents in Q–F–V Groups, by Religion and Sex*

	N	Abst.	In- freq.	Light + Mod.	Heavy	% Heavy of All Drinkers
Total sample	2746	32	15	41	12	18
Conservative Protestant	1305	48	14	31	7	13
Methodist and similar[a]	515	34	17	39	10	15
Baptist	521	53	11	29	7	17
Other conservative Protestant	269	64	12	21	3	8
Liberal Protestant[b]	471	20	15	52	13	16
Lutheran	207	19	14	52	15	19
Presbyterian	159	25	16	47	12	16
Episcopalian	80	9	13	66	12	13
Protestant, no denomination	46	35	10	35	20	29
Catholic	764	17	15	49	19	23
Jewish	73	8	26	56	10	11
No religion; not ascertained	69	21	13	46	20	25
Miscellaneous	18					
Men						
Conservative Protestant	550	35	13	39	13	20
Methodist and similar	219	26	16	40	18	24
Baptist	226	37	9	41	13	21
Other conservative Protestant	105	49	15	32	4	8
Liberal Protestant	193	13	8	56	23	26
Lutheran	84	14	7	54	25	29
Presbyterian	69	17	8	55	20	24
Episcopalian	32	2	8	65	25	26
Catholic	330	9	6	52	33	36
Jewish	27	4	11	60	25	26
Women						
Conservative Protestant	755	58	14	25	3	7
Methodist and similar	296	40	18	38	4	7
Baptist	295	66	13	18	3	9
Other conservative Protestant	164	75	10	13	2	8
Liberal Protestant	278	24	20	50	6	8
Lutheran	123	23	20	50	7	9
Presbyterian	90	31	21	41	7	10
Episcopalian	48	13	17	67	3	3
Catholic	434	22	22	47	9	10
Jewish	46	11	36	53	0	0

[a] Methodists, United Church of Christ, Congregationalist, Disciples of Christ, Evangelical, United Brethren.

[b] Liberal Protestants include a few persons of miscellaneous denominations in addition to the three denominations listed.

aggregate rate masks the fact of a fairly high number of heavy drinkers among Jewish men offset by the scarcity of such drinkers among Jewish women. These findings must be interpreted with caution because they are based on small samples. It would require further research with larger samples to test the finding of such a large difference between Jewish men and women, as well as any conclusions concerning their relative acculturation, but these findings do illustrate the necessity of analyzing data on drinking separately by sex.

The attempt to classify Protestants into conservative and liberal groups involved some arbitrary classifications, since some denominations differ from one congregation to another in their stand regarding abstinence. However, it will be seen that the liberal or conservative classification has practical usefulness in terms of distinguishing between abstainers and nonabstainers; for in all tabulations conservative Protestants were consistently higher in the proportion of abstainers than were those classified as liberal Protestants.

Those who belonged to the conservative Protestant denominations had the highest proportions of abstainers and relatively low rates of heavy drinking, although there was considerable range among the individual denominations in this group (e.g., materially more of the Baptists than of the Methodists were abstainers, although the proportion of heavy drinkers among those who drank was about the same in both groups).

Catholics had relatively high proportions of both drinkers and heavy drinkers. Liberal Protestants showed a pattern of drinking that was remarkably close to that of the Catholics as regards proportions of drinkers, but with fewer heavy drinkers.

The data of Table 26 have been restated in Table 27, which

TABLE 27.—*Sex Differences in the Percentage of Drinkers and Heavy Drinkers, by Religion*

	DRINKERS			HEAVY DRINKERS		
	Men	Women	% Difference	Men	Women	% Difference
Total sample	77	60	17	21	5	16
Conservative Protestants	65	42	23	13	3	10
Liberal Protestants	87	76	11	23	6	17
Catholics	91	78	13	33	9	24
Jews	96	89	7	25	0	25

draws some comparisons between men and women of the various religious groups:

(1) Jews showed highest similarity (i.e., least difference) between men and women in percentage of drinkers but great contrast in the rate of heavy drinkers. (2) Conservative Protestants showed the greatest difference in the proportions of men and women drinkers, but the least difference in heavy drinkers (because both groups were low). (3) Liberal Protestants and Catholics were intermediate in the similarity of men and women drinkers. There was relatively more difference among Catholics than among Protestants in the proportions who were heavy drinkers.

2. *Religion by Sex, Age and Social Position* (Table 28). Since this and other studies have established that both religious affiliation and drinking are interrelated with sex, age and socioeconomic status,[10] a special analysis was made to control for these factors in assessing drinking practices by different religious groups. Dividing respondents into eight sex–age–ISP groups as was done for the analyses of marital status and urbanization, we determined the Q–F–V classification of each of the three major religious groups within each subgroup. The results, as shown in Table 28, were as follows:

(1) Among men, when sex, age and ISP were controlled, the Catholics invariably had the highest proportions of heavy drinkers; the liberal Protestants were next, and the conservative Protestants generally had the smallest proportions. This difference was most marked among men of lower ISP in the 45-and-older group. (2) Among the women, the same relationship held in the higher ISP groups but not in the lower. The proportion of heavy drinkers was very low among conservative Protestant women, although the highest proportion of women heavy drinkers in any group was only 14% (among younger Catholic women of higher ISP). (3) In all subgroups, the conservative Protestants had the highest proportions of persons who drank less than once a month (abstainers and infrequent drinkers). Among older men, the liberal Protestants had more abstainers and infrequent drinkers than did the Catholics. (4) Among men, conservative Protestants had about the same proportion of abstainers and infrequent drinkers in both the upper

[10] In the present study, for example, 50% of the Jews and 40% of the Presbyterians had incomes of $10,000 or more, compared with only about 10% of Baptists and other conservative Protestants.

TABLE 28.—*Percentage of Respondents in Q-F-V Groups, by Sex, Index of Social Position, Religion and Age*

	MEN				WOMEN			
	N	Abst. + Infreq.	Light + Mod.	Heavy	N	Abst. + Infreq.	Light + Mod.	Heavy
Total sample	1177	33	46	21	1569	58	37	5
Higher ISP								
Conservative Protestants	239	46	42	12	325	64	34	2
Liberal Protestants	128	14	60	26	179	36	59	5
Catholics	165	10	58	32	185	33	56	11
Lower ISP								
Conservative Protestants	311	49	37	14	428	78	19	3
Liberal Protestants	65	36	48	16	99	59	34	7
Catholics	165	21	46	33	248	54	41	5
Age 21–44								
Conservative Protestants	286	38	46	16	366	66	30	4
Liberal Protestants	83	9	66	25	148	37	55	8
Catholics	197	12	57	31	232	39	51	10
Age 45+								
Conservative Protestants	264	58	32	10	387	79	20	1
Liberal Protestants	110	30	49	21	130	53	43	4
Catholics	133	21	44	35	201	52	43	5

[Continued on next page]

TABLE 28—continued

	MEN				WOMEN			
	N	Abst. + Infreq.	Light + Mod.	Heavy	N	Abst. + Infreq.	Light + Mod.	Heavy
Age 21–44								
Higher ISP								
Conservative Protestants	129	40	48	12	168	56	41	3
Liberal Protestants	64	7	67	26	102	33	61	6
Catholics	113	9	59	32	104	23	63	14
Lower ISP								
Conservative Protestants	157	36	44	20	198	73	21	6
Liberal Protestants	19	a	a	a	46	47	43	10
Catholics	84	16	54	30	128	51	42	7
Age 45+								
Higher ISP								
Conservative Protestants	110	53	35	12	157	74	25	1
Liberal Protestants	64	20	54	26	77	40	56	4
Catholics	52	13	55	32	81	45	48	7
Lower ISP								
Conservative Protestants	154	63	29	8	230	83	16	1
Liberal Protestants	46	44	42	14	53	70	25	5
Catholics	81	27	37	36	120	57	39	4

a Too few cases for analysis.

and lower ISP groups, but the liberal Protestants and Catholics had a relatively lower proportion of abstainers and infrequent drinkers in the upper social group. (5) Among men of upper social status, the proportion of heavy drinkers in each religious group was the same for those aged 21 to 44 and those 45 or older. But among men in the lower ISP group, the older Catholics had a slightly higher proportion of heavy drinkers than did the younger ones. Thus it is clear that, within comparable sex–age–ISP groups, relatively more Catholics are drinkers (and heavy drinkers) than are liberal Protestants; and the conservative Protestants are the most abstemious of all.

The findings in Tables 26 to 28 underscore the point that religious affiliation is indeed correlated significantly with drinking behavior and that there are sociologically interesting variations in these general patterns when the findings are further analyzed by sex, age and ISP.

3. *Church Attendance* (Tables 29–31). As shown in Table 29, there was a negative relationship between frequency of church attendance and heavy drinking—i.e., those who said they never go to church had the highest rate of heavy drinkers (22%). Correspondingly, the proportion of abstainers was relatively high among those who attended church most frequently.

In view of the findings on religious affiliation, the correlation between church attendance and drinking behavior would be expected to vary by specific religion and by sex. Table 30 presents a summary of drinking behavior separately for men and women who reported going to church weekly and those who went less often, in the three major categories of Christians.

Among the regular church-going conservative Protestant men,

TABLE 29.—*Percentage of Respondents in Q–F–V Groups, by Church Attendance*

	N	Abst.	Infreq.	Light + Mod.	Heavy	% Heavy of All Drinkers
Total sample	2746	32	15	41	12	18
Go to church once a week or more often	1285	38	15	37	10	16
Once or twice a month	445	28	16	45	11	15
A few times a year	431	22	16	51	11	14
Rarely	384	27	12	44	17	23
Never	201	31	14	33	22	32

TABLE 30.—Percentage of Respondents in Q–F–V Groups, by Church Attendance, Religion and Sex[a]

	MEN				WOMEN			
	N	Abst. + Infreq.	Light + Mod.	Heavy	N	Abst. + Infreq.	Light + Mod.	Heavy
Total sample	1177	33	46	21	1569	58	37	5
Conservative Protestants								
Weekly attendance	177	71	23	6	351	84	14	2
Less than weekly	373	37	46	17	404	62	34	4
Liberal Protestants								
Weekly attendance	61	18	69	13	116	57	40	3
Less than weekly	132	23	50	27	162	35	57	8
Catholics								
Weekly attendance	230	14	52	34	333	45	49	6
Less than weekly	100	19	51	30	101	44	42	14

[a] Omits groups with insufficient cases to permit tabulation of religion by sex and church attendance (e.g., Jews, Protestants of no specified denomination).

TABLE 31.—*Percentage of Respondents in Q-F-V Groups, by Church Attendance, Index of Social Position, Age and Sex*

	MEN				WOMEN			
	N	Abst. + Infreq.	Light + Mod.	Heavy	N	Abst. + Infreq.	Light + Mod.	Heavy
Total sample	1177	33	46	21	1569	58	37	5
Age 21–44								
Higher ISP								
Once a week or more	159	24	53	23	209	46	48	6
Less often	175	19	59	22	196	33	60	7
Lower ISP								
Once a week or more	97	35	41	24	188	67	29	4
Less often	178	24	51	25	197	57	34	9
Age 45+								
Higher ISP								
Once a week or more	112	41	43	16	183	64	33	3
Less often	144	26	49	25	171	48	48	4
Lower ISP								
Once a week or more	104	50	32	18	231	77	22	1
Less often	208	49	33	18	191	69	27	4

71% were either abstainers or infrequent drinkers; moreover, even the conservative Protestants who did not attend church regularly were more likely than either group of Catholics or of liberal Protestants to be abstainers or infrequent drinkers. There was not much difference in the rate of drinking by Catholic women according to their church attendance; but among both the conservative and liberal Protestant women, those who attended church weekly were considerably more likely to be abstainers or infrequent drinkers than those who attended seldom if at all.

Among all groups except Catholic men, those who went to church every week had materially fewer heavy drinkers. Among Catholic men, there was a slightly higher proportion of heavy drinkers among the weekly churchgoers; this proportion was not much higher than for less-than-weekly Catholic men churchgoers, but was materially higher than for all other groups.

Table 31 shows that the combined proportion of abstainers and infrequent drinkers (less than once a month) was generally higher among those who went to church once a week or more often, even when sex, age and social position are controlled. The difference was particularly marked among women (especially those of higher status) and in older men of higher status.

Chapter 3

Wine, Beer and Distilled Spirits

QUESTIONS on the drinking of the three specific types of alcoholic beverages were asked primarily to assess whether the various beverages had somewhat different social utilities, as well as to accumulate information on the total consumption of alcohol. No details were obtained on the brands purchased, their cost or other marketing considerations. However, it will be seen that the few questions asked on the three types of beverages yielded useful information on the tastes and life styles of various subgroups.

Quantity–Frequency–Variability of Drinking Three Types of Beverages (Table 32)

In Table 32, drinking of the three beverages[1] is cross-analyzed by the over-all Q–F–V groupings. While only 32% of the total population sampled drank no alcoholic beverage as often as once a year, 61% drank no wine, 50% no beer, and 43% no distilled spirits. Most of those who did drink wine were infrequent or light drinkers of wine, while both beer and spirits drinkers tended to drink larger quantities of these beverages more often.[2] As can be seen, the heavy drinkers were more likely to be heavy drinkers of beer (62%) than of spirits (49%) or wine (5%).[3] Those whose general classifications were light, moderate or infrequent drinkers were more likely to drink spirits than wine or beer.

The timing of the national survey (October through March) may have resulted in some understatement of beer drinking, since beer is likely to be drunk less often in winter than in summer.

---

[1] As mentioned in Chapter 1, the three beverages were identified in the questions as "Wine (or a punch containing wine)," "Beer," and "Drinks containing whisky or liquor (such as martinis, manhattans, highballs, or straight drinks)."

[2] Fink (20, 22) has analyzed the use of the three types of beverages in considerable detail from intensive interviews in the Oakland, Calif., area. His findings are congruent with those of this national survey.

[3] The finding that heavy drinkers were more likely to be heavy drinkers of beer than of other beverages should be borne in mind when reading later analyses. However, there is a considerable overlap here, with nearly 80% of the heavy drinkers reporting that they drank both beer and spirits (Table 34).

TABLE 32.—*Percentage of Respondents in Q–F–V Groups Drinking Wine, Beer and Distilled Spirits*[a]

		Drinking	Classification	on	Specific	Beverages
	N	Abst.	Infreq.	Light	Moderate	Heavy
			WINE			
Total sample	2746	61	23	13	2	1
Abstainers	898	100	0	0	0	0
Infrequent drinkers	404	48	52	0	0	0
Light	766	41	28	31	0	0
Moderate	354	37	35	22	6	0
Heavy	324	48	26	15	6	5
			BEER			
Total sample	2746	50	14	21	8	7
Abstainers	898	100	0	0	0	0
Infrequent	404	51	49	0	0	0
Light	766	28	15	57	0	0
Moderate	354	14	13	23	50	0
Heavy	324	5	8	16	9	62
			DISTILLED	SPIRITS		
Total sample	2746	43	18	23	10	6
Abstainers	898	100	0	0	0	0
Infrequent	404	30	70	0	0	0
Light	766	16	19	65	0	0
Moderate	354	10	9	23	58	0
Heavy	324	11	10	11	19	49

[a] Table should be read as follows: Of the total sample, 61% drank no wine, 23% were infrequent drinkers of wine, 13% light wine drinkers, etc. Of those classified on their over-all consumption as heavy drinkers, 48% drank no wine, 26% were infrequent drinkers of wine, etc.

While the question was asked in terms of quantity and frequency with which the person "usually" drank the various beverages, it is likely that people would tend to answer in terms of current drinking patterns. Mulford and Miller (55) reported this phenomenon in observing a lower level of beer drinking in an Iowa survey conducted in March than in one conducted several summers previously (54).

Drinking of Specific Beverages (Tables 33–35)

Wine was drunk least frequently: Only 6% of the total sample (15% of wine drinkers) said they drank it once a week or more. Beer and spirits, on the other hand, were drunk with much greater regularity: About a fifth of the sample (40% of beer drinkers and

32% of spirits drinkers) reported drinking the respective beverages once a week or more. Frequency of drinking the various beverages is shown in Table 33.

Table 34 summarizes the respondents' drinking (at least once a year) of various combinations of the three types of beverages: A quarter of the sample said they drank all three of the beverages at least once a year. Men reported the combinations of all three beverages and of beer and spirits more frequently than women, while women more frequently reported drinking only spirits (or drinks containing spirits) or wine and spirits, and less frequently beer and combinations with beer.

The implication of Table 34 that women differ from men more in their drinking of beer than of wine or spirits is borne out by Table 35, which shows the totals drinking each beverage. While fewer women than men among the total sample drank each of the beverages as often as once a year, among drinkers (of any beverage) the proportion drinking wine was slightly higher among women than among men, about equal for spirits, and much higher among men for beer.

Among men who drank any of the three beverages, the pattern of drinking of specific beverages was similar in all Q–F–V groups: Somewhat fewer drank wine, and larger (fairly similar) proportions drank beer and spirits. Among women, however, relatively more of the infrequent drinkers tended to drink wine than beer, with beer higher in popularity among the heavier-drinking women.

Highlights of other group divisions[4] both on the basis of the total sample and of drinkers only (generally true with either per-

TABLE 33.—*Frequency of Drinking Three Specific Beverages, in Per Cent (N=2746)*

	Wine	Beer	Spirits
Have never had	33	31	25
Less than once a year	28	19	18
1–11 times a year	23	14	18
Once a month	6	8	11
2–3 times a month	4	8	10
Once a week or more	6	20	18
Total drinkers of beverage	39	50	57
Total nondrinkers of beverage	61	50	43

[4] Reported in full in Detail Table A-35; see *Headnote*, p. 229.

TABLE 34.—*Percentage of Respondents Drinking Wine, Beer and Distilled Spirits Only and in Combinations, by Sex and Q-F-V Group*[a]

	N	Abst.	Wine Only	Beer Only	Spirits Only	Wine & Beer	Beer & Spirits	Wine & Spirits	Wine, Beer & Spirits	Misc.
Total sample	2746	32	2	6	7	3	16	9	25	[b]
Men	1177	23	1	8	4	2	23	4	35	[b]
Women	1569	40	3	5	9	3	10	12	18	[b]
Men										
Abstainers	268	100	0	0	0	0	0	0	0	0
Infrequent drinkers	121	0	7	22	13	6	17	8	25	2
Light	324	0	2	12	6	3	30	6	41	0
Moderate	212	0	[b]	5	2	3	30	4	56	0
Heavy	252	0	0	8	2	2	37	2	49	0
Women										
Abstainers	630	100	0	0	0	0	0	0	0	0
Infrequent	283	0	13	6	25	7	14	21	13	1
Light	442	0	3	8	12	4	16	24	33	0
Moderate	142	0	0	7	11	4	20	14	44	0
Heavy	72	0	0	11	6	4	33	4	42	0

[a] More detailed data for various subgroups are given in Detail Tables which are numbered to correspond to the selective-data tables included in this report. To obtain the Detail Tables, see Headnote, p. 229. The results of other groupings besides sex and Q-F-V are reported in Detail Table A-34.
[b] Less than 0.5%.

TABLE 35.—*Percentage of Respondents Drinking Wine, Beer and Distilled Spirits, by Sex and Q–F–V Group*[a]

	N	Wine	Beer	Spirits
Total sample	2746	39	50	57
Total drinkers	1848	57	74	83
Men: total	1177	42	68	65
Drinkers only	909	54	87	85
Women: total	1569	36	36	49
Drinkers only	939	60	59	82
Men				
Infrequent drinkers	121	47	69	63
Light	324	52	85	84
Moderate	212	63	93	91
Heavy	252	53	96	90
Women				
Infrequent	283	54	40	72
Light	442	64	61	85
Moderate	142	62	75	89
Heavy	72	50	90	85

[a] The results in other groups are reported in Detail Table A-35; see Headnote, p. 229.

centage base but easier to see in the data on drinkers only) are as follows:

Index of Social Position: Among drinkers, a larger proportion of those in the upper ISP groups drank wine and spirits than those in the lower ISP groups. Fairly uniform proportions of the various ISP groups, however, reported drinking beer.

Age: Older women drinkers were more likely to drink wine than younger women drinkers, while relatively more of the younger drank beer and spirits. More younger men than older drank beer; and more men in their 30s and 40s drank spirits.

Region: The proportion of wine drinkers was highest in the wine-producing Pacific and the Middle Atlantic states and lowest in the Mountain states and southeastern areas. Beer and spirits drinkers showed somewhat less regional fluctuation, with relatively more spirits than beer drinkers in all regions except the generally low-drinking areas of the East South Central and Mountain states.

Urbanization: Analysis by size of city shows drinking of wine reported by proportionately more persons in the larger suburbs outside metropolitan areas, beer more in smaller towns, and spirits more in urban than rural areas.

National identity: The Italians led in wine drinking, followed by the Russian–Baltic–Polish group; the Latin-American–Caribbean and Italian groups led in beer drinking; while no particular differences in nationality groups were found in spirits drinking.

Relative Drinking of Beer and Spirits

Table 36 shows the great similarity in classifications of respondents on their drinking of beer and spirits. Generally speaking, the people who drank little or none of one beverage also drank little or none of the other, and the light and moderate drinkers of one were likely to be similar drinkers of the other. Only small proportions were heavy drinkers of either beverage.

TABLE 36.—*Relative Drinking of Beer and Distilled Spirits, in Per Cent (N=2746)*

Beer Drinking	SPIRITS DRINKING			
	Infreq. or None	*Light or Mod.*	*Heavy*	*Total Sample*
Infrequent or none	49	14	1	64
Light or moderate	10	16	3	29
Heavy	2	3	2	7
Total Sample	61	33	6	100

Chapter 4

Behavioral Correlates of Drinking

ANALYSIS of social behavior and attitudes related to drinking should help to facilitate understanding of the reasons why some people drink moderately, some drink heavily and some do not drink at all. Alcohol is a key concern in the mores of many groups, including some which counsel total abstinence, some which advocate moderation, and some which do not discourage heavy drinking. As ingredients of the culture, alcoholic beverages have acquired many affectively tinged connotations which can be expected to vary widely from one group to another, particularly in the United States which has so many ethnic groups in various stages of assimilation.

Some of the group differences in behavior concerning alcohol have been discussed earlier in this report, in relation to the kinds and amounts of alcoholic beverages drunk by various subgroups. We have seen how drinking varies greatly according to such factors as sex, age, social position, degree of urbanization, religion and national origin. In the light of these variations, it would be expected that values and behavior surrounding the occasions of drinking would also vary greatly from group to group.

That alcohol is a "social" phenomenon is self-evident—most people (a two-thirds majority) drink at least occasionally and seem to recognize drinking as normal behavior. Most drinking behavior is social behavior, as is indicated by the fact that drinking in America appears to vary more by social groupings (e.g., sex, age, socioeconomic status, religion or ethnic origin) than it does by personality variables. Therefore, in this section primary emphasis is put on social-psychological variables related to the circumstances of drinking, leaving for a later section a discussion of such personality indices as might help to account for deviations from the norms of drinking behavior.

While the national survey could not cover all aspects of the social acceptability of various kinds and circumstances of drinking, it included many questions about behavior from which social drinking norms can be inferred. The present section of the report deals with the following correlates of drinking, in this order: (a) social

71

activities of the individual, including some activities only tangential-
ly related to drinking; (b) family background regarding drinking
by parents and spouses; and (c) usual circumstances of drinking:
with whom, under what circumstances and where people drink.

Social Activities

The several indices of social activities included in the survey
were not intended to constitute a complete list but rather a representative selection of the major social activities which might be
associated with drinking. Most of the questions were asked as
casual "warm-up" items prior to discussion of drinking behavior;
others related certain kinds of social behavior to drinking.

Three groups of questions about social activities were asked.
These included participation in various types of recreational activities in the evening, sources of close friends (e.g., from work, neighborhood and family), and frequency of getting together with people from work, from the neighborhood and from church.

1. Participation in Evening Recreational Activities (Tables 37, 38)

The respondents were asked whether they participated in each
of seven activities "often," "sometimes," "rarely," or "never." Table
37 presents the frequency of participation in each of the seven
activities and the percentage participating in the three activities
which are most likely to entail contact with other people—visiting
friends or relatives, having visitors in one's home, and going out
somewhere for entertainment. As might be expected, heavy drinkers of both sexes were noticeably less likely than other people to
engage in evening church activities. A higher proportion of the
heavy drinkers reported engaging in all three of the primarily
interpersonal activities, and they were somewhat less prone than
others to take part in recreation which might be less compatible
with drinking (such as pursuing a hobby, reading or going to
church).

A stronger indication of the relationship between a person's
drinking and his level of social activity is provided by an analysis
of the drinking practices of those who often participated in two
or more of the three interpersonal activities, with the variables of
sex, age and ISP held constant. The findings, presented in Table
38, show that those with a higher social-activity level were some-

TABLE 37.—Percentage of Respondents "Often" Participating in Evening Activities, by Sex and Q-F-V Group

	N	a Watch TV	b Read	c Hobby	d Church	e Visit Friends, Relatives	f Have Visitors in Home	g Go Out for Entert.	Often on e, f and g
Total sample	2746	48	42	20	21	29	35	16	7
Men	1177	45	42	19	19	27	34	18	7
Women	1569	51	42	21	23	30	37	15	6
Men									
Abstainers	268	45	43	19	35	25	30	12	7
Infrequent drinkers	121	44	33	16	19	25	35	9	1
Light	324	38	43	18	17	27	34	18	6
Moderate	212	45	45	19	11	26	35	15	4
Heavy	252	53	42	22	11	33	36	30	11
Women									
Abstainers	630	51	41	21	35	30	37	7	5
Infrequent	283	53	38	20	19	30	33	13	5
Light	442	48	44	22	15	31	36	20	8
Moderate	142	49	43	21	12	32	43	29	8
Heavy	72	62	37	27	9	30	46	29	11

TABLE 38.—*Percentage of Respondents in Q–F–V Groups, by Social Activity, Index of Social Position, Age and Sex*

	MEN				WOMEN			
	N	Abst. + Infreq.	Light + Mod.	Heavy	N	Abst. + Infreq.	Light + Mod.	Heavy
Total sample	1177	33	46	21	1569	58	37	5
Social Activity Level[a]								
Higher	275	26	47	27	398	50	44	6
Lower	902	34	46	20	1168	61	35	4
Age 21–44								
Higher ISP								
Higher activity	89	21	48	31	113	29	63	8
Lower activity	245	21	59	20	292	44	50	6
Lower ISP								
Higher activity	72	26	41	33	95	61	33	6
Lower activity	203	29	50	21	290	62	31	7
Age 45+								
Higher ISP								
Higher activity	54	23	51	26	98	54	40	6
Lower activity	202	36	45	19	256	58	40	2
Lower ISP								
Higher activity	60	38	46	16	92	63	36	1
Lower activity	252	52	30	18	330	76	21	3

[a] Higher social activity = often participated in two or more of the following: visiting friends or relatives, having visitors in own home, and going out somewhere for entertainment.

what less likely to be abstainers or infrequent drinkers than those who were less active. This finding holds for most subgroups examined. Moreover, among men under 45 years and men of higher ISP, the more socially active were also more likely to be heavy drinkers; among other groups, however, where the incidence of heavy drinking was generally low, no such tendency was apparent. These findings suggest that greater social activity would be likely to lead to heavier drinking if a sizable proportion of the peer group were heavy drinkers, but not if only a few of the group drank heavily.

Obviously, since much drinking is done in company with others, one who participates more actively in interpersonal relationships is likely to find himself more often in a situation where drinking is done. The results do indicate, however, that additional study of the relationship of social activity and drinking—utilizing a broader range of activities and more detailed analyses of group pressures —should be profitable in analyzing influences on drinking.

2. Sources of Close Friends (Table 39)

Table 39 shows the proportions who reported having close friends they had come to know from five different sources, as well as a combined index of variety of friendships including those who men-

TABLE 39.—*Sources of Close Friends, by Sex and Q–F–V Groups, in Per Cent*

	N	From Work	From Neighb.	From School	Through Family	Other Ways	4 or 5 Sources
Total sample	2746	55	61	39	67	51	27
Men	1177	67	60	39	66	52	31
Women	1569	45	62	40	68	51	23
Men							
Abstainers	268	67	70	35	67	47	34
Infrequent drinkers	121	65	59	38	68	44	27
Light	324	66	60	39	70	49	29
Moderate	212	71	50	42	62	55	30
Heavy	252	67	58	40	61	61	33
Women							
Abstainers	630	44	70	38	72	46	26
Infrequent	283	43	64	39	68	55	24
Light	442	45	56	41	66	52	21
Moderate	142	48	48	48	61	55	22
Heavy	72	58	49	37	65	58	17

tioned at least four of the five sources. The principal differences between the various Q–F–V groups on sources of friends were as follows: (1) Among the men, fewer moderate and heavy drinkers than others had met their close friends through their families. More heavy drinkers reported having met close friends in "other ways" not listed, e.g., in bars or taverns and through recreation. (2) Among women, the pattern was similar to that of the men, except that women, of course, were less likely than men to have friends from work, and that the heavier drinkers among the women were materially less likely than male heavy drinkers to have friends from a variety of sources; thus the woman who drinks heavily, having a narrower range of friends, may be more likely to be a social isolate than is the heavy-drinking man.

3. Social Meetings (Table 40)

Table 40 shows the proportions who said they met socially "fairly often" with people from work, from their neighborhood or from church. The major group differences were as follows: (1) Among both men and women, the abstainers were most likely to report meeting socially with people they met through church activities.

TABLE 40.—*Sources of Persons with Whom Respondents Fairly Often Met Socially, by Sex and Q–F–V Group, in Per Cent*

	N	From Work	From Neigh- borhood	From Church[a]
Total sample	2746	19	22	17
Men	1177	21	20	13
Women	1569	17	24	20
Men				
Abstainers	268	17	22	23
Infrequent drinkers	121	13	19	14
Light	324	18	17	11
Moderate	212	30	16	8
Heavy	252	24	26	9
Women				
Abstainers	630	13	24	25
Infrequent	283	16	25	15
Light	442	20	24	18
Moderate	142	24	20	15
Heavy	72	34	27	12

[a] Not asked of respondents who said they "only rarely" or "never" attend religious services.

This appears to be a reflection not only of greater religiosity on the part of the abstainers, but also of their often limited social contacts. (2) The heavier drinkers, both men and women, were more likely than others to meet with people from work rather than with people from the neighborhood or from church. This finding is interpreted as reflecting a tendency on the part of the heavier drinkers to be relatively less subject than others to the social controls implied in having close social relationships with those in one's neighborhood or from one's church.

DRINKING HABITS OF PARENTS AND SPOUSE

Several questions were asked to test the expectation of a positive relationship between the respondents' drinking practices and the drinking habits or attitudes of their parents and of their husbands or wives. The findings are presented in Table 41.

Four out of 10 reported their fathers as drinking twice a month or more often. A higher proportion of women reported their hus-

TABLE 41.—*Drinking Habits and Attitudes of Parents and Spouse, by Sex and Q–F–V Group, in Per Cent*[a]

		FATHER		MOTHER		SPOUSE	
		Drank at Least Twice a Month	Approved of Drinking	Drank at Least Twice a Month	Approved of Drinking		Drinks at Least Twice a Month
	N					N	
Total sample	2746	38	43	12	23	2027	41
Men	1177	42	43	12	22	971	33
Women	1569	35	43	12	24	1056	49
Men							
Abstainers	268	30	30	3	7	221	3
Infrequent drinkers	121	27	29	9	17	99	6
Light	324	44	47	11	23	273	30
Moderate	212	45	47	14	29	174	52
Heavy	252	58	55	22	34	204	64
Women							
Abstainers	630	22	25	3	10	397	18
Infrequent	283	34	47	8	24	203	32
Light	442	46	55	19	35	315	79
Moderate	142	54	64	25	44	96	87
Heavy	72	49	55	22	37	45	95

[a] The results in other groups are reported in Detail Table A-41; see Headnote, p. 229.

bands as drinking this often (49%) than reported their fathers as drinking this often (35%). Husbands may well drink more now than fathers in the past (before respondents were aged 16). But it will be noted that a higher percentage of men than of women reported their fathers as drinking twice a month or more often. One reason for this disparity may be that some of the women may either have been unaware of or chose to minimize their fathers' drinking, while men may have had better recollection of their fathers' drinking or tended to report it more in line with their own.

Men and women agreed in the percentage reporting their mothers' drinking twice a month or more often (12%), and in reporting whether their fathers or mothers approved of drinking (more than 40% of fathers approved, less than 25% of mothers).

Abstainers and infrequent drinkers, both men and women, were much less likely than others to report either parent drinking twice a month or more; conversely, the moderate or heavy drinkers were noticeably more likely to say their parents drank that often. Among the married heavy drinkers, 64% of the men and 95% of the women reported that their spouses drank at least twice a month. There is also a fairly clear relationship between level of drinking and parents' approval: the abstainers and infrequent drinkers were much less likely than others to say either of their parents had approved of drinking.

The more important findings from detailed analyses of age and ISP[1] are as follows: In general, the higher the ISP, the higher the proportion reporting more frequent drinking by spouse and (to a lesser extent) by parents, and also the higher the parental approval of drinking; in general, the younger the respondent, the more likely to report higher rates of parents' (and, for women, spouse's) drinking, and the higher the parental approval.

Looking at the findings in another way, the drinking behavior of respondents whose fathers or mothers drank frequently can be compared with that of respondents whose fathers or mothers drank infrequently or not at all. This analysis is presented in Table 42.

Particularly among male respondents, frequent drinking on the part of the father was found to be highly correlated with later heavy drinking on the part of the son. Of male respondents who reported that their fathers drank three or more times a week, 35%

[1] Reported in Detail Table A-41; see *Headnote*, p. 229.

TABLE 42.—*Percentage of Drinkers and Heavy Drinkers, by Parents' Frequency of and Attitudes toward Drinking*[a]

		MEN			WOMEN	
	N	Drinkers	Heavy Drinkers	N	Drinkers	Heavy Drinkers
Father's Frequency						
3 times a week or more	246	84	35	299	80	7
2–3 times a month to 1–2 times a week	242	84	24	237	71	6
1–12 times a year	244	81	19	296	70	3
Less than once a year or never	345	64	12	586	40	3
Mother's Frequency						
3 times a week or more	53	89	44	69	89	8
2–3 times a month to 1–2 times a week	87	97	39	104	88	9
1–12 times a year	204	94	33	274	83	5
Less than once a year or never	759	70	15	1038	49	4
Father's Attitude						
Approved	495	84	28	663	77	6
Did not care	217	84	23	209	65	4
Disapproved	353	63	12	546	41	3
Mother's Attitude						
Approved	262	93	33	368	84	7
Did not care	185	87	29	212	81	4
Disapproved	638	69	15	901	45	4

[a] Excluding those who did not know their parents' frequency of or attitude toward drinking.

were heavy drinkers, compared to 12% of men who reported that their fathers never drank or drank less than once a year. Corresponding differences according to mothers' drinking were even more marked: 44% compared to 15%.

The same tendency was true of parents' reported attitudes toward drinking alcoholic beverages. Among men who reported their fathers approved of drinking, 28% were heavy drinkers; among men who said their fathers disapproved, 12% were heavy drinkers. Again the differences according to mothers' attitude were even more marked: 33% compared to 15%.

Both these findings also hold consistently for women. The findings that differences in general were less marked for fathers' drinking and attitudes than for mothers' suggest that mothers' examples and attitudes are more influential than those of fathers. It is also possible that in households where the general societal taboos against heavy drinking by women were flouted by the mothers, the environment (because of the mother's influence) would be more likely to be one of relative indifference to sanctions against heavy drinking.

It must be pointed out that parental drinking may not be as strong a determinant of respondents' drinking habits as might appear from these findings. It may well be that the similarities in parents' and children's drinking may result as much from the fact that individual communities and neighborhoods have well-established norms for drinking that influenced both generations as from parental influence per se. However, it is clear from this relationship that if parents' drinking habits are known, forecasting of the drinking habits of their children is thereby improved materially.

The question on husbands' and wives' drinking affords an excellent opportunity for a special type of validation by comparing the reported frequency of spouse's drinking with the frequency of drinking by persons of the spouse's sex reporting on their *own* drinking. Table 43 shows this comparison.

The results showed practically identical distributions in women respondents and in wives of male respondents. The results in men were similar, but indicated a tendency toward underreporting of husbands' drinking on the part of wives: a slightly higher proportion of wives reported that their husbands drank less than once a year than did male respondents reporting their own drinking,

TABLE 43.—*Comparison of Frequency of Drinking Reported by Respondents for Selves and for Husbands or Wives, in Per Cent*[a]

	Married Men's Frequency of Drinking Reported by		Married Women's Frequency of Drinking Reported by	
	Married Men	Married Women	Married Women	Married Men
N	971	1056	1056	971
Three times a week or more	29	21	11	11
Once or twice a week to 2–3 times a month	29	28	23	22
About once a month to at least once a year	19	23	26	28
Less than once a year	23	28	40	39
Have no idea	0	b	0	b
Totals	100	100	100	100

[a] Comparison limited to married men and women reporting on selves and on wives or husbands (spouses were not interviewed).
[b] Less than 0.5%.

and a lower proportion of wives than husbands reported the men drinking 3 times a week or more. The slight difference in reliability of drinking reports for men is in the expected direction: it is more reasonable that wives would know less about their husbands' drinking than the converse, since men spend more time away from home, and women (who generally drink less) do relatively more drinking in company with their husbands. In any event, the results do not indicate that one is more likely to get a realistic picture of drinking habits from a spouse than from the person himself, in the average case.

The data on the drinking habits of wives or husbands can be rearranged so as to compare the drinking habits of wives whose husbands drink frequently or infrequently, and the same for husbands whose wives drink with varying frequencies. This analysis is presented in Table 44 which indicates that wives who drink frequently are much more likely to have husbands who are heavy drinkers, and vice versa. A much larger proportion (63%) of the men who reported their wives drank three or more times per week were classified as heavy drinkers than of those who said their wives drank less than once a year (6%). Similarly, among women respondents who reported their husbands drank three times a week or more, 17% were heavy drinkers, while less than 0.5% of those who

TABLE 44.—*Percentage of Respondents in Q–F–V Groups, by Frequency of Spouse's Drinking*[a]

| | N | RESPONDENTS' Q–F–V GROUP | | | | |
		Abst.	Infreq.	Light	Mod.	Heavy
Frequency of Wives' Drinking		M E N				
3 times a week or more	104	3	1	13	20	63
2–3 times a month to 1–2 times a week	210	2	2	32	33	31
1–12 times a year	277	7	16	38	21	18
Less than once a year, never	378	52	12	23	7	6
Frequency of Husbands' Drinking		W O M E N				
3 times a week or more	220	11	11	43	18	17
2–3 times a month to 1–2 times a week	294	16	14	52	16	2
1–12 times a year	247	32	44	20	4	b
Less than once a year, never	291	83	10	6	1	b

[a] Excludes those not married and the six persons who said they did not know the frequency of their spouses' drinking.
[b] Less than 0.5%.

said their husbands drank less than once a year were classified as heavy drinkers themselves. The relationship of a wife's drinking to that of her husband is underscored by the finding that among those women who reported that their husbands drank less than once a year, 93% were themselves classified as abstainers or infrequent drinkers (less than once a month), whereas only 22% of those whose husbands drank three times a week or more were in these two categories.

USUAL CIRCUMSTANCES OF DRINKING

To describe some of the more usual aspects of drinking practices, the drinkers were asked a series of questions concerning the circumstances of their drinking. These questions covered the serving of drinks on social occasions when they got together with people they had met in various ways (people they had known at work or from their husbands' work, or from the neighborhood, or their close friends); whether they themselves drank more or less when they were with people from these various sources; how many of their social acquaintances drank "quite a bit"; how often they drank with friends, members of the family or by themselves; and how often they drank on weekdays as against weekends.

1. Serving of Drinks on Social Occasions (Table 45)

Table 45 (based on those who ever met socially with people from the specified groups) shows that alcoholic beverages were reported as served relatively more often on the occasions when people met socially with persons from work than at social meetings with neighbors or church acquaintances or even close friends.

Fewer women than men reported that drinks were served when they met socially with people from each of the various sources (work, neighborhood, church, close friends). Particularly interesting is the finding on serving drinks at social meetings with people from the neighborhood: while it was shown earlier (Table 40) that women met people from the neighborhood at least as often as men, only half as many women as men reported that drinks were served on such occasions.

Heavier drinkers consistently more frequently than lighter drinkers reported serving drinks in meetings with people from any of these types of sources. But it is also notable that, even among

TABLE 45.—*Percentage of Respondents Reporting that Drinks Were Served More than Half the Time on Social Occasions with Various People, by Sex and Q–F–V Group*[a]

	N	Close Friends	N[b]	People from Work	N[b]	Neighbors	N[b]	Church People
Total sample	2746	23	1454	36	1562	16	1222	5
Men	1177	30	678	41	667	22	484	8
Women	1569	17	776	31	895	11	738	3
Men								
Abstainers	268	4	128	11	168	2	151	1
Infrequent drinkers	121	7	64	18	73	7	53	3
Light	324	23	178	30	181	21	131	10
Moderate	212	41	143	56	103	27	73	15
Heavy	252	66	165	71	142	49	76	19
Women								
Abstainers	630	2	257	10	374	2	354	1
Infrequent	283	8	143	21	166	10	117	3
Light	442	27	248	46	246	16	202	5
Moderate	142	48	82	59	70	31	46	8
Heavy	72	64	46	58	39	33	19	15

[a] The results in other groups are reported in Detail Table A-45; see Headnote, p. 229.
[b] Respondents who said they "almost never" get together socially with people from these groups are excluded. The item concerning people from church was not asked of respondents who said they "only rarely" or "never" attend religious services.

the abstainers and infrequent drinkers, a substantial number reported that drinks were served in social gatherings with people from work.

Detailed group analyses[2] showed considerable variation in the serving of drinks with different types of people, including the following highlights: More persons in the higher ISP groups, in general, reported serving drinks. Differences by region and urbanization were sizable and in line with the over-all level of drinking in the various areas. Serving drinks at social meetings was reported most frequently among those from the Middle Atlantic and Pacific areas with three of the four types of people (work, neighborhood and close friends), and was highest of all at meetings with people from work. The serving of drinks on different occasions again was most common in the large cities and larger suburbs.

2. Drinking with Certain Kinds of People (Table 46)

Table 46 presents findings on the minority who reported that they adapted their drinking to the social circumstances by drinking either more or less when they were with certain kinds of people. It is seen that more respondents said they drank less than usual (than said they drank more than usual) in social meetings with neighbors, people from church or members of their own families. On the other hand, a larger proportion said they drank more than usual, rather than less, when with close friends (30 vs 13%).

Women drinkers were less likely than men to report drinking greater amounts than usual when with close friends or people from work, but more likely to report drinking more than usual with members of their immediate families.

The heavier-drinking men and women were more inclined than others to report drinking more than usual when with people from work or with close friends and less than usual when with people from the neighborhood or from church. This is consistent with the likelihood that a heavier-than-average drinker will find some of his fellow workers and his close friends to be more permissive about heavy drinking than people from the neighborhood, the church or his family.

Detailed group analyses[3] show the following: More men drinkers of higher ISP than lower tended to drink more than usual when

[2] Reported in Detail Table A-45; see Headnote, p. 229.
[3] Reported in Detail Table A-46; see Headnote, p. 229.

TABLE 46.—Drinkers Drinking More or Less When with Certain Kinds of People, by Sex and Q-F-V Group, in Per Cent[a]

	N	People from Work		From Neighborhood		From Church		Close Friends		Immediate Family	
		More	Less	More	Less	More	Less	More	Less	More	Less
Total drinkers[b]	1848	13	14	5	14	1	11	30	13	14	35
Men	909	17	14	7	16	1	13	34	12	11	42
Women	939	9	15	5	11	1	9	26	14	18	29
Men											
Infrequent drinkers	121	13	11	5	10	0	7	13	14	11	39
Light	324	10	13	5	13	1	8	26	12	8	42
Moderate	212	25	14	6	21	1	17	42	13	13	46
Heavy	252	21	18	10	19	2	16	48	8	14	40
Women											
Infrequent	283	8	12	3	10	c	6	18	14	12	30
Light	442	7	15	5	11	1	10	23	13	18	26
Moderate	142	13	17	6	11	c	10	35	15	24	29
Heavy	72	18	19	8	22	1	14	55	14	29	38

[a] The results in other groups are reported in Detail Table A-46; see Headnote, p. 229.
[b] The 32% of the total sample who were abstainers are excluded. However, the base includes individuals who do not get together socially with one or more of the five groups. The item concerning people from church was not asked of respondents who said they "only rarely" or "never" attend religious services.
c Less than 0.5%.

they were with people from work or close friends, and to drink less when they were with people from the immediate neighborhood or from church. The youngest men drinkers drank more than usual (to a greater extent than older men) when with people from work or close friends, and less than usual—by a considerable margin—with members of their immediate families. Results by age in women were much the same as in men, but less pronounced in relation to people from work and close friends. Women in their 40s and 50s were more likely than men of similar ages to drink more than usual when with members of their immediate families. The inference is that many of these reported drinking "more than usual" because they drank infrequently except in the company of their husbands.

3. Social Acquaintances Who Drink "Quite a Bit" (Table 47)

Relatively small percentages of respondents reported that more than half of their acquaintances drink "quite a bit"; and more re-

TABLE 47.—*Drinking "Quite a Bit" by Social Acquaintances,*[a] *by Sex and Q–F–V Group, in Per Cent*[b]

	N	Close Friends	N	Work People	N	Neigh-bors[c]
Total sample	2746	8	1454	16	1562	6
Men	1177	11	678	20	667	10
Women	1569	5	776	13	895	5
Men						
Abstainers	268	3	128	7	168	4
Infrequent drinkers	121	7	64	12	73	7
Light	324	6	178	16	181	7
Moderate	212	12	143	23	103	11
Heavy	252	29	165	34	142	21
Women						
Abstainers	630	1	257	7	374	1
Infrequent	283	2	143	9	166	6
Light	442	6	248	15	246	3
Moderate	142	11	82	20	70	14
Heavy	72	37	46	38	39	20

[a] More than half of social acquaintances drink "quite a bit."

[b] The results in other groups are reported in Detail Table A-47; see Headnote, p. 229.

[c] Respondents who said they "almost never" get together socially with people from this group are excluded. Percentages shown may be on the low side in a few cases, since the question was not asked of those who said drinks are never served when they meet socially with such people; such respondents were not deleted from the base because it was felt that to do so would have differential effects on the data of the various Q–F–V groups, resulting in a distorted comparison.

ported such drinking in people from work than in their own close friends or people from their own neighborhoods. A higher proportion of heavy drinkers than of lighter drinkers reported that more than half their social acquaintances from all three sources drink "quite a bit." Both men and women in the heavy-drinking category reported this more frequently about their close friends than about persons from the neighborhood.

4. With Whom Respondents Drink Wine or Beer (Table 48)

All respondents who reported drinking wine or beer as often as once a month (43% of the total sample) were asked whether they drank wine or beer "most often" with friends, their families, or by themselves. They were also asked how often they drank wine or beer in each circumstance. The results show (Table 48) that the largest proportions of respondents drank wine or beer most often with friends, the next largest with their families; the smallest proportions drank them when alone. In terms of absolute rather than relative frequency, drinking wine or beer "fairly often" with members of the family was mentioned as frequently as drinking with friends.

A majority of men who drank wine or beer at least once a month said they most often drank it with their friends; a majority of the women said they most often drank wine or beer with members of the family. Similarly, men were more likely to drink wine or beer fairly often with friends, women with their families.

The heavy drinkers among the men of this group differed little from other drinkers in the relative proportion reporting drinking wine or beer most often with friends, family or by themselves, although they had a higher rate of drinking these beverages fairly often in each of the three circumstances. But among the women of this group, the heavy drinkers were more likely to drink, both most often and fairly often, with friends, while other women drinkers drank more often with their families. The results may reflect a relatively greater tolerance of heavy drinking by women on the part of their friends, as compared to their families. Heavy drinkers were also more likely to drink alone.

Analyses by age and ISP[4] showed that while younger men tended to drink wine and beer most often with friends, older persons most

[4] Reported in Detail Table A-48; see *Headnote*, p. 229.

TABLE 48.—*Percentage of Respondents who Drink Wine or Beer at Least Once a Month and with Whom They Most Often and Fairly Often Drink Wine or Beer, by Sex and Q–F–V Group*[a]

	N	At Least Once a Month	Most Often with[b]				Fairly Often with[b]		
			N	Friends	Family	Self	Friends	Family	Self
Total sample	2746	43	1143	49	39	14[c]	23	24	14
Men	1177	58	677	55	29	19	27	21	17
Women	1569	30	466	40	54	7	18	29	8
Men									
Light drinkers	324	79	255	51	29	22	12	12	11
Moderate	212	87	185	56	31	14	24	22	13
Heavy	252	95	237	58	27	19	45	29	28
Women									
Light	442	68	297	35	59	8	10	23	5
Moderate	142	72	105	44	53	4	19	37	10
Heavy	72	87	64	57	34	10	48	40	17

[a] The results in other groups are reported in Detail Table A-48; see Headnote, p. 229.
[b] The three columns under "Most Often" represent responses to a single question: "When you have wine or beer, with whom do you have them most often?" The columns under "Fairly Often" represent separate questions for each situation: "How often do you have wine or beer with friends?" etc. The N in each case is the number of respondents who drink wine or beer at least once a month.
[c] These three groups add to a little more than 100% of those drinking wine or beer because a few drinkers named more than one situation where wine or beer was drunk most often.

often drank these beverages with other members of the family. Younger people, both men and women, less often drank wine or beer alone than did older people. The proportion of persons drinking wine or beer most often by themselves (rather than with friends or family) was generally highest in the lowest ISP groups. Differences in drinking most often with family and friends, however, varied according to sex and age levels more than it did by ISP.[5]

Among younger men (21 to 39 years) there was little difference by ISP in the drinking of wine or beer under the three circumstances. However, among middle-aged and older men, more of those of higher ISP reported drinking most often with their families and relatively fewer drinking by themselves than did those of lower status.

Among younger women, more of those in the lowest ISP group than in the other ISP groups, drank beer or wine most often with friends or by themselves rather than with members of the family. Among older women, relatively more of the higher ISP groups most often drank wine or beer with friends; relatively more of the lower ISP groups did so with family members.

The finding that substantial percentages of less well-to-do persons, especially among older persons, reported that they drank wine, beer or spirits by themselves casts doubt on the utility of the "solitary drinker" label for identifying problem drinkers (or alcoholics). It may well be that many of those who drink alone do so only because there is no one at hand with whom to drink. Whether drinking alone constitutes problem drinking depends upon the frequency and amount drunk, the circumstances of the drinking (e.g., whether relaxing, brooding, reading, watching TV) and, also, upon the reason the individual has for drinking. Reasons for drinking are analyzed in detail later.

5. With Whom Respondents Drink Spirits (Table 49)

Those who drank any spirits (or drinks containing spirits) as often as once a month (39% of the total sample) were asked both

[5] It should be borne in mind that the comparisons by ISP are somewhat artificial in that the question was asked about wine and beer together, so the results may not follow the same pattern as if the two beverages had been asked about separately (for example, wine is drunk by fewer people in total but relatively more by men and women of higher ISP; while, among women, beer tends to be drunk more by those of medium or lower ISP).

TABLE 49.—*Percentage of Respondents who Drink Distilled Spirits at Least Once a Month and with Whom they Most Often and Fairly Often Drink Distilled Spirits, by Sex and Q–F–V Group*[a]

	N	At Least Once a Month	MOST OFTEN WITH[b]				FAIRLY OFTEN WITH[b]		
			N	Friends	Family	Self	Friends	Family	Self
Total sample	2746	39	1046	63	31	7[c]	29	19	6
Men	1177	48	566	63	28	11	31	18	9
Women	1569	30	480	64	34	3	27	20	3
Men									
Light drinkers	324	63	205	62	24	16	13	8	6
Moderate	212	78	162	67	26	7	34	16	6
Heavy	252	80	199	60	34	8	47	31	15
Women									
Light	442	68	305	64	33	4	18	13	2
Moderate	142	85	119	62	39	1	36	30	4
Heavy	72	78	56	67	29	4	53	36	5

[a] The results in other groups are reported in Detail Table A-49; see Headnote, p. 229.

[b] The three columns under "Most Often" represent responses to a single question; those under "Fairly Often" separate questions for each situation. See footnote to Table 48.

[c] These three groups add to a little more than 100% of those drinking spirits because a few drinkers named more than one situation where spirits were drunk most often.

the relative and absolute questions on the frequency with which they drank spirits with friends, with their families, or by themselves. The findings shown in Table 49 differed from those for wine or beer in that the drinking of spirits with friends was considerably more frequent than with family or by oneself.

Relatively larger proportions of both men and women drank spirits most often with friends than was the case with wine or beer. This undoubtedly reflects the role of spirits as more of a party drink.

With minor exceptions, subgroup differences in the relative drinking of spirits under various circumstances[6] followed the same general pattern as for wine and beer.

6. Where People Drink (Tables 50–52)

All who drink either wine or beer, or spirits, at least once a month were asked where they drank most often—in their own homes, at friends' homes, or in restaurants or bars. They were then asked how often they drank the beverages in the three localities. Table 50 presents the results of the latter series of questions.

Both men and women who drank wine or beer, or spirits, at least once a month drank relatively less often in restaurants and bars than at friends' or their own homes. Wine or beer was drunk by higher proportions at home than in either of the other locations; spirits were drunk by about equal proportions at home and at friends' homes. Women were much less likely than men of the same drinker group to drink wine or beer in restaurants or bars.

The findings on where people most often and fairly often drink wine or beer at various places are shown by Q–F–V group in Table 51. Among the heavier drinkers, both men and women most often drank wine or beer relatively more at restaurants and bars and less in their own homes or with friends than was the case with the lighter drinkers. On an absolute basis, the heavy drinkers drank all beverages more often at each of the three locations than did others.

Detailed analysis[7] shows the following results among once-a-month-or-more wine or beer drinkers: Relatively higher proportions of older persons than younger drank wine or beer most often at

---

[6] Reported in Detail Table A-49; see *Headnote*, p. 229.
[7] Reported in Detail Table A-51; see *Headnote*, p. 229.

TABLE 50.—*Where People Drink Wine or Beer or Distilled Spirits, by Sex, in Per Cent*

	Total	Men	Women
N	2746	1177	1569
Wine or Beer			
At least once a month	43	58	30
N	1143	677	466
In own home			
Fairly often	36	35	36
Once in a while	51	49	55
Almost never	13	16	9
At friends' homes			
Fairly often	11	12	10
Once in a while	57	59	54
Almost never	32	29	36
At restaurants or bars			
Fairly often	15	20	8
Once in a while	38	41	33
Almost never	47	39	59
Distilled Spirits			
At least once a month	39	48	30
N	1046	566	480
In own home			
Fairly often	24	24	24
Once in a while	58	56	60
Almost never	18	20	16
At friends' homes			
Fairly often	17	15	18
Once in a while	64	65	64
Almost never	19	20	18
At restaurants or bars			
Fairly often	21	22	19
Once in a while	42	39	47
Almost never	37	39	34

home. Relatively higher proportions of younger persons than older drank these beverages most often in restaurants or bars. Among men of the various ISP groups, especially younger men, relatively more of the well-to-do than of the lower ISP groups said they most often drank beer or wine at home and relatively fewer at restaurants or bars. Young men in the lowest ISP groups were more likely than those at other levels to report drinking wine or beer most

TABLE 51.—Where People Drink Wine or Beer, by Sex and Q–F–V Group, in Per Cent[a]

	N	At Least Once a Month	N	Most Often At[b]			Fairly Often At[b]		
				Own Home	Friends' Homes	Bars, Rest.	Own Home	Friends' Homes	Bars, Rest.
Total sample	2746	43	1143	68	12	22[c]	36	11	15
Men	1177	58	677	63	12	28	35	12	20
Women	1569	30	466	75	13	13	36	10	8
Men									
Light drinkers	324	79	255	70	12	20	21	6	6
Moderate	212	87	185	60	14	27	34	13	17
Heavy	252	95	237	58	10	38	53	17	38
Women									
Light	442	68	297	77	15	8	30	7	3
Moderate	142	72	105	74	11	18	44	13	10
Heavy	72	87	64	69	7	24	50	24	26

[a] The results in other groups are given in Detail Table A-51; see Headnote, p. 229.
[b] The three columns under "Most Often" represent responses to a single question; those under "Fairly Often" separate questions for each location. See footnote to Table 48.
[c] These three groups add to a little more than 100% of those drinking wine or beer because a few drinkers named more than one place where wine or beer was drunk most often.

often at friends' homes. No particular patterns by ISP group were discernible among women.

Where people reported they usually drank spirits (including mixed drinks) is shown in Table 52. In general, the findings were much the same as for where people drink wine or beer, with these exceptions:

Within the ISP groups,[8] the younger men (21 to 39 years) showed no particular differences by ISP as to where they drank spirits most often. Among men aged 40 to 59, relatively more of the lowest social group than of the upper groups drank spirits most often at home (and relatively more of the highest ISP drank spirits most often in restaurants and bars). With wine and beer the situation was reversed: relatively fewer of those in the lower ISP than in the upper groups within the 40 to 59 age level drank wine or beer most often at home. Among women there were again no clear-cut patterns by ISP as to where spirits were most often drunk.

7. Weekday and Weekend Drinking (Tables 53, 54)

All respondents who drank as often as once a month were asked how often they drank wine or beer and spirits on weekdays and on weekends. From Table 53 it can be seen that two-thirds of those who drank wine or beer at least once a month drank on weekdays at least once in a while, and that about 90% drank wine or beer on weekends at least once in a while. Somewhat fewer reported drinking spirits (or drinks containing spirits) on weekdays, but 92% drank spirits on weekends at least occasionally. There was relatively little difference between men and women in the proportion drinking spirits at least once in a while on weekdays and weekends; but somewhat more men than women reported drinking wine or beer fairly often on both weekdays and weekends.

Table 54 shows the proportions of once-a-month-or-more drinkers who said they drank wine-or-beer and spirits fairly often on weekdays and weekends. The pattern of weekday and weekend drinking appears to be about the same in both men and women and within each Q–F–V group.

Subgroup comparisons on weekday and weekend drinking must be drawn with caution, since respondents were asked separately about each, and not which they did most often (as was done re-

[8] Reported in Detail Table A-52; see *Headnote*, p. 229.

TABLE 52.—Where People Drink Distilled Spirits, by Sex and Q-F-V Group, in Per Cent[a]

	N	At Least Once a Month	N	Most Often At[b]			Fairly Often At[b]		
				Own Home	Friends' Homes	Bars, Rest.	Own Home	Friends' Homes	Bars, Rest.
Total sample	2746	39	1046	48	26	29[c]	24	17	21
Men	1177	48	566	49	23	30	24	15	22
Women	1569	30	480	45	29	27	24	18	19
Men									
Light drinkers	324	63	205	51	26	23	10	5	9
Moderate	212	78	162	45	26	30	20	12	21
Heavy	252	80	199	49	18	37	41	27	37
Women									
Light	442	68	305	44	36	22	15	10	10
Moderate	142	85	119	51	20	34	36	28	28
Heavy	72	78	56	47	13	43	50	39	53

[a] The results in other groups are reported in Detail Table A-52; see Headnote, p. 229.
[b] The three columns under "Most Often" represent responses to a single question; those under "Fairly Often" separate questions for each location. See footnote to Table 48.
[c] These three groups add to a little more than 100% of those drinking spirits because a few drinkers named more than one place where spirits were drunk most often.

TABLE 53.—*Percentage who Drink Wine or Beer or Distilled Spirits on Weekdays and at Weekends, by Sex*

	Total	Men	Women
N	2746	1177	1569
Wine or Beer			
At least once a month	43	58	30
N	1143	677	466
On weekdays			
Fairly often	22	25	16
Once in a while	44	43	46
Almost never	34	32	38
On weekends			
Fairly often	40	45	33
Once in a while	48	44	54
Almost never	12	11	13
Distilled Spirits			
At least once a month	39	48	30
N	1046	566	480
On weekdays			
Fairly often	16	18	14
Once in a while	41	43	39
Almost never	43	39	47
On weekends			
Fairly often	37	38	36
Once in a while	55	52	58
Almost never	8	10	6

garding various types of drinking companions and locations for drinking). Therefore, comparisons must take into account the relative mention of weekends and weekdays as times when drinking was done fairly often, to compensate for the fact that some sub-groups drank more than others on both weekends and weekdays. Analysis by age and ISP groups[9] revealed that young men of lower ISP tended to drink wine or beer (but not spirits) relatively more often on weekends than did others. Among middle-aged and older men, the lower ISP groups did not differ from the upper in their relative drinking of wine or beer or of spirits on weekends; but the upper ISP groups (of all ages) were relatively more likely than the lower to drink spirits on weekdays. No major differences by ISP were apparent among the women. Although all groups drank

[9] Reported in Detail Table A-54; see *Headnote*, p. 229.

TABLE 54.—*Percentage who Drink Wine or Beer or Distilled Spirits "Fairly Often" on Weekdays and at Weekends, by Sex and Q–F–V Group*[a]

	N	Wine or Beer at Least Once a Month	Spirits at Least Once a Month	N	Wine or Beer Fairly Often on		N	Spirits Fairly Often on	
					Weekdays	Weekends		Weekdays	Weekends
Total sample	2746	43	39	1143	22	40	1046	16	37
Men	1177	58	48	677	25	45	566	18	38
Women	1569	30	30	466	16	33	480	14	36
Men									
Light drinkers	324	79	63	255	13	23	205	9	21
Moderate	212	87	78	185	18	41	162	13	32
Heavy	252	95	80	237	43	71	199	31	59
Women									
Light	442	68	68	297	11	25	305	6	25
Moderate	142	72	85	105	20	39	119	20	46
Heavy	72	87	78	64	36	63	56	38	65

[a] The results in other groups are reported in Detail Table A-54; see Headnote, p. 229.

more on weekends, older people were relatively more likely than younger to drink on weekdays. This age pattern was true of both men and women.

SUMMARY

The findings of this chapter show that there are substantial differences between heavy drinkers and others, and between men and women and the various age and socioeconomic groups, in their social associations and the circumstances in which they usually drink. Among the differences are the following:

Heavy drinkers were more likely than others to get together socially with people from work rather than with people from their neighborhood or church. This finding suggests that heavy drinkers are less subject to the special controls implied in social relationships with persons from the neighborhood and the church. This does not imply, of course, that lack of such social controls "caused" the heavy drinking; it is just as plausible to expect that a person who is a heavy drinker will gravitate toward the company of other heavy drinkers and away from that of persons from the neighborhood and the church, who may be less congenial.

The reported drinking behavior and attitudes of parents and spouses were found to be rather strongly associated with respondents' own drinking. The examples and attitudes regarding drinking set by mothers were more strongly associated with heavy drinking than were the drinking behavior and attitudes of fathers. The cause of this difference cannot be known without more detailed research. However, it might stem from the mother's presumed stronger influence upon the child, or it might be attributable in part to the likelihood, in a society which is not very permissive toward women's heavy drinking, that a home in which the mother drinks heavily is more likely to have a higher degree of disorganization and indifference to sanctions against heavy drinking, with consequent lessening of social controls upon the children in the family.

Regardless of the cause of the strong association between parental attitudes and drinking and the drinking of the children, knowledge of parents' attitudes and behavior regarding drinking (and particularly, the attitudes and behavior of the mother) is of material help in predicting the later drinking behavior of their children.

Both men and women drank more often in their own homes or in friends' homes than in restaurants or bars. Among the differences noted in various groups was the finding that a majority of men who drank beer or wine at least once a month said they drank it most often with their friends, while a majority of women who drank beer or wine at least once a month said they drank it most often with other members of the family. Those of upper socioeconomic status, especially the younger men, drank beer or wine most often at home rather than in restaurants or bars.

Chapter 5

Retrospective Reports of Changes in Drinking

L ITTLE IS KNOWN at present about recent increases or decreases in the proportions of heavy drinkers in the population. However, evidence was presented earlier (Chapter 2) which indicates fairly conclusively that there has been a material increase in the proportion of persons who drink at least a little; and the evidence from trends in surveys conducted over a period of years indicates that a considerable part of the apparent increase in the size of the drinking population is accounted for by the rise in the number of women who drink (Chapter 2). Only through longitudinal studies can a conclusive measurement of changes in drinking be attained.[1] Retrospective reports of one's past drinking activity are always suspect because they are subject to forgetfulness, distortion and rationalization. Such information, however, can be useful in providing clues as to the forces operating to increase or decrease the level of drinking. At minimum, such retrospective information helps to define both the respondents' perceptions of themselves in relation to drinking and the social climate which may influence future changes in drinking habits.

The national survey covered several areas of inquiry related to changes in amount of drinking, on a retrospective basis: How old was the person when he started to drink? Did he ever drink more than at present, and at what age? Did he consider himself a heavy drinker when he drank more? What are his reasons for drinking less now? Did he ever drink less at any time since he reached maturity, and at what age? What are his reasons for drinking more now? Has he noticed any changes in the drinking of people in general during the last 5 years, and does he think people are drinking more or less than 5 years ago? If now an abstainer, did he ever drink as often as once a year? At what age did he quit? What were the reasons for quitting?

---

[1] The case for longitudinal studies and an enumeration of the shortcomings of retrospective and anecdotal efforts to measure change has been presented succinctly by Knupfer (40).

Age at Starting to Drink (Tables 55, 56)

Table 55 shows the ages when respondents reported starting to drink (disregarding small "tastes" of alcoholic beverages when younger). More than half of the drinkers began before age 21, 16% before age 18. More men than women drinkers (21% vs 11%) started to drink before age 18. More heavy-drinking men than other groups started drinking before age 18.

Detailed analyses by age and ISP[2] reveal the following highlights: One-third of the men drinkers now aged 21 to 29 recalled having started drinking before age 18, compared to only 19% of those 50 years and older. A similar pattern was found in women (21 vs 5%). If the memories of the older and younger respondents are equally reliable, these reports would suggest that people are now drinking at an earlier age than they did a generation ago. However, these findings are to be taken with caution, both because it may well be that those over age 50 have less accurate memories of their earliest drinking than have those in their 20s, and also because the findings are affected by the artifacts that (1) the tabulations of drinkers in their 20s automatically exclude from the base those who will start drinking later and (2) the base for drinkers in their 50s by definition excludes all those who used to drink before they were aged 50 but no longer do so. Drinkers of highest ISP generally started drinking at a later age than did others.

Since early drinking appears to be related to a tendency toward later heavy drinking, a special analysis was made within sex, age and ISP subgroups of the Q–F–V classifications of drinkers who said they started to drink before they reached age 21, as against those who started later (Table 56). In all age and ISP groups, particularly those aged 45 and over, men who started drinking before age 21 were considerably more likely than others to be heavy drinkers. This was not true of women, however.

Present and Former Drinking (Table 57)

More than a third (37%) of the sample said they used to drink more than they do now, while 20% said they used to drink less; these include a few who said they had drunk both more and less in the past (Table 57). Just about half reported that their drinking habits were different now than in the past. Changes in drinking were

[2] Reported in Detail Table A-55; see *Headnote*, p. 229.

TABLE 55.—Age at Which Drinkers First Drank, by Sex and Q-F-V Group, in Per Cent[a]

	N	<18	18–20	21–24	25–29	30–34	35–39	40+	Not Known
					AGE				
Total drinkers	1848	16	37	26	10	5	2	3	1
Men	909	21	40	26	7	4	1	1	b
Women	939	11	33	28	13	6	3	4	2
Men									
Infrequent drinkers	121	16	43	27	5	7	b	1	1
Light	324	19	38	27	8	4	2	2	0
Moderate	212	15	44	29	6	3	3	b	0
Heavy	252	31	39	19	7	2	1	1	0
Women									
Infrequent	283	8	34	27	16	7	2	4	2
Light	442	10	32	29	12	6	3	6	2
Moderate	142	19	35	26	10	6	2	1	1
Heavy	72	16	34	27	11	6	3	3	0

[a] The results in other groups are reported in Detail Table A-55; see Headnote, p. 229.
[b] Less than 0.5%.

TABLE 56.—*Percentage of Drinkers in Q-F-V Groups, by Whether They Started to Drink Before Age 21, by Index of Social Position, Sex and Age*

	MEN				WOMEN			
	N	Infreq.	Light + Mod.	Heavy	N	Infreq.	Light + Mod.	Heavy
Total drinkers	909	13	59	28	939	30	62	8
Age 21–44								
Higher ISP								
Before age 21	199	9	62	29	178	22	70	8
Not before 21	93	10	70	20	148	29	63	8
Lower ISP								
Before age 21	167	11	57	32	124	33	53	14
Not before 21	53	9	66	25	106	36	56	8
Age 45+								
Higher ISP								
Before age 21	75	9	50	41	55	28	69	3
Not before 21	114	9	71	20	151	29	64	7
Lower ISP								
Before age 21	111	22	46	32	47	44	51	5
Not before 21	96	26	52	22	116	31	62	7

TABLE 57.—*Percentage of Respondents who Formerly Drank More or Less, by Sex and Q-F-V Group*[a]

| | | ABSTAINERS | | DRINKERS | | | | (2, 3, 5) | (4, 5) | (2, 3, 4, 5) |
| | | (1) | (2) | (3) | (4) | (5) | (6) | Total | Total | Total |
	N	Never Drank	Drank Formerly	Drank More	Drank Less	Drank More & Less	No Change	Ever More	Ever Less	Changers
Total sample	2746	22	10	21	14	6	27	37	20	51
Men	1177	9	13	29	15	10	24	52	25	67
Women	1569	32	8	14	13	3	30	25	16	38
Men										
Abstainers	268	41	59	0	0	0	0	59	0	59
Infrequent drinkers	121	0	0	55	3	3	39	58	6	61
Light	324	0	0	38	16	9	37	47	25	63
Moderate	212	0	0	36	20	14	30	50	34	70
Heavy	252	0	0	29	29	21	21	50	50	79
Women										
Abstainers	630	81	19	0	0	0	0	19	0	19
Infrequent	283	0	0	27	10	1	62	28	11	38
Light	442	0	0	20	25	6	49	26	31	51
Moderate	142	0	0	25	30	6	39	31	36	61
Heavy	72	0	0	23	37	17	20	40	54	77

[a] The results in other groups are reported in Detail Table A-57; see Headnote, p. 229.

much more evident among men than among women, and among heavy drinkers compared to others. Also notable is the fact that 59% of the men abstainers said they used to drink, compared to only 19% of the women abstainers.

Among the various Q–F–V groups, more men who drink infrequently said they used to drink more than did men who drink heavily. But among women, more of the heavy drinkers said they formerly drank more than did women in the infrequent, light and moderate categories.

Findings by age and ISP level[3] show no particular differences among younger men (21–39 years); but among men 40 years and over, fewer of those in higher ISP levels reported having drunk more in the past than did those of lowest ISP.

Reasons for Currently Drinking More (Tables 58, 59)

The 20% of the total sample who said they used to drink less represent 30% of all drinkers. Table 58 presents reasons given, by

TABLE 58.—*Reasons for Drinking More than Formerly, by Sex, in Per Cent*

	Total	Men	Women
N drinking more	553	288	265
Social reasons (including influence of spouse)	27	20	36
Have more money	18	21	15
Go out more	14	9	20
Enjoy drinking more	12	13	10
Have more time	7	8	6
More need for relaxation	7	7	7
Business reasons	7	10	2
Have more opportunity	5	9	1
Older (more able to drink)	5	3	7
Better health	4	6	1
Prescribed by doctor	4	3	5
Have fewer problems	4	2	6
Alcohol not illegal now	2	3	a
Have more problems or responsibilities	1	1	2
In military service now	a	1	0
Miscellaneous reasons	9	10	8
Not ascertained	3	1	4
Totals	129[b]	127[b]	130[b]

a Less than 0.5%.

b Adds to more than 100% because some respondents gave more than one reason for drinking more now.

[3] Reported in Detail Table A-57; see *Headnote*, p. 229.

men and women who used to drink less, for drinking more now than formerly. The most frequently mentioned reason for drinking more now was social influences, including the effects of increased visiting and entertaining and the influence or example of one's husband, wife or associates. Women who had increased their drinking gave this and other social reasons more often than did men, perhaps reflecting the more socially oriented nature of their drinking in general. Women also mentioned more often that they are going out more now than before. Men relatively more often than women cited financial considerations (having more money now) and business reasons.

Table 59 analyzes the differences in the frequency with which the leading reasons for drinking more were mentioned by various subgroups. The heavier drinkers among men mentioned more often than did other men that they enjoy drinking more now than they used to and that they drink more for business reasons.[4] They mentioned social reasons much less often than did other men. More heavier-drinking women than other women said that they have more time now to drink and that they have a greater need for relaxation now than before.

Analysis of the major reasons for increased drinking by age and ISP[5] shows that younger people tended relatively more often than older ones to say they now go out more. The upper ISP groups, both men and women, tended to mention financial reasons more than did the lower groups.

Reasons for Currently Drinking Less (Tables 60, 61)

Table 60 gives the reasons cited for drinking less now by those who used to drink more. The chief emphases implied little in the way of guilt or anxiety about drinking—the respondents said they drink less now because of more responsibilities or problems or for financial reasons or because they go out less than formerly. Relatively few mentioned guilt-related or moral or religious reasons,

---

[4] This finding is consistent with the results of a special cross-analysis by self-rating of present drinking. The analysis showed that those who classified their drinking as "fairly heavy" or "heavy" put greater emphasis than others upon business reasons for drinking more than previously, while those who rated their present drinking as "very light" put greater emphasis than others on social reasons (including influence of spouse) for the increase.

[5] Reported in Detail Table A-59; see *Headnote*, p. 229.

TABLE 59.—*Reasons for Drinking More than Formerly, by Sex and Q–F–V Group, in Per Cent*[a]

	N	DRINK MORE %	DRINK MORE N	Social Reasons	More Money	Go Out More	Enjoy Drink More	More Time	More Need to Relax	Busi-ness
Total drinkers	1848	30	553	27	18	14	12	7	7	7
Men	909	32	288	20	21	9	13	8	7	10
Women	939	27	265	36	15	20	10	6	7	2
Men										
Infrequent drinkers	121	6	7	78	0	29	0	0	0	0
Light	324	25	81	24	23	5	11	9	10	7
Moderate	212	34	76	21	28	5	7	7	7	11
Heavy	252	50	124	14	17	13	19	8	6	13
Women										
Infrequent	283	11	34	42	3	23	0	0	3	0
Light	442	31	138	33	16	25	11	4	7	2
Moderate	142	36	53	41	25	12	7	4	7	1
Heavy	72	56	40	31	12	6	16	21	13	5

[a] The results in other groups are reported in Detail Table A-59; see Headnote, p. 229.

TABLE 60.—*Reasons for Drinking Less than Formerly, in Per Cent*

	Total	Men	Women
N drinking less	741	455	286
Have more responsibilities or problems	21	24	16
Financial reasons	17	20	11
Go out less	17	10	29
Less need or desire	17	17	15
Social reasons (including influence of spouse)	14	12	18
Older, more mature	13	16	9
Fewer opportunities to drink	11	13	8
Bad health; was in better health formerly	11	11	11
Military service then or now (mostly then)	8	12	a
Fewer problems	5	4	7
Do not like smell or taste of alcohol	4	3	7
Drinking bad for job or business	3	3	1
Did not like effects drinking had on my behavior	3	3	3
Alcohol nauseates me	2	1	4
Was exposed to bad examples then	2	2	2
Drinking sets bad example for children, community	1	1	2
Hangovers, headaches	1	a	1
Religious or moral reasons	a	a	1
Miscellaneous negative reasons	6	6	6
Not ascertained	a	1	a
Totals	156[b]	159[b]	151[b]

[a] Less than 0.5%.

[b] Adds to more than 100% because some respondents gave more than one reason for drinking less now.

such as not wanting to set a bad example, concern about one's own behavior, or that drinking was bad for one's job or business.

Table 61 presents findings in various subgroups of drinkers on the eight most frequently mentioned reasons for drinking less. The heavier drinkers among the men were more likely than others to mention having more responsibilities now, financial reasons or the process of aging. Relatively few of the heavy drinkers among women who used to drink more said they reduced their drinking because they were going out less—although among women as a whole this was the major reason for cutting down. The women heavy drinkers who reported drinking less now were more likely than others to give as a reason that they now had fewer opportunities; and they were less likely to name social influences.

Detail analysis by other subgroups[6] yielded the following high-

[6] Reported in Detail Table A-61; see *Headnote*, p. 229.

TABLE 61.—*Reasons for Drinking Less than Formerly, by Sex and Q-F-V Group, in Per Cent*[a]

	N	Drink Less %	Drink Less N	More Resp. or Prob.	Financial Reasons	Go out Less	Less Need or Desire	Social Reasons	Older, More Mature	Less Opportunity	Bad for Health
Total drinkers	1848	40	741	21	17	17	17	14	13	11	11
Men	909	50	455	24	20	10	17	12	16	13	11
Women	939	29	286	16	11	29	15	18	9	8	11
Men											
Infrequent drinkers	121	58	70	17	21	7	25	13	11	9	17
Light	324	47	154	21	19	11	22	14	14	11	13
Moderate	212	50	109	25	17	10	18	9	16	20	9
Heavy	252	50	122	29	24	12	8	9	21	11	7
Women											
Infrequent	283	29	86	15	12	35	14	18	10	5	13
Light	442	26	121	12	11	29	14	22	10	7	10
Moderate	142	30	48	29	6	24	18	12	11	12	10
Heavy	72	42	31	16	19	12	17	9	0	17	10

[a] The results in other groups are reported in Detail Table A-61; see Headnote, p. 229.

lights: Young men tended to emphasize increased responsibilities and financial factors as reasons for drinking less now. Older men and women mentioned health reasons more frequently than did younger people. Women 60 years or older were more likely than younger ones to say they drink less because they go out less now, and mentioned financial and social reasons (including their spouse's influence) much more often than did older men. Among the men, those of lower ISP tended to mention financial reasons and increased responsibilities relatively more often than did others, as well as a decreased need or desire to drink.

Drinking Turn-Over (Table 62)

Additional inferences regarding turn-over in drinking habits can be gleaned from the analysis shown in Table 62. Of the total sample, 22% said they had always been abstainers and 41% that they had never drunk any more in the past than they were now drinking. The remaining 37% had either reduced or quit drinking since some earlier period.

TABLE 62.—*Percentage of Respondents who Formerly Drank More, by Sex and Age*

| | | ABSTAINERS | | DRINKERS | | Drank More within Past 5 Years[a] |
	N	Never Drank	Used to Drink	Drank More	Never Drank More	
Total sample	2746	22	10	27	41	13
Men	1177	9	13	39	39	15
Women	1569	32	8	17	43	11
Men						
Age 21–29	216	9	7	46	38	30
30–39	243	6	8	42	44	15
40–49	264	7	14	42	37	11
50–59	197	11	16	33	40	11
60+	257	14	21	30	35	11
Women						
Age 21–29	256	25	5	24	46	29
30–39	345	23	5	21	51	13
40–49	333	26	9	17	48	7
50–59	265	42	8	12	38	3
60+	367	46	10	13	31	4

[a] Base: total sample.

Half of the men and a quarter of the women said either that they used to drink more or that they used to drink but had quit. This supports the other evidence that there is high turn-over in drinking practices, particularly among men. Relatively more older than younger men had quit drinking, and relatively more younger men had cut down. Among the women, only 25% of those aged 21 to 29 said they had never drunk, compared to 46% of those 60 years or older. This finding supports other indications that the proportion of drinkers among women is growing.[7]

An additional tabulation of when respondents drank more than at present (also shown in Table 62) reveals that 15% of the men and 11% of the women said they used to drink more (or, among present nondrinkers, drank more than once a year) within 5 years prior to the time of interview. The proportion was close to 3 out of 10 among those in the 21 to 29 age group. Hence it appears that a substantial number of people go into and out of the various classifications of users of alcohol over a period of time.

"Fairly Heavy" Drinking by Those Who Used to Drink More (Table 63)

As shown in Table 63, only 15% of the drinkers said they used to drink more and reported that they had thought of themselves as at least "fairly heavy" drinkers at the time they were drinking more. The proportion was 24% among the men and 6% among the women. The heavier drinkers (according to their present level of drinking) were readier than others to say that they had considered themselves to be heavy drinkers when they drank more than they do now. Although it will be shown later that only small proportions of those classified as drinking heavily at present are willing to call themselves heavy drinkers, the finding that two-thirds of the heavy-drinking men and half of the heavy-drinking women who used to drink more said they had then considered themselves as being at least fairly heavy drinkers may be indicative of at least a certain degree of recognition if not self-consciousness or concern about drinking on their part.

[7] These findings are consistent with the other reports (see Chapter 2) which indicate that the proportion of drinkers is increasing among women, and with the findings of a short-term longitudinal study in Hartford, Conn., that the proportion of drinkers among younger women is increasing (10).

TABLE 63.—*Self-Rating of Past Drinking by Drinkers who Used to Drink More, by Sex and Q–F–V Group, in Per Cent*[a]

	N	Drank More	Drank More When Under 25	Had Considered Self at Least a Fairly Heavy Drinker
Total drinkers	1848	40	21	15
Men	909	50	28	24
Women	939	29	14	6
Men				
Infrequent drinkers	121	58	37	18
Light	324	47	25	19
Moderate	212	50	29	21
Heavy	252	50	28	34
Women				
Infrequent	283	29	15	1
Light	442	26	11	4
Moderate	142	30	16	14
Heavy	72	40	20	21

[a] The results in other groups are reported in Detail Table A-63; see Headnote, p. 229.

Detailed analysis of subgroups[8] gives these additional findings: Persons aged under 30 who formerly drank more reported more often than did those aged 60 or over that they had considered themselves as at least fairly heavy drinkers in the past. While this may reflect a tendency on the part of older persons to forget or to reinterpret earlier concerns about heavy drinking, it is also possible that this finding may be an indication that there actually is a higher level of heavy drinking among those now in their 20s than there was within older age groups at an equivalent age in the past.

Among men aged 40 years and older who used to drink more, those of lower ISP had a larger proportion reporting that they then thought of themselves as at least fairly heavy drinkers than did those of higher status. This may be a reflection of an actual fact that those of lower ISP do have a larger proportion who once drank heavily; or it may be that those of higher ISP formerly drank as much but are less willing to say they were heavy drinkers than are those of lower status.

[8] Reported in Detail Table A-63; see *Headnote,* p. 229.

An additional finding relevant to age, shown in Table 63, was that men drinkers were materially more likely than women drinkers to have drunk more before age 25 than at present. Men infrequent drinkers and women heavy drinkers were more likely than others to have drunk more before age 25.

Past Drinking of Abstainers (Tables 64–66)

Table 64 summarizes drinking practices in terms of those who now drink (once a year or more), those who used to drink, and those who said they had never had any kind of beverage containing alcohol.

The group of special interest here is the 10% who used to drink but are now abstainers (drink not at all or less than once a year). The fact that one-third of the present abstainers said they used to drink is another indication of the relatively high rate of turn-over in drinking practices discussed above (see Table 62).

Differences in the proportions of former drinkers, revealed by detailed subgroup analysis,[9] were as follows: Relatively more older than younger persons were former drinkers. This relationship undoubtedly reflects primarily the fact that older people have had a greater span of time in which to get into and out of the drinker group. There is a notable difference in age variations by sex, however: men 50 years and older had higher proportions saying they used to drink than said they never drank, while among women much larger proportions never drank than used to drink in all age groups. In general those of lower ISP tended more often than the upper ISP groups to report themselves as former drinkers. Larger

TABLE 64.—*Present and Past Drinking of Respondents, by Sex, in Per Cent*[a]

	N	Present Drinkers	Used to Drink	Never Drank
Total sample	2746	68	10	22
Men	1177	77	13	10
Women	1569	60	8	32
Abstainers				
Men	268	0	59	41
Women	630	0	19	81

[a] The results in other groups are reported in Detail Table A-64; see Headnote, p. 229.

[9] Reported in Detail Table A-64; see *Headnote*, p. 229.

proportions of conservative Protestants (Methodists, Baptists and others), fewer of whom were drinkers than those of other religious groups, both used to drink and never drank, but they were in about the same proportions relative to each other as for the sample as a whole.

1. *Age When Abstainers Stopped Drinking* (Table 65). As seen above, of the one-third of the total sample who were abstainers at the time of the interview, about one-third said they used to drink at least once a year. The age at which former drinkers said they stopped drinking, as shown in Table 65, was fairly evenly distributed over a wide range, with 7% saying they stopped at age 45 or older. The fact that relatively more men than women gave it up after they were 45 is primarily (but not exclusively) a function of the fact that more of the men abstainers formerly drank.

The tabulation by age groups suggests that many of those classified as abstainers may not have withdrawn permanently from the ranks of those who drink at least once in a while. It will be noted that a relatively large proportion within each age group up to age 45—particularly among men—said they stopped drinking within the past 10 years. One-fourth to one-third of the men in their 50s or older said they stopped drinking after the age of 45. Perhaps some of those who stopped drinking fairly recently may return to the ranks of drinkers later.

Another point of interest in the responses of abstainers is that a relatively smaller proportion of the older men abstainers said they had never drunk than was true of men aged 21 to 29, whereas about 8 out of 10 women abstainers in all age groups said they had never drunk. The findings suggest that some factor such as personal or social constraints may be operating fairly uniformly to keep women abstainers at the various age levels from drinking, while men abstainers, whose likelihood of having drunk at one time or another increases with age, may abstain less often for reasons of social pressure than is the case with women; the reasons given for abstaining (see Table 67) bear out this assumption.

Men of above-average ISP who were abstainers had a somewhat higher percentage who said they had never drunk than did men of below-average status. Thus, while men of higher ISP had a higher proportion of drinkers, men abstainers in this group apparently included a higher proportion who had never drunk than did lower-

TABLE 65.—*Age when Abstainers Stopped Drinking, by Sex, Age and Index of Social Position, in Per Cent*

| | N | Never Drank | Age when Stopped Drinking | | | | | | | Not Known |
			<21	21–24	25–29	30–34	35–39	40–44	45+	
Total abstainers	898	68	5	4	4	4	4	3	7	1
Men	268	41	9	10	7	6	7	3	16	1
Women	630	81	3	2	2	3	3	3	3	ª
Men										
Age 21–29	37	56	22	21	0	0	0	0	0	1
30–39	32	45	12	14	20	6	3	0	0	0
40–49	55	35	9	14	12	7	10	8	4	1
50–59	52	40	4	6	7	7	10	3	23	0
60+	92	39	4	6	2	8	7	2	31	1
Women										
Age 21–29	75	82	9	5	3	0	0	0	0	1
30–39	93	82	2	5	5	4	2	0	0	0
40–49	115	74	3	3	5	5	5	2	2	1
50–59	133	83	0	0	3	2	4	7	1	0
60+	213	82	2	ª	0	2	3	2	9	ª

ª Less than 0.5%.

[Continued on next page]

TABLE 65.—continued

		Never Drank				Age when Stopped Drinking				Not Known
Men	N		<21	21-24	25-29	30-34	35-39	40-44	45+	
Age 21-44										
Higher ISP	42	47	14	17	12	2	7	0	0	1
Lower ISP	55	45	9	21	12	9	2	2	0	0
Age 45+										
Higher ISP	66	46	5	13	4	7	6	4	15	0
Lower ISP	105	34	3	6	6	5	10	4	31	1
Women										
Age 21-44										
Higher ISP	78	77	5	6	4	2	5	0	0	1
Lower ISP	153	78	2	5	5	5	2	1	0	2
Age 45+										
Higher ISP	141	82	2	0	1	1	4	4	5	1
Lower ISP	257	82	1	1	1	2	2	4	6	1

status abstainers. Lower-status older men abstainers were more likely than upper-status men of this group to have quit after age 45.

2. *Self-Rating on Fairly Heavy Drinking by Abstainers Who Used to Drink* (Table 66). Abstainers who used to drink more than once a year were also asked whether they had ever considered themselves fairly heavy drinkers. Table 66 shows that relatively few

TABLE 66.—*Self-Rating of Past Drinking by Abstainers who Formerly Drank, by Sex, Age and Index of Social Position, in Per Cent*

	N	Formerly Drank	Stopped Before 25	Had Considered Self at Least a Fairly Heavy Drinker
Total abstainers	898	32	9	5
Men	268	59	19	14
Women	630	19	5	1
Men				
Age 21–29	37	44	43	3
30–39	32	55	26	14
40–49	55	65	23	21
50–59	52	60	10	13
60+	92	61	10	14
Women				
Age 21–29	75	18	14	0
30–39	93	18	7	3
40–49	115	26	6	1
50–59	133	17	0	0
60+	213	18	2	1
Men				
Age 21–44				
Higher ISP	42	53	31	11
Lower ISP	55	55	30	11
Age 45+				
Higher ISP	66	54	18	14
Lower ISP	105	66	9	16
Women				
Age 21–44				
Higher ISP	78	23	11	0
Lower ISP	153	22	7	2
Age 45+				
Higher ISP	141	18	2	1
Lower ISP	257	18	2	1

abstainers (only 5%) said that there was ever a time when they had rated themselves as fairly heavy drinkers (this compares with 15% of the drinkers who used to drink more and considered themselves fairly heavy drinkers, as shown in Table 63).

While this group of self-nominated former fairly heavy drinkers among the abstainers was relatively small, it is of special interest because further study may provide some clues as to the process whereby the heavy drinker who does quit drinking happens to quit. Table 66 shows that those abstainers who considered themselves as formerly fairly heavy drinkers were almost all men and more likely to be found among those aged over 30, particularly among men in their 40s.

Reasons for Abstainers Not Drinking (Tables 67, 68)

Abstainers (those who did not usually drink as often as once a year) were asked, "What are the main reasons that you don't drink?" As shown in Table 67, the leading reason given by abstainers for not drinking was religious or moral grounds. The next

TABLE 67.—*Reasons for Abstainers Not Drinking, in Per Cent*

	Total Abstainers	Men	Women
N	898	268	630
Religious or moral reasons	31	26	33
Just do not like to drink	26	21	28
No need or desire	26	22	28
Drinking bad for health	20	27	16
Exposed to bad example in the past	20	15	22
Upbringing was against drinking	19	12	23
Financial reasons	12	18	9
Sets a bad example	4	4	3
Do not like the effects of drinking	3	6	1
Social reasons (including influence of spouse)	3	4	2
Drinking is nauseating	2	3	2
Bad for job or business	1	1	a
Have more problems	a	1	a
Older, more mature	1	1	1
Miscellaneous reasons	14	15	13
Not ascertained	a	a	a
Total	182[b]	176[b]	181[b]

a Less than 0.5%.

b Adds to more than 100% because some abstainers gave more than one reason.

two leading reasons reflect primarily a lack of desire or need for alcohol; the next reason was that drinking is bad for health, followed by two somewhat moralistic reasons (was exposed to bad examples of drinking in the past, or was brought up not to drink). It will be noted that men abstainers put relatively greater emphasis upon health and financial reasons, while abstaining women mentioned religious or moral reasons (including being exposed to bad example, being brought up not to drink) and lack of need or desire to drink, more often than did men.

Table 68 shows the major reasons offered by abstainers from various subgroups.

Age: Relatively more abstainers aged 30 to 59, both men and

TABLE 68.—*Major Reasons for Abstainers Not Drinking, by Sex, Age and Index of Social Position, Region and Religion, in Per Cent*

	N	Relig. or Moral	Don't Care for It	No Need or Desire	Bad for Health	Exposed to Bad Example in Past	Brought up Not to Drink	Finan- cial Reasons
Total abstainers	898	31	26	26	20	20	19	12
Men	268	26	21	22	27	15	12	18
Women	630	33	28	28	16	22	23	9
Men								
Age 21–29	37	15	22	25	21	27	14	18
30–39	32	35	26	30	14	17	12	26
40–49	55	35	16	19	30	12	9	23
50–59	52	30	18	16	31	12	15	15
60+	92	19	24	22	30	13	11	13
Women								
Age 21–29	75	28	52	24	6	23	15	11
30–39	93	37	29	38	17	21	23	9
40–49	115	36	31	23	13	26	22	13
50–59	133	36	22	27	21	19	23	7
60+	213	30	20	28	18	20	27	6
Men								
Age 21–44								
Higher ISP	42	29	30	28	17	30	17	14
Lower ISP	55	29	16	23	20	13	6	30
Age 45+								
Higher ISP	66	32	26	17	29	13	12	13
Lower ISP	105	20	16	22	33	12	13	16

[Continued on next page]

TABLE 68.—*continued*

Women	N	Relig. or Moral	Don't Care for it	No Need or Desire	Bad for Health	Exposed to Bad Example in Past	Brought up Not to Drink	Finan- cial Reasons
Age 21–44								
Higher ISP	78	34	32	34	10	27	20	9
Lower ISP	153	31	40	28	14	19	18	14
Age 45+								
Higher ISP	141	34	19	27	17	19	28	4
Lower ISP	257	34	23	26	20	23	24	8
Region								
New England	36	3	17	22	10	11	11	7
Middle Atlantic	93	6	26	18	15	11	10	3
South Atlantic	149	40	24	23	20	11	20	11
E. South Central	158	42	16	28	16	21	27	10
E. North Central	158	24	25	26	28	20	18	14
W. South Central	95	38	38	23	18	31	16	12
W. North Central	84	22	26	33	9	24	23	10
Mountain	37	55	16	23	9	34	20	19
Pacific	88	32	29	18	21	13	11	18
Religion								
Conserv. Prot.	633	40	23	26	16	20	21	11
Liberal Prot.	85	32	34	34	31	23	38	18
Catholic	130	4	35	29	30	21	10	12

women, than of the youngest and oldest groups, mentioned religious and moral grounds for not drinking. Relatively more older women than younger said that drinking was bad for health and that they were brought up not to drink. The leading reasons given by men aged 21 to 29 for not drinking were that they had been exposed to bad examples in the past or had no need or desire to drink. Men aged 40 and older gave health reasons more often than did younger men.

Index of Social Position: Relatively more of the upper-ISP men than of the lower mentioned religious or moral reasons, having been exposed to bad example, or just not caring for alcohol as reasons for not drinking; more of the lower-ISP men gave financial reasons.

Region: Abstainers from the Mountain and Southern states very often mentioned religious and moral grounds for not drinking, while those in the New England and Middle Atlantic areas did not mention this reason very often. Health reasons were mentioned most often in the East North Central region.

Religion: More conservative Protestants among the abstainers mentioned religious or moral reasons for not drinking. Liberal Protestant abstainers emphasized being brought up not to drink relatively more than did others. Catholic and liberal Protestant abstainers mentioned health and "just don't care for it" more than did conservative Protestants.

Opinion on Whether People are Drinking More or Less
(Tables 69, 70)

All respondents—drinkers and nondrinkers alike—were asked a direct question on whether they thought people were drinking more or less now than they were 5 years ago. They were also asked an open-ended question on what changes (if any) they had noticed in people's drinking in the last 5 years. The purpose of these questions was to obtain a partial assessment of the "climate of permissiveness," on the presumption that drinkers who believed more people were drinking would tend also to assume that the social climate was becoming more tolerant of drinking.

Table 69 shows that, in answer to the direct question, a majority said they thought people are drinking more than they were 5 years ago; only 5% said they thought people were drinking less. But in response to the open-ended question about changes they had noticed in people's drinking in the last 5 years, a majority did not indicate they had noticed any changes. Of the minority who thought they had seen changes, about half (i.e., about one-fourth of the total) volunteered either that they thought people were drinking more (larger quantities) or that more people were drinking. Very few answers implied that people were now drinking less.

The difference in results on the two questions is interpreted as indicating that the question of recent changes in people's drinking practices is not a very salient one to a majority of people, but that when respondents are pressed to say whether people are drinking more or less now than 5 years ago, the weight of opinion is that people are drinking more.[10]

[10] There was some confusion among respondents as to whether the issue concerned the number of people drinking or the average quantity consumed per person.

TABLE 69.—*Changes Observed in People's Drinking in Last 5 Years, by Sex, in Per Cent*

	Total	Men	Women
N	2746	1177	1569
Results of direct question[a]			
People are drinking more	56	55	56
People are drinking less	5	7	4
Drinking about same	20	23	17
No opinion	19	15	23
Results of open-ended question[b]			
People in general drinking more	24	23	25
More people are drinking	4	5	4
Younger people drinking more; more young people drinking	9	9	9
Women drinking more; more women drinking	2	2	2
More public drinking	4	4	4
More private drinking	1	2	1
More alcoholics, problem drinkers	1	1	1
People drinking more wisely	6	8	4
People drinking relatively more of the weaker beverages	1	2	c
People drinking relatively more of the stronger beverages	1	2	1
Miscellaneous answers	2	2	2
Had not noticed any changes; answer not ascertained	55	52	57
Totals[d]	110	112	110

[a] "Do you think people are drinking more or less now than they were five years ago?"
[b] "What changes, if any, have you noticed in people's drinking in the last five years?"
[c] Less than 0.5%.
[d] Add to more than 100% because some respondents named more than one kind of change.

Table 70 shows the results in various subgroups of the direct question on whether people are drinking more or less than 5 years ago. Men and women differed little in their opinions. If those with no opinion are set aside, relatively more of the women than of the men said people were drinking more than they were 5 years ago. This finding is another indirect indication that the proportion of women drinking has increased within recent years.

A higher proportion of both men and women abstainers, compared to nonabstainers, said they thought people were drinking more. This appears to reflect the greater view-with-alarm among abstainers. More abstainers and heavy drinkers than the infrequent, light and moderate said that people were drinking more now. The

TABLE 70.—*Respondents' Beliefs on whether People Are Drinking More or Less, by Sex and Q–F–V Group, in Per Cent*[a]

	N	More	Less	Same	No Opinion
Total sample	2746	56	5	20	19
Men	1177	55	7	23	15
Women	1569	56	4	17	23
Men					
Abstainers	268	65	5	12	18
Infrequent drinkers	121	50	4	24	22
Light	324	51	7	28	14
Moderate	212	50	9	30	11
Heavy	252	56	9	24	11
Women					
Abstainers	630	60	3	9	28
Infrequent	283	54	5	17	24
Light	442	52	4	25	19
Moderate	142	53	2	30	15
Heavy	72	58	6	22	14

[a] The results in other groups are reported in Detail Table A-70; see Headnote, p. 229.

differences may simply reflect the different outlooks by opposite groups. The abstainer notices more drinking; the heavy drinker does more drinking—so both may have a greater consciousness of drinking than do the light to moderate Q–F–V groups, to whom drinking is probably a normal part of their life pattern and no special cause for concern.

SUMMARY

The retrospective questions on past changes in drinking behavior have shown the following:

More of the heavy-drinking men than of other men started drinking before age 18; and those of the highest ISP started drinking later in life and also continued drinking to a later period in life than did those of lower status. The latter finding is consistent with general differences in the phasing of various activities by those of upper and lower class—e.g., upper-class persons generally start their sexual activity at a later age but continue a relatively high level of activity to an older age than do lower-class persons (36).

The principal reasons for drinking less than before centered around the incurring of more responsibilities or problems, or financial or social considerations; relatively few mentioned guilt-related, moral or religious reasons. The findings are consistent with those of an intensive inquiry in a community study (also retro-spective), in which social reasons (rather than personal or moral-istic) were given most frequently both for past increases or de-creases in drinking.[11]

In their reasons for not drinking, men abstainers emphasized health and financial reasons, while women emphasized religious or moral grounds and the lack of a need or desire to drink.

Half (51%) of the total sample reported that they had changed their drinking patterns at some time in their lives, either by drink-ing and then quitting, or by having drunk more or less in the past. More of the men (67%) had changed than of the women (38%), the difference stemming primarily from the larger percentage of women than of men who said they had never drunk (32% vs 9%). These findings, as well as those from other polls (Chapter 2) which indicate a sharp tapering off of drinkers after about age 50, empha-size the fact that there is a substantial turn-over in the drinking population going on much of the time. This conclusion is further supported by the results of two recent independently conducted short-term longitudinal community studies, in which Cahalan (10) and Williams (72) reported that about one-fourth of each of two probability samples of adults showed a material change in their drinking over a period of about 3 years.[12]

Reports of the abstainers (those not currently drinking as often as once a year) showed that one-third used to drink. This finding, plus the fact that many said they had stopped drinking within the last 10 years (thus including at least some who may be only temporarily abstainers) is further indication of a sizable turn-over in drinker status.

[11] See Cahalan (10); his study of 325 persons also found that in their retrospec-tions, persons speaking of their 30s or 40s tended to say they increased their drinking at that time (relatively more than persons reporting on an older or younger age span) as a means of coping with the heavier responsibilities and problems to which they felt themselves to have been subjected at this age. Another finding from the same study was that older persons appeared to reduce their drinking partly because of health and also as a result of the interaction of the lessening of social influences to drink and of responsibilities and interpersonal pressures, as well as because of an increased emphasis on health by older persons. These findings are consistent with the indications of the present national study regarding both turn-over in the drinking population and the sharp reduction in consumption at about age 50.

[12] A national study of turn-over in drinking over a 3-year period also has been completed by the authors and will be published shortly. A longer-term longitudinal study of turn-over, directed by Genevieve Knupfer, will be completed in the early 1970s.

Chapter 6

Personal Correlates of Drinking

W HILE it is clear from the findings presented in previous chapters that drinking is very much a part of the day-to-day life of many people, the function of alcohol varies a great deal from one person to another. Some of the variations can be accounted for simply by the different circumstances under which people live. Other differences are more deeply related to attitudes toward and reasons behind drinking and to differences in personality or physiological makeup. Findings of the national survey in these general areas are presented in the present chapter.

Effects and Implications of Drinking

Effects of Drinking During Previous Year (Tables 71-73)

Table 71 presents the responses of men and women drinkers to the question, "During the past year, what kinds of effects—if any—resulted from your drinking?" This was a free-answer question, without prompting.

The major finding is that two-thirds of the drinkers said that they did not recall any effects; men and women gave very similar responses on this point. The positive and negative aspects of drinking were mentioned approximately equally often by respondents who drank at least once a year.

It is probable that more intensive probing would uncover a higher level of both positive and negative effects than came to light in response to this single free-answer question. The results may well indicate, however, that a very large percentage of those who drink do not have any noteworthy effects from their drinking.

Table 72 presents subgroup comparisons on the effects which were mentioned most often. Heavy drinkers gave somewhat greater emphasis than others to having hangovers or headaches, becoming nauseated (women), and miscellaneous negative effects such as becoming more nervous or jittery (men).

The chief difference by age[1] was that younger drinkers were

---

[1] Reported in Detail Table A-72; see *Headnote*, p. 229.

TABLE 71.—*Effects of Drinking Noted in Past Year, by Sex, in Per Cent*

	Both Sexes	Men	Women
N drinkers	1848	909	939
Negative Effects			
Hangover, headache	9	9	9
Nausea	6	6	5
Passing out, blackout, becoming intoxicated (negative implications)	1	2	1
Aggressiveness, irritation	1	1	ª
Sadness, loneliness	1	ª	1
Miscellaneous negative effects (e.g., nervous feeling)	4	5	4
Positive Effects			
Social stimulation	6	6	7
Relaxation	5	5	6
Mildly pleasant effects (e.g., physiological)	3	4	2
Made me sleep well	1	1	1
Medicinal effects	1	1	1
Feeling of being high, intoxicated (positive implications)	1	1	1
Lessened inhibitions (positive implications)	ª	ª	1
Miscellaneous (cannot tell whether positive or negative, e.g., sleepiness)	4	3	4
None, or do not recall any effects	68	66	69
Totals[b]	111	110	112

ª Less than 0.5%.
[b] Add to more than 100% of drinkers because some mentioned more than one effect.

more likely than older to report hangovers or headaches. Differences by ISP were not great.

Table 73 gives a tabulation of those mentioning only favorable effects, only unfavorable effects, or both favorable and unfavorable effects. There is little difference by sex. There is a sharp difference, however, in the balance of reports from the lighter and heavier drinkers. It might be expected that the heavier drinkers would have more favorable than unfavorable things to say about drinking, if solely hedonistic considerations were applicable; but, to the contrary, a higher proportion of heavy drinkers mentioned only unfavorable effects.

The apparent paradox may stem simply from the greater physical effects felt by those who drink larger quantities of alcohol, or

TABLE 72.—*Most Frequently Mentioned Effects of Drinking, by Sex and Q–F–V Group,*[a] *in Per Cent*

	N	No Effects	NEGATIVE EFFECTS			POSITIVE EFFECTS			
			Hang-over, Head-aches	Nausea	Misc.	Social Stimu-lation	Relax-ation	Pleasant Physio-logical	Misc.
Total drinkers	1848	68	9	6	4	6	5	3	4
Men	909	66	9	6	5	6	5	4	3
Women	939	69	9	5	4	7	6	2	4
Men									
Infrequent drinkers	121	87	2	4	3	1	1	1	2
Light	324	76	4	4	1	4	6	5	2
Moderate	212	57	13	9	5	9	6	3	4
Heavy	252	51	17	8	12	8	4	3	5
Women									
Infrequent	283	82	3	2	4	3	1	1	3
Light	442	73	7	4	2	7	7	1	4
Moderate	142	53	19	8	5	12	10	1	3
Heavy	72	35	19	13	7	10	9	5	9

[a] The results in other groups are reported in Detail Table A-72; see Headnote, p. 229.

TABLE 73.—*Favorable vs Unfavorable Effects from Drinking, by Sex and Q–F–V Group,*[a] *in Per Cent*

	N	None	Favor- able Only	Unfavor- able Only	Both Favor- able & Unfavor- able	Un- classi- fiable
Total drinkers	1848	68	12	15	3	2
Men	909	66	12	17	3	2
Women	939	69	12	14	3	2
Men						
Infrequent drinkers	121	87	4	8	0	1
Light	324	76	13	7	2	2
Moderate	212	57	16	23	2	2
Heavy	252	51	9	31	6	3
Women						
Infrequent	283	82	8	8	1	1
Light	442	73	12	11	2	2
Moderate	142	53	14	26	5	2
Heavy	72	35	22	35	5	3

[a] The results in other groups are reported in Detail Table A-73; see Headnote, p. 229.

it may result from psychological factors, such as a tendency on the part of heavy drinkers who drink to escape from their problems to blame the alcohol when the problems recur.

Results of the subgroup analysis[2] reveal the following differences: Among both men and women, a much larger proportion of the younger drinkers (under 40 years) reported adverse effects than did older drinkers. Since younger drinkers are somewhat less likely than older to be classified as heavy drinkers, this result presumably does not stem from heavier drinking by young people; older drinkers, in general, appear to have learned either to drink within their capacities or to spread out their drinking more evenly. Further light is cast on this question by the analysis of variability of drinking in Appendix I, which shows that younger people do tend to drink larger quantities sporadically (hence ostensibly getting unpleasant reactions relatively more often), while older people generally drink smaller amounts more regularly. Drinkers, especially men, of lower ISP tended to report a larger ratio of negative to positive effects than did those of upper status.

[2] Reported in Detail Table A-73; see *Headnote*, p. 229.

Implications of One's Own Drinking (Table 74)

The following questions were asked to measure drinkers' perceptions of the implications of their own drinking: Whether the person worried about his own drinking; whether he considered himself at least a fairly heavy drinker; whether he would miss drinking if he had to give it up; whether others (spouse, friends, neighbors, employer, or co-workers) had tried to get him to drink less at some time during the last year. The results are summarized in Table 74.

A small proportion (9%) of drinkers said they worried about their own drinking, and 12% said that others had tried to get them to drink less at some time during the past year. Only 3% considered themselves to be at least fairly heavy drinkers. On the other hand, a much larger proportion (35%) of drinkers said they would miss drinking at least "a little." The proportions giving all these responses were consistently higher among men than among women drinkers, although even among men only 5% would rate themselves as fairly heavy drinkers.

TABLE 74.—*Perception of One's Own Drinking, by Sex and Q–F–V Group,*[a] *in Per Cent*

	N	Worry about Own Drinking	Consider Self at Least Fairly Heavy Drinker	Would Miss Drinking	Advised to Reduce Drinking in Past Year[b]
Total drinkers	1848	9	3	35	12
Men	909	11	5	45	16
Women	939	7	1	24	7
Men					
Infrequent drinkers	121	3	0	9	17
Light	324	6	c	32	11
Moderate	212	11	2	52	21
Heavy	252	21	16	70	19
Women					
Infrequent	283	7	0	6	7
Light	442	6	c	23	4
Moderate	142	13	1	45	7
Heavy	72	22	15	65	24

  [a] The results in other groups are reported in Detail Table A-74; see Headnote, p. 229.
  [b] By one or more of the following: friends, neighbors, spouse, boss, other people where respondent works.
  [c] Less than 0.5%.

Heavy drinkers among both men and women showed greater involvement with drinking on all these points except on whether others had tried to get them to drink less during the last year. Here a larger percentage of heavy-drinking women conceded this than did other women; but there was no particular difference by Q–F–V group among men. This contrast reflects the greater social pressures against heavy drinking by women compared to heavy drinking by men in this culture.

The item on how much the respondent would miss drinking if he had to give it up altogether is seen to be highly related to drinking behavior, since 70% of the men heavy drinkers and 65% of the women heavy drinkers said they would miss it at least "a little," whereas less than 10% of both men and women in the infrequent drinker group said they would miss it. It may be, however, that the would-miss-drinking item reflects two types of situations in varying degrees: instances in which the person is dependent upon alcohol for its psychic effects, and situations in which alcoholic beverages are simply part of one's general life-style or standard of living which one would be reluctant to change.

That the would-miss-drinking response is at least partially related to the individual's life style is indicated by differences among groups by ISP.[3] Those of higher social status (particularly the men) had materially higher proportions saying they would miss drinking. Another social difference is that those of lower status (particularly men) more often reported that someone had tried to get them to drink less during the last year—perhaps reflecting lesser autonomy and independence among those who are less well-off, compared to the well-to-do. Results by age level show little difference except that drinkers 60 years and over (both men and women) were less likely than younger drinkers to say they would miss drinking and less likely to report that someone had tried to get them to drink less during the past year.

OPINIONS ABOUT DRINKING

The items under this general heading, asked of all respondents, drinkers and nondrinkers, included questions as to whether drinking in general does more harm than good or more good than harm, whether the respondent considers alcoholism a serious problem,

---

[3] Reported in Detail Table A-74; see *Headnote*, p. 229.

whether he ever had a close relative or friend with a serious drinking problem, and what good and bad things can be said about drinking.

Drinking as a General Problem (Table 75)

In response to these general questions, over 75% said that drinking does "more harm than good," and the same proportion regarded alcoholism as either a "very serious" or "fairly serious" problem compared to other public health problems. Fairly large proportions of respondents said that they had had a close relative (41%) or a friend (31%) with a serious drinking problem.[4] A larger percentage of women than of men rated drinking as

TABLE 75.—*Respondents' Beliefs about Drinking as a General Problem, by Sex and Q–F–V Group,[a] in Per Cent*

	N	More Harm than Good	Alcoholism a Serious Problem	Close Relative with Serious Problem	Close Friend with Serious Problem
Total sample	2746	78	75	41	31
Men	1177	72	68	39	38
Women	1569	83	80	43	24
Men					
Abstainers	268	92	84	50	40
Infrequent drinkers	121	82	70	40	37
Light	324	71	67	32	37
Moderate	212	68	64	35	32
Heavy	252	53	58	39	42
Women					
Abstainers	630	93	83	51	22
Infrequent	283	86	79	41	20
Light	442	75	80	36	26
Moderate	142	66	77	36	36
Heavy	72	60	76	44	31

[a] The results in other groups are reported in Detail Table A-75; see Headnote, p. 229.

[4] Those who had a close relative or friend with a serious drinking problem were asked whether knowing this person had affected the amount of their drinking in any way. Of the total sample, 13% said knowing such a person had affected their drinking: 1% by making them start drinking or increase their drinking, 4% by making them stop or decrease their drinking, 8% in miscellaneous ways; 43% said knowing such a person had not affected their drinking; and the remaining 44% said they had not known such persons.

doing more harm than good and rated alcoholism as being a serious problem. Relatively more men than women reported having a close friend with a serious drinking problem; since women drink less than men, it is logical that they would be less likely than men to have heavy or problem drinkers among their friends. Almost equal proportions of men and women reported having a close relative with a serious drinking problem.

As would be expected, heavy drinkers were less inclined than others to rate drinking as doing more harm than good and to consider alcoholism a serious problem. Among both men and women, however, relatively more abstainers than drinkers reported having a close relative with a serious drinking problem; and only slightly fewer abstainers reported having a close friend with such a problem. These apparently inconsistent findings may result from a semantic difficulty: what is a serious drinking problem to an abstainer may not seem serious to a heavy drinker.

Among ISP groups[5] the attitudes toward drinking of lower-status respondents were generally more negative than were those of upper-status groups. Responses on having relatives or friends with drinking problems were more varied; the main contrast to be noted is that among men 40 years and over the higher-status groups were much more likely to report having had friends with drinking problems, whereas among younger men, those in the upper groups were less likely to have had such friends. Findings on relatives with drinking problems were much less clear-cut. Women aged 40 to 59 in the lower-status groups had a slightly higher proportion saying they had a close relative with a serious drinking problem than was true of women in the same age class in the highest social group. Among men aged 40 to 59 the picture was reversed: slightly more upper-level men than lower reported having a close relative with a drinking problem.

Good Things about Drinking (Tables 76, 77)

Table 76 summarizes the good things that people had to say about drinking in response to a free-answer question. One of the two leading attributes, mentioned by a quarter of the sample as a good thing, was that it helps people mix socially; about the same proportion said that drinking helps people to relax. The next most

---

[5] Reported in Detail Table A-75; see *Headnote,* p. 229.

TABLE 76.—*Good Things Said about Drinking, by Sex, in Per Cent*

N	Total Sample 2746	Men 1177	Women 1569
Helps people mix socially	26	28	24
Helps people to relax	25	28	22
Medicinal uses	19	20	18
Tastes good; helps appetite	12	16	8
Makes you cheerful; a pickup	6	6	5
Beverage industry provides jobs	3	4	1
Lessens inhibitions	3	3	3
Good if not abused (qualified answer)	3	2	3
Depends upon the individual (qualified answer)	1	1	1
Miscellaneous answers	3	4	2
Nothing good can be said	35	28	40
Totals	136[a]	140[a]	127[a]

[a] Adds to more than 100% because some respondents named more than one good thing.

frequently mentioned positive feature of drinking was its medicinal functions. One-third of the total sample found nothing good to say about drinking.

A separate cross-tabulation was made of the good things to be said about drinking on the part of those who said alcohol does more good than harm, as against those saying it does more harm than good. The results are not presented here because they showed no particular difference between the two groups in the rank order of mentioning good things about drinking, although more of the more-good-than-harm group naturally mentioned all the individual aspects, and the more-harm-than-good group was much more likely to see nothing good about it.

Table 77 presents differences by sex and Q–F–V group in mentions of the leading favorable aspects of drinking. Men and women gave parallel responses, except that relatively more women saw nothing good about it. Heavier drinkers mentioned "helps people mix socially" and "helps people to relax" more often than others. Among lighter drinkers and abstainers of both sexes, medicinal uses were seen as the greatest advantage.

Subgroup analyses[6] showed the following highlights: Younger people tended to emphasize the advantages of drinking to help

[6] Reported in Detail Table A-77; see *Headnote*, p. 229.

TABLE 77.—*Most-Frequent Mentions of Good Things to be Said about Drinking, by Sex and Q–F–V Group,*[a] *in Per Cent*

	N	Helps Mix Socially	Helps Relax	Medi-cinal Uses	Taste; Appe-tite	Makes Cheer-ful	Noth-ing Good
Total sample	2746	26	25	19	12	6	35
Men	1177	28	28	20	16	6	28
Women	1569	24	22	18	8	5	40
Men							
Abstainers	268	8	9	20	2	2	60
Infrequent drinkers	121	19	14	29	12	3	34
Light	324	27	32	21	19	8	22
Moderate	212	42	41	12	27	5	16
Heavy	252	45	40	20	20	11	12
Women							
Abstainers	630	8	5	20	1	2	64
Infrequent	283	24	20	21	6	7	38
Light	442	37	35	19	16	7	21
Moderate	142	47	44	12	13	9	12
Heavy	72	45	49	8	14	9	14

[a] The results in other groups are reported in Detail Table A-77; see Headnote, p. 229.

people mix socially and to relax, while older people mentioned the medicinal values of drinking more than did others. Those of higher ISP emphasized more than others the aspects of drinking that help people to mix socially and to relax. Relatively more of both men and women of lower than of upper ISP had nothing good to say about drinking; but these groups usually gave fewer responses on free-answer questions.

Bad Things about Drinking (Tables 78, 79)

Table 78 shows, first, that many more bad than good aspects of drinking were mentioned: only 3% could think of no bad things to say about drinking, while 35% could mention no good things (Table 77). The chief aspects mentioned as "bad" were generally of a nonmoralistic nature, even though the term might well have encouraged moralistic replies. The leading bad things mentioned were that it was bad for health and family life; that it causes accidents; that it is expensive; that it leads to loss of control or judgment; and that it can lead to alcoholism or drunkenness. Responses of men and women on this question were quite similar.

TABLE 78.—*Bad Things Said about Drinking, by Sex, in Per Cent*

	Total Sample	Men	Women
N	2746	1177	1569
Bad for health (long-term)	33	33	32
Bad for family life	31	29	32
Causes accidents	26	25	26
Expensive; causes poverty	24	26	23
Causes loss of control or judgment	24	22	25
Causes fights, obnoxious behavior	19	18	19
Leads to alcoholism, drunkenness	18	20	16
Habit-forming	8	7	9
Affects work, business	7	10	4
Bad physical effects (short-term, e.g., hangovers)	7	8	7
Bad mental effects	4	5	4
Leads to crime, trouble with the law	4	4	4
Hurts friendships, reputations	4	4	4
Causes loss of pride or self-respect	4	4	5
Fosters sexual misbehavior; hurts morals	3	3	3
Bad influence for children, others	3	3	3
Religious, moral issues	1	1	2
Cannot think of any bad things	3	3	3
Miscellaneous responses	5	5	5
Totals	228[a]	230[a]	226[a]

[a] Adds to more than 100% because some respondents named more than one bad thing.

A separate cross-tabulation of the bad things to be said about drinking by those who thought alcohol did more harm than good, in contrast to those who said alcohol did more good than harm, found both groups mentioning the various problems in about the same rank order. Differences in degree, however, were less pronounced than was the case with good things to be said by these two groups—in other words, those favorable to alcohol appeared to be more willing to recognize its bad points than those unfavorable were to recognize its good points. Those who saw more harm than good in drinking were particularly likely to stress its alleged bad effects on family life, while those who saw more good than harm were relatively more concerned with accidents resulting from drinking.

Table 79 shows results for the major categories of this question by sex and Q–F–V groups. The Q–F–V groups differed on this item primarily in that the heavy drinkers tended to mention relatively

TABLE 79.—*Most-Frequent Mentions of Bad Things to be Said about Drinking, by Sex and Q–F–V Group,[a] in Per Cent*

	N	Bad for Health	Bad for Family	Causes Accidents	Expensive	Causes Loss of Control	Causes Fights	Leads to Alcoholism
Total sample	2746	33	31	26	24	24	19	18
Men	1177	33	29	25	26	22	18	20
Women	1569	32	32	26	23	25	19	16
Men								
Abstainers	268	33	35	27	32	20	15	13
Infrequent drinkers	121	32	37	28	30	15	14	18
Light	324	33	25	20	25	21	16	26
Moderate	212	33	26	29	28	29	19	22
Heavy	252	33	25	23	19	23	25	20
Women								
Abstainers	630	32	38	26	27	25	16	10
Infrequent	283	36	37	26	27	23	21	16
Light	442	33	25	26	18	27	21	22
Moderate	142	27	27	27	17	26	25	21
Heavy	72	27	23	27	10	24	24	23

[a] The results in other groups are reported in Detail Table A-79; see Headnote, p. 229.

more often that drinking led to fights and obnoxious behavior, and the heavier-drinking women mentioned alcoholism and drunkenness more often than did other women. More abstainers and infrequent drinkers mentioned the problems of expense and resulting poverty and of disruption of family life.

Subgroup analyses[7] revealed the following: More men of upper ISP mentioned the expense of drinking and its relation to poverty, to loss of judgment and control, and to alcoholism and drunkenness. More men and women of lower status mentioned its relationship to fights and obnoxious behavior. These social-class differences are consistent with the presumed greater concern of the upper classes to maintain appropriate decorum, and the supposedly greater incidence of fights and acting-out of aggression among the lower classes.

PERSONALITY CORRELATES OF DRINKING

A number of items in the interview schedule dealt with the personality attributes of the respondent, measuring values or habit patterns which might be related to drinking behavior and, hence,

[7] Reported in Detail Table A-79; see *Headnote*, p. 229.

relevant to drinking patterns. Such personality attributes may operate through "moderator" variables (such as sex, age, social status and urbanization) in affecting the dependent variable—the kind and amount of drinking. The items included the following: General outlook on one's own fortunes, and optimism or pessimism, as reflected in recall of experiences during the past year; Principal life goals, and level of satisfaction in achieving these goals; Attitudes on mobility, indicated by preference for a different occupation or different neighborhood, or whether more education would have helped a lot in attaining one's life goals; Health; Utilization of oral outlets for tension (smoking, etc.) and of nonoral outlets such as hard work or religious activity; Personality characteristics, as determined from a number of brief scales measuring such attributes as neurotic tendencies, feelings of alienation, tendencies toward impulsivity or rigidity.

Preliminary to a discussion of the relationship of personality and drinking, we will report the differences in attitudes, values and other characteristics among the various Q–F–V groups.[8]

General Outlook on Own Fortunes and Values (Tables 80–85)

This group of items includes the following: Free-answer question on good things that happened during the past year; Bad things that happened during the year; Perceptions of one's own fortunes: whether last year was a good or bad year, whether respondent was happily married, whether one's childhood was mostly happy, and whether one has had more than a usual share of problems; Main things respondent has wanted out of life; Preferences for different occupation, neighborhood, or education level.

1. *Good Things during the Past Year.* A wide variety of occurrences were offered in response to the question on good things which happened during the past year. The eight leading types are presented in Table 80. It will be noted that only 8% said that they could not think of anything good about the preceding year. The chief emphasis reflected first an appreciation that one remained healthy, followed by mention of favorable things about one's family's health, then financial improvement or material acquisitions (such as a car or a house), some success by a family

---

[8] See Tables 92–94 for individual and moderator variables which appear to be correlated with drinking.

TABLE 80.—*Principal Mentions of Good Things that Happened during Past Year, by Sex and Q-F-V Group, in Per Cent*

	N	Own Health Good	Family Health Good	Finances Improve	Material Things	Progress or Success of Relative	Steady Work (Resp. or Spouse)	Personal Progress	Trips, Vacations	Nothing Good
Total sample	2746	36	21	19	13	12	12	10	10	8
Men	1177	33	19	25	11	9	13	10	7	9
Women	1569	39	23	15	14	15	10	9	1	7
Men										
Abstainers	268	39	18	22	7	8	13	7	5	9
Infrequent drinkers	121	29	18	17	11	6	12	12	6	16
Light	324	33	22	23	13	9	10	12	10	7
Moderate	212	32	18	31	12	11	14	13	7	9
Heavy	252	31	18	28	14	9	17	10	7	8
Women										
Abstainers	630	43	20	13	13	13	12	8	8	8
Infrequent	283	40	30	18	16	16	8	8	11	7
Light	442	36	24	14	14	16	10	8	15	6
Moderate	142	27	26	16	16	16	7	18	17	4
Heavy	72	29	8	30	14	14	17	9	11	11

member, and the fact that the respondent (or spouse) had had steady work. Many of the comments were family oriented. It is noteworthy that while responses of men and women were somewhat similar, the women laid greater emphasis upon health and matters concerning the family, while work and financial improvements were relatively more salient to the men. Among women, fewer of the heavier drinkers mentioned that their family's health or their own health had been good throughout the year.

2. *Bad Things during the Past Year* (Table 81). While many kinds of untoward events were mentioned as "bad" things, onethird of the sample said that nothing really bad had happened to them during the last year. Again the two most frequent responses concerned health—one's own health or aging, or illnesses or accidents within the immediate family. Again the responses of men and women were similar, with women mentioning family-related items somewhat more often than men.

Responses of the various Q–F–V groups showed very little difference except that the abstainers, both men and women, men-

TABLE 81.—*Principal Mentions of Bad Things that Happened during Past Year, by Sex and Q–F–V Group, in Per Cent*

	N	Respondent's Health, Aging	Immediate Family Illness, Accident, Death	Lack of Money	Relatives' Illness, Accident, Death	Financial Problems	Nothing Bad
Total sample	2746	15	13	11	10	7	36
Men	1177	13	11	11	8	9	37
Women	1569	15	15	10	11	6	35
Men							
Abstainers	268	20	10	8	7	10	36
Infrequent drinkers	121	14	15	13	3	10	36
Light	324	13	13	10	7	9	36
Moderate	212	10	10	14	8	4	39
Heavy	252	10	9	14	10	9	39
Women							
Abstainers	630	21	16	11	9	7	35
Infrequent	283	12	18	11	13	7	30
Light	442	13	13	9	14	5	38
Moderate	142	10	12	12	12	5	38
Heavy	72	12	14	9	4	6	33

tioned their own health problems more frequently than did those who drank (as they also did under "good" things). This is consistent with the generally greater age of the abstainers.

3. *Perceptions of Own Fortunes* (Table 82). Large majorities— from 60 to 80% of the total sample—said that last year had been a good year for them, that their marriages (if any) were very happy, that their childhoods were mostly happy and that they had not had more than their share of problems.

The various Q–F–V groups differed in their responses as follows: The heavier drinkers had a higher proportion of those saying they had had a good year than was true of the abstainers; however, relatively fewer of the heavy drinkers among married men or women said they were very happily married. Both heavy drinkers and abstainers, particularly among the women, were more likely than those in the middle drinking groups to say that they had had more than their share of problems.

4. *Life Goals and Satisfaction* (Tables 83, 84). Table 83 presents the detailed responses of men and women on the questions of what are the main things they have wanted out of life and their level of satisfaction in attaining them. As can be seen, the leading categories of goals were concerned with family life and friendships (or pri-

TABLE 82.—*Perceptions of One's Own Fortunes, by Sex and Q–F–V Group, in Per Cent*

	N	No Unusual Share of Problems	Last Year Good	Child- hood Mostly Happy	Total Married N	Very Happily Married
Total sample	2746	74	66	82	2027	62
Men	1177	74	66	83	971	64
Women	1569	74	67	81	1056	61
Men						
Abstainers	268	72	61	83	221	67
Infrequent drinkers	121	75	61	83	99	58
Light	324	76	68	83	273	64
Moderate	212	78	71	87	174	68
Heavy	252	71	69	81	204	61
Women						
Abstainers	630	68	61	84	397	60
Infrequent	283	77	69	79	203	57
Light	442	80	71	79	315	64
Moderate	142	78	72	77	96	68
Heavy	72	67	65	70	45	55

TABLE 83.—*Main Things Respondent Has Wanted out of Life and Satisfaction with their Attainment, by Sex, in Per Cent*

	Total Sample	Men	Women
N	2746	1177	1569
Main Things Wanted Out of Life			
Family life: happy home, marriage, children; friends	55	48	61
Financial or job security	48	58	41
Health (family or self)	30	28	32
Material things (car, own home)	27	26	27
Emotional security; happiness	18	14	20
Self-improvement (e.g., change in jobs, advancement)	10	13	7
Recreation or leisure	10	9	10
Altruistic or religious goals (live good life)	9	8	9
Good job; interesting work	7	10	5
Prestige, respect, status	2	4	1
All other wishes	7	8	7
Cannot think of any; not ascertained	2	3	1
Totals	225[a]	229[a]	221[a]
Satisfaction in Attaining Goals			
Very satisfied	41	36	43
Fairly satisfied	46	50	44
Not very satisfied	13	14	13
Totals	100	100	100

[a] Adds to more than 100% because some respondents named more than one item.

mary-group-related goals), financial or job security, health, and possessions. The women gave somewhat greater emphasis than the men to matters pertaining to the family, while the men laid relatively more emphasis than the women upon financial or occupational matters.

The general level of expressed satisfaction with attaining one's life goals was fairly high: only 13% said they were "not very" satisfied. A slightly higher proportion of the women than of the men reported themselves as very satisfied in meeting their life goals.

The principal stated life goals of persons in the various Q–F–V groups are shown in Table 84. The heavy drinkers had almost as high a level of over-all satisfaction in meeting their goals (in terms of proportions "very satisfied") as did the lighter drinkers or nondrinkers.

The groups differed primarily in these respects concerning their

TABLE 84.–Principal Mentions of Goals and Proportion "Very Satisfied" with Attainment, by Sex and Q-F-V Group, in Per Cent

	N	Family Life, Friends	Financial or Job Security	Health for Family or Self	Material Things	Emotional Security, Happiness	Self Improvement	Recreation, Leisure	Very Satisfied in Attaining Goals
Total sample	2746	55	48	30	27	18	10	10	41
Men	1177	48	58	28	26	14	13	9	36
Women	1569	61	41	32	27	20	7	10	43
Men									
Abstainers	268	42	54	21	30	15	11	8	38
Infrequent drinkers	121	42	60	24	29	13	11	8	38
Light	324	51	57	33	25	11	16	10	39
Moderate	212	51	59	31	26	14	14	12	32
Heavy	252	50	60	29	23	19	13	8	35
Women									
Abstainers	630	54	41	28	27	19	6	8	42
Infrequent	283	61	42	39	27	22	9	9	47
Light	442	68	40	35	27	20	7	10	44
Moderate	142	65	41	27	27	19	12	16	45
Heavy	72	63	40	20	36	24	8	13	40

stated goals: (1) The heavier drinkers laid more emphasis upon family life and friends as goals than did abstainers and infrequent drinkers; (2) The heavy-drinking women mentioned health as a goal less often than did other women, while among men the abstainers and infrequent drinkers mentioned health less often than did other men; (3) A somewhat higher percentage of heavy-drinking women mentioned desire for material things (e.g., car, home, clothes) than did other women, while a lower percentage of heavy-drinking men mentioned material things than did other men.

5. *Preference for Different Occupation, Neighborhood or Education.* Response to four questions—whether one would prefer a different occupation for oneself (or one's husband), worries about getting ahead at work, would prefer a different neighborhood, or thinks that more education would have helped "a lot" in attaining life goals—may be taken as a rough index of dissatisfaction with one's lot in life. The findings given in Table 85 show little difference among men heavy and lighter drinkers, but somewhat more of the women heavy drinkers reported dissatisfaction than did other women.

TABLE 85.—*Preference for Different Occupation, Neighborhood or Education, by Sex and Q–F–V Group, in Per Cent*

	N	Different Occupation (Self or Spouse)	Different Neighborhood	More Education	Total Self or Spouse Employed N	Worried about Getting Ahead in Work (Self or Spouse)
Total sample	2746	30	28	62	2264	41
Men	1177	35	29	65	1007	49
Women	1569	26	27	60	1257	35
Men						
Abstainers	268	34	26	66	204	49
Infrequent drinkers	121	32	30	62	92	55
Light	324	37	29	65	279	49
Moderate	212	37	33	62	194	47
Heavy	252	36	27	70	238	47
Women						
Abstainers	630	25	22	65	442	36
Infrequent	283	26	28	61	232	39
Light	442	25	29	53	386	28
Moderate	142	29	31	51	132	39
Heavy	72	35	39	73	65	40

Health and Weight (Tables 86–88)

In the self-rating of health, as shown in Table 86, the abstainers had the lowest proportion of all Q–F–V groups stating they were in excellent or good health (at least in part, this difference may be attributed to the older age and lower social status of abstainers). Among those who drank at all, the heavy drinkers were not materially different from others in their self-ratings of health.

To check on the relationship, if any, between drinking and being overweight or underweight, each respondent was asked his height and weight. This information was transformed into a weight rating according to standards of the Metropolitan Life Insurance Company.[9] The results are shown in Table 87. In terms of conformity to approved weight ranges, only 30% of the sample fell into the "de-

TABLE 86.—*Health and Hospitalization of Respondents, by Sex and Q–F–V Group, in Per Cent*

	N	Health Excellent or Good	Health Better or Same as Last Year	Not Hospitalized Last Year
Total sample	2746	76	92	90
Men	1177	79	92	90
Women	1569	74	92	89
Men				
Abstainers	268	66	89	87
Infrequent drinkers	121	75	91	93
Light	324	82	94	92
Moderate	212	88	96	89
Heavy	252	82	93	91
Women				
Abstainers	630	64	90	88
Infrequent	283	78	96	89
Light	442	82	91	90
Moderate	142	80	94	88
Heavy	72	76	92	94

[9] *Statistical Bulletin*, November–December 1959. The ratings in the present survey were computed after deducting 2 inches from women's reports of height, and 1 inch from men's, as an allowance for height of heels. Since some must have reported their height without heels (as suggested in the interviewer instructions), the adjustment may be too great; and therefore the rating of weight in relation to height may overstate somewhat the proportion rated as overweight. The ratings also do not take account of variations in body frame.

TABLE 87.—*Respondents' Conformity to Desirable Weight Range,*[a] *by Sex, Index of Social Position and Q–F–V Group, in Per Cent*

	N	Desir-able	Over-weight	Under-weight	Not Classi-fiable
Total sample	2746	30	52	18	b
Men	1177	26	61	12	1
Women	1569	33	45	22	b
Men					
Age 21–39, Higher ISP	251	30	58	11	1
Lower ISP	208	34	51	14	1
40–59, Higher ISP	247	24	67	8	1
Lower ISP	214	18	72	10	0
60+ Higher ISP	92	32	54	13	1
Lower ISP	165	20	60	19	1
Women					
Age 21–39, Higher ISP	318	44	20	36	b
Lower ISP	283	37	38	25	b
40–59, Higher ISP	281	40	40	20	b
Lower ISP	317	23	64	12	1
60+ Higher ISP	160	22	56	22	0
Lower ISP	207	24	64	11	1
Men					
Abstainers	268	29	57	13	1
Infrequent drinkers	121	24	61	14	1
Light	324	24	64	11	1
Moderate	212	32	57	11	b
Heavy	252	23	67	9	1
Women					
Abstainers	630	27	52	20	b
Infrequent	283	37	44	18	1
Light	442	37	39	24	b
Moderate	142	40	30	30	0
Heavy	72	35	42	23	0

[a] See text for source and correction.
[b] Less than 0.5%.

sirable" category, three times as many being overweight as underweight.[10] Relatively more men than women were overweight.

It must be emphasized that it is difficult to establish any causal connection between drinking and overweight, because so many factors enter into the correlations. Sex, age and social status, how-

[10] This is not out of line with Metropolitan Life's own findings, which show well over half the people in most age groups to be at least 10% over the "best" weight.

ever, are among the factors related to overweight, as can be seen in Table 87. Older women in both upper and lower ISP groups were more likely to be overweight than younger women. Women of all ages in the lower ISP groups were more likely than those in the upper groups to be overweight; among men under 40 years, however, those in the lower ISP groups tended to be underweight more than did the upper groups.

The relationship of weight category and Q–F–V group is also shown in Table 87: relatively more of the men heavy drinkers than of other groups were overweight. Among women, however, relatively more abstainers than heavy drinkers were overweight.

Bearing these group contradictions in mind, it might still be suspected that a factor behind the difference between men and women in the drinking–weight relationship may be differences in type rather than quantity of beverages consumed. For example, men drink much more beer than do women. Beer might be associated with overweight, among other reasons, because of a tendency for people to eat food when they drink beer more often than when they drink spirits. However, Table 88 shows that differential drinking of beer and spirits does not go far toward explaining group differences in the proportions who were overweight. Men who drank relatively more beer than spirits[11] were no more frequently overweight than other men. But women who drank relatively more beer than spirits were more likely to be overweight. Men who drank neither beer nor spirits were slightly less likely than drinkers of these beverages to be overweight, while women who drank neither beer nor spirits were more likely to be overweight.

Because of the complex interrelationships of the many social, psychological and physical factors involved, it is difficult to pin down the connection between drinking and being overweight or underweight. These findings indicate, however, that a relationship does exist, apparently operating in different ways within various subgroups. A full understanding of the relationships is possible only through additional clinical studies to supplement more precise anthropometric measurements.

[11] That is, light or moderate for beer as against infrequent or never for spirits; heavy for beer as against moderate, light, infrequent or never for spirits. Wine was omitted from this table to simplify the analysis and because it is drunk by relatively few compared to the other two beverages.

TABLE 88.—*Relationship of Weight Range to Drinking of Beer and Distilled Spirits, by Sex, in Per Cent*

	MEN					WOMEN				
	N	Desir-able	Over-weight	Under-weight	Not Class.	N	Desir-able	Over-weight	Under-weight	Not Class.
Total sample	1177	26	61	12	1	1569	33	45	22	a
Neither beer nor spirits	268	29	57	13	1	630	27	53	20	a
Both spirits and beer infrequent or never	141	24	62	14	a	328	37	43	19	1
More Beer than Spirits										
Spirits infrequent or never, beer light or moderate	152	28	62	10	a	115	26	52	22	0
Spirits less than heavy, beer heavy	121	24	65	10	1	28	27	54	19	0
More Spirits than Beer										
Spirits light or moderate, beer infrequent or never	126	30	60	10	0	251	40	31	28	1
Spirits heavy, beer less than heavy	78	23	69	7	1	33	36	36	27	0
Both spirits and beer light or moderate	250	26	60	13	1	175	40	35	25	0
Both spirits and beer heavy	41	17	72	11	0	9	b	b	b	b

a Less than 0.5%.
b Too few cases for analysis.

Relationship between Smoking and Drinking (Table 89)

The Hartford community survey which was conducted as a prelude to this national survey found a high correlation between cigarette smoking and drinking (8, *p. 66*). The same relationship was found in this national study, both in respect to cigarette smoking as a whole and heavier smoking (more than a pack—20 cigarettes—a day). Table 89 shows the results.

Among both men and women, there was a marked relationship between drinking and smoking—the more a respondent drank, the more likely he was to smoke cigarettes. The relationship was especially high among women: while only 19% of women who abstained from drinking reported smoking cigarettes at present, 81% of the women in the heavy-drinking group smoked cigarettes. The relationship held for heavy smoking also: the heavy drinkers among both men and women were most likely to smoke more than one pack a day and the abstainers least likely.

The Berkeley (39) and Hartford (8) studies pointed out that both smoking and drinking are oral activities, and adduced evidence to show that there is a connection between drinking and a number of other oral activities. This "oral activity" factor is discussed in the next section.

TABLE 89.—*Cigarette Smoking by Respondents, by Sex and Q–F–V Group, in Per Cent*

	N	Smoke Cigarettes at Present	Smoke More than a Pack a Day
Total sample	2746	43	15
Men	1177	50	22
Women	1569	37	10
Men			
Abstainers	268	38	14
Infrequent drinkers	121	47	24
Light	324	49	18
Moderate	212	58	27
Heavy	252	60	31
Women			
Abstainers	630	19	5
Infrequent	283	39	10
Light	442	41	7
Moderate	142	71	27
Heavy	72	81	36

It is assumed that the reasons for the relationship between drinking and smoking lie within a mixture of cultural and individual attributes. Part of the connection may be due to relative permissiveness or nonpermissiveness for both smoking and drinking in different cultural environments. Part of it may stem from a greater tension level on the part of those who smoke and drink (although, as will be seen later, the limited evidence we have on neurotic tendencies does not indicate any greater degree among men who drink heavily, and only a slightly higher degree among women who drink heavily).

Activities to Relieve Depression or Nervousness (Table 90)

The extent to which drinking and eight other activities were reported as being useful for allaying depression or nervous tensions is shown in Table 90, which also shows the proportions naming one or more of four "oral" activities other than drinking (including smoking, eating, taking a tranquilizer, or taking some other kind of pill or medicine) as being "very" or "fairly" helpful. The results serve a comparative rather than quantitative purpose because the question assumes that everyone is subject to depression or nervousness at some time but makes no allowance for frequency.

Looking at the full list of suggested activities, it can be seen that "having a drink such as a highball or cocktail or some wine or beer" was found helpful when depressed or nervous by more people than was taking tranquilizers or pills, but by fewer than reported smoking or eating to be helpful. Each of these oral activities was considerably below other types of activities (such as going to church, talking with friends, working harder, or just trying to forget) in reported effectiveness.

As anticipated, much larger proportions of heavier drinkers than of others reported they found having a drink to be helpful in relieving depression or nervousness; the proportion was 71% among both men and women heavy drinkers. Consistent with the relationship reported earlier between smoking and drinking, a higher percentage of heavy drinkers, both men and women, reported that smoking was helpful in alleviating depression and nervousness. Again, the difference was more pronounced in the women than in the men.

More men abstainers and infrequent drinkers than heavier drinkers reported eating helpful for depression or nervousness, while

TABLE 90.—Activities Very or Fairly Helpful when Depressed or Nervous, by Sex and Q-F-V Group,[a] in Per Cent

	N	Having a Drink	Smoking	Eating	Tranquilizer	Other Pill or Med.	Index of Oral Activity[b]	Work Harder	Church, Prayer	Talk with Friends, Relatives	Try to Forget
Total sample	2746	29	34	40	13	23	71	69	71	71	48
Men	1177	39	41	36	7	16	67	62	59	64	46
Women	1569	21	28	42	17	29	74	75	81	77	50
Men											
Abstainers	268	5[c]	32	43	12	23	70	57	67	60	51
Infrequent drinkers	121	11	40	43	8	22	73	61	62	60	57
Light	324	40	38	33	8	17	64	62	55	64	44
Moderate	212	59	46	33	3	12	63	66	60	70	39
Heavy	252	71	50	31	6	12	69	64	50	66	47
Women											
Abstainers	630	1[c]	15	42	17	31	72	77	86	78	53
Infrequent	283	9	30	40	21	29	74	76	81	79	49
Light	442	36	33	44	15	25	73	75	78	76	50
Moderate	142	61	56	36	19	31	82	74	70	78	43
Heavy	72	71	59	50	19	28	83	71	77	61	47

[a] The results in other groups are reported in Detail Table A-90; see Headnote, p. 229.
[b] Index of Oral Activity: The proportion who mentioned one or more of the nondrinking oral activities (smoking, eating, taking a tranquilizer or taking other pills or medicines) as being "very helpful" or "fairly helpful" when depressed or nervous.
[c] Abstainers were defined as persons who now report usually drinking less than once a year or not at all.

the women heavy drinkers were somewhat more likely than other women to rate eating as helpful.

Two other oral activities (taking tranquilizers and taking other pills or medicines) showed parallel patterns of differences among men: the abstainers found these helpful more often than did those who drank. Among women, however, there were no consistent differences on helpfulness of tranquilizers or other medicines by Q–F–V groups. In general, the level of helpfulness of tranquilizers and other medicines was higher among women than among men.

When the four oral activities other than drinking (smoking, eating, tranquilizers, other pills or medicines) are considered together, the proportion finding at least one of the four helpful was higher among women than among men; and among women, higher on the part of heavy and moderate drinkers than others.

Among the nonoral activities tested, the only consistent patterns in the various Q–F–V groups were that abstainers (both men and women) relied much more than heavy drinkers upon going to church or saying a prayer, and fewer of the heavy-drinking women than other women said they found talking it over with a friend or relative to be helpful for depression or nervousness. The results on prayer and churchgoing are consistent with the finding reported earlier that heavier drinkers went to church less often than did others.

The fact that heavy-drinking women seemed to rely less than other women upon talking their problems over with friends or relatives is in line with the finding (see Table 92) that such women scored much higher than other women (except abstainers) on an "alienation" scale (which included among others the items "Sometimes I feel very lonesome," "I have the feeling that I am different," and "Sometimes life just isn't worth living"). Thus the evidence accumulates that the heavy-drinking woman tends to be more out of joint with society, and less amenable to the support and controls of primary groups, than is true of heavy-drinking men.

The results in other demographic groups[12] on activities to relieve depression showed that men and women 60 years and over were somewhat less likely than other age groups to say having a drink was helpful and much more likely to report help from pills other than tranquilizers. Younger women were very much more likely

[12] Reported in Detail Table A-90; see *Headnote*, p. 229.

than women 60 years and over to find smoking helpful. Up to age 60, both men and women of the higher ISP groups were more likely than those of lower ISP to say that having a drink was helpful. Among men the reverse was true on smoking: men of lower ISP at all ages were more likely than those in the upper groups to say smoking was helpful.

Both having a drink and smoking were considered helpful by relatively high proportions in the New England, Middle Atlantic and Pacific regions. Residents of the southeastern states gave relatively more emphasis to pills and churchgoing. Having a drink was mentioned as helpful relatively more often by residents of suburbs outside cities under 1 million than by respondents living elsewhere, while big-city residents were more likely than others to mention tranquilizers and other pills, and residents of rural and farm areas put relatively more emphasis on eating than did others. More respondents with no religious preference found drink helpful, followed by liberal Protestants and Catholics; least likely were conservative Protestants, more of whom mentioned going to church and working harder. Nonwhite respondents were no more likely than others to say having a drink was helpful, but they were considerably more likely to find tranquilizers and other pills helpful, as well as going to church. Jewish respondents were a little below average in reporting drinking to be helpful and much lower than all other religious groups on finding help in religious services; they led all others on helpfulness of tranquilizers.

While the range of activities to alleviate depression and nervousness covered by the questions in this survey was suggestive rather than exhaustive, the findings show enough differences in the preferred palliatives of various groups to make it clear that various social and cultural groupings have distinctly different ways of coping with their problems. These behavioral patterns have broad implications for mental health, since some groups may show a greater preference than others for socially adaptive ways of dealing with their tensions.[13]

[13] In recognition of the existence of these group differences, the current series of community surveys and the national survey of drug use being conducted by the Social Research Group (in collaboration with the Family Research Center, Langley-Porter Neuropsychiatric Clinic, California Department of Mental Hygiene) is designed to study intensively the incidence of various types of emotionally based problems and the ways in which people cope with them.

Relationship of Personality Measures to Drinking (Tables 91–94)

Eight sets of items were devised to measure personality, in the sense of being directly concerned with affective and attitudinal or evaluative aspects of the individual.[14] One set of items dealt with the respondent's mode of expressing anger. The other seven sets consisted of short scales (containing four or five items) designed to measure neurotic tendencies, tendencies toward alienation, empathy, impulsivity, rigidity, religious fundamentalism, and subscription to a "Protestant ethic" set of values.

1. Expression of Anger (Table 91). One index of adaptation to stress is whether—and how—one relieves tensions by expressing anger. The survey questions bearing on this point asked how often the respondent became angry (often, sometimes, rarely or never) and how he usually expressed his anger (by keeping it to himself, showing it but not losing his temper, or losing his temper). Only 3% of the respondents said they never became angry, and the re-

TABLE 91.—*Usual Mode of Expression of Anger, by Sex and Q–F–V Group, in Per Cent*

	N	Never Get Angry	Keep it to Self	Show it but Do Not Lose Temper	Lose Temper
Total sample	2746	3	29	38	30
Men	1177	4	31	42	23
Women	1569	3	26	35	36
Men					
Abstainers	268	6	34	38	22
Infrequent drinkers	121	2	36	42	20
Light	324	3	31	41	25
Moderate	212	4	29	47	20
Heavy	252	2	32	40	26
Women					
Abstainers	630	5	31	36	28
Infrequent	283	3	24	37	36
Light	442	1	24	35	40
Moderate	142	1	20	33	46
Heavy	72	5	22	24	49

[14] Although put together specifically for the purposes of this study, most of the individual items were drawn from other sources and have been utilized in other research. Sources used include the Minnesota Multiphasic Personality Inventory, *The Authoritarian Personality*, the neurotic inventory used in *The American Soldier* studies. Most of the questions were asked in a self-administered form at the end of the interview.

mainder were fairly evenly divided among the three modes of re-
pressing or expressing their anger. A higher percentage of women
than men admitted that they lost their temper, and the abstainers
were somewhat more likely than others to say they kept their anger
to themselves. More of the heavier drinkers among women reported
that they lost their tempers. The results can be interpreted to mean
that the heavy-drinking woman (a) has a greater-than-average
tension level which she relieves both by drinking and by losing
her temper, or (b) tends to be a self-indulgent person who both
drinks and loses her temper to excess, or (c) operates in a milieu
in which both heavy drinking and losing one's temper are accepted
as part of the way of life.

2. *Relationship of Personality Scales to Drinking.* Seven scales,
each containing four or five items, were used in this limited assessment. The items in the seven scales were as follows:[15]

Neurotic Tendencies. Frequency of the following symptoms in past
year: upset stomach; headaches; felt tense or nervous; worried about
things; felt depressed.

Alienation. Agreement with following statements: "This world has
more pain than pleasure"; "Sometimes I feel so lonesome"; "I have the
feeling that I am different"; "Sometimes life just isn't worth living."

Empathy. Agreement with following statements: "When someone in
my family has a misfortune, it upsets me as much as it does them";
"When I see an underdog win, I feel almost as good as if I had won";
"When I hear of a man who stole because his family was hungry, I
can easily understand how he felt"; "When I go to a movie or watch
TV, I live right along with the characters."

Impulsivity. Agreement with following statements: "I react quickly
to other people's remarks"; "I often spend more money than I think I
should"; "I often act on the spur of the moment without stopping to
think"; "I often change my mind rather quickly."

Rigidity. Agreement with following statements: "I am happiest when
I have a place for everything and everything in its place"; "In whatever
one does, the 'tried and true' ways are always best"; "I always finish
things I start, even if they aren't very important"; "A person who seldom
changes his mind can usually be depended upon to have good judgment."

Religious Fundamentalism. Agreement with following statements:
"The Bible is the word of God and all of it is absolutely true"; "Almost
everything that happens can be understood by studying the Bible";
"Obedience to the word of God is one of the most important virtues that

---

[15] Five of the seven scales conformed to the Guttman model in that each item
in the scale was drawn from a single universe of content and that the scale meets
the criterion of reproducibility of .90 or higher. The coefficients of reproducibility
for the other two (Neurotic Tendencies and Alienation) were .89 and .87.

children should learn"; "There are many things in the universe that only religion, and not science, can explain."

Protestant Ethic. Agreement with following statements: "A person is always wiser to save his money for future needs"; "There is nothing like good hard work to help you get ahead in life"; "The only way to get ahead in this world is to get a good education"; "In getting ahead in the world, it is important to mingle with the very best class of people."

Hypotheses concerning the likely relationship of each of the seven personality scales to heavy (and hence, presumably, to "problem") drinking were set up as follows:

Neurotic Tendencies scale: those with higher scores would be more prone than others to be problem drinkers, because of their greater need to find relief from their anxieties and depression.

Alienation scale: those who have a feeling of being apart from society will be more likely than others to be problem drinkers, because they are more likely than others to be out of touch with the values of society and may also have a higher-than-average tendency toward paranoia and depression, which may be correlated with alcoholismic tendencies. These feelings are related to the deep-seated maladjustment between the individual and society which Durkheim called "anomie."

Empathy scale: those with lower empathy scores (less-than-average tendency to take the role of the other person) would tend more than others to be problem drinkers because of their presumed greater degree of concern for themselves rather than for the feelings of others.[16]

Impulsivity scale: those who tend to act upon the spur of the moment would tend more than others to be heavy drinkers because of a greater emphasis upon short-term gratification.

Rigidity: it would be predicted that abstainers would have higher Rigidity scores because of a greater-than-average tendency to be uncompromising.

Religious Fundamentalism: while the scale items are concerned only with religious faith, it would be expected that those with high scores on this scale would be more likely than others to be abstainers because most churches with fundamentalist religious tenets also take a stand against drinking.

Protestant Ethic: those with high scores would be less likely than others to be heavy drinkers because of a greater concern for long-term goals rather than short-term gratifications.

The results by sex and Q–F–V group on the seven scales are shown in Table 92. On the Neurotic Tendencies scale there was no important difference between men who did not drink, drank little or drank more heavily; but, as expected, more women who drank

[16] It could also be argued that empathic people are more outgoing, would tend to socialize more and, hence, drink more.

TABLE 92.—*Percentage of Respondents with High Scores[a] on Seven Personality Scales, by Sex and Q–F–V Group*

	N	Neurotic	Alien-ation	Em-pathy	Impul-sivity	Rigid-ity	Fundamen-talism	Prot-estant Ethic
Total sample	2746	34	34	58	33	44	43	62
Men	1177	25	32	53	29	42	36	59
Women	1569	42	37	62	37	45	50	64
Men								
Abstainers	268	26	36	54	25	48	55	64
Infrequent drinkers	121	28	35	44	25	47	40	57
Light	324	24	29	54	31	44	37	66
Moderate	212	24	31	53	29	36	24	50
Heavy	252	24	31	54	34	35	21	55
Women								
Abstainers	630	43	45	61	34	54	68	68
Infrequent	283	43	29	61	34	42	40	67
Light	442	38	32	63	37	39	39	59
Moderate	142	41	30	65	49	29	31	57
Heavy	72	51	42	66	47	48	32	68

[a] High scores = 4 or 5 out of 5 on Neurotic Tendencies scale; 3 or 4 out of 4 on Empathy, Impulsivity, Rigidity and Protestant Ethic; 2 to 4 out of 4 on Alienation; 4 out of 4 on Religious Fundamentalism.

heavily had high scores than did other women. More women abstainers and heavy drinkers had high Alienation scores than other groups, but there was little difference by Q–F–V group among men. The high proportion of women abstainers is undoubtedly attributable to their generally higher age level: abstainers among women tend to be older than women drinkers, and women of 60 years and older had above-average Alienation scores. Heavy drinking seems to be resorted to more often by women who feel alienated from life than by men. From another viewpoint, since heavy drinking by women is less accepted by society than is heavy drinking by men, the woman who does drink heavily is more likely than others to have social problems.

The Empathy scale showed no differences of importance by Q–F–V group, although more women than men had high scores. More of the heavier-drinking men and women (particularly the women) had high scores on the Impulsivity scale. It was expected that more heavy drinkers would have high Impulsivity scores because of a general tendency toward more immediate gratification of their own desires. The results are in line with the expectation. More men and women abstainers, than other groups, had high Rigidity scores. The men and women differed in that fewer heavy drinkers among men had high Rigidity scores, while more women heavy drinkers than infrequent, light or moderate drinkers had high scores.

Consistent with the earlier-noted connection between membership in "conservative" religious groups and abstinence, and between churchgoing and abstinence, more abstainers had high scores on the Religious Fundamentalism scale. The hypothesis was that the Protestant Ethic scale (postponing immediate self-gratification in the interest of longer-term goals) would be related to abstinence or moderation in drinking, but little relationship was found. While fewer moderate drinkers (both men and women) had high scores on the scale, the differences were small and the trend was not consistent.

3. *Personality as a Moderator Variable.* It is possible that the differences in personality-scale findings in the various Q–F–V groups are attributable to the correlations between sex, age and social class and drinking rather than to drinking per se. Accordingly special tabulations were made to control for these three factors (Table 93). When sex, age and social status were controlled, Neurotic

TABLE 93.—*Percentage of Respondents in Q–F–V Groups, by Personality Scale Scores, Index of Social Position, Age and Sex*

	MEN				WOMEN			
	N	Abst. + Infr.	Light + Mod.	Heavy	N	Abst. + Infr.	Light + Mod.	Heavy
Total sample	1177	33	46	21	1569	58	37	5
NEUROTIC TENDENCIES								
Age 21–44								
Higher ISP								
Lower score (0–3)	261	23	53	24	234	34	60	6
Higher score (4–5)	73	15	66	19	171	48	45	7
Lower ISP								
Lower score	185	28	50	22	177	65	30	5
Higher score	90	29	43	28	208	58	34	8
Age 45+								
Higher ISP								
Lower score	210	33	47	20	247	58	40	2
Higher score	46	34	44	22	107	54	41	5
Lower ISP								
Lower score	235	45	35	20	254	71	26	3
Higher score	77	61	24	15	168	77	21	2
ALIENATION								
Age 21–44								
Higher ISP								
Lower score (0–1)	250	22	56	22	302	41	54	5
Higher score (2–4)	84	18	56	26	103	38	53	9

Lower ISP								
Lower score	180	30	47	23	224	65	30	5
Higher score	95	25	49	26	161	57	33	10
Age 45+								
Higher ISP								
Lower score	186	29	49	22	251	54	43	3
Higher score	70	43	39	18	103	64	32	4
Lower ISP								
Lower score	175	46	34	20	199	67	29	4
Higher score	137	53	30	17	223	79	20	1
EMPATHY								
Age 21–44								
Higher ISP								
Lower score (0–2)	183	23	57	20	158	42	53	5
Higher score (3–4)	151	19	55	26	247	38	55	7
Lower ISP								
Lower score	130	31	43	26	162	62	30	8
Higher score	145	26	52	22	223	62	33	5
Age 45+								
Higher ISP								
Lower score	115	34	44	22	137	60	39	1
Higher score	141	32	48	20	217	54	41	5
Lower ISP								
Lower score	135	52	32	16	135	79	21	ᵃ
Higher score	177	47	33	20	287	71	26	3

ᵃ Less than 0.5%.

[Continued on next page]

TABLE 93.—Continued

		MEN				WOMEN		
	N	Abst. + Infr.	Light + Mod.	Heavy	N	Abst. + Infr.	Light + Mod.	Heavy
IMPULSIVITY								
Age 21–44								
Higher ISP								
Lower score (0–2)	239	23	56	21	251	44	51	5
Higher score (3–4)	95	17	56	27	154	34	57	9
Lower ISP								
Lower score	200	31	48	21	235	66	29	5
Higher score	75	20	47	33	150	55	36	9
Age 45+								
Higher ISP								
Lower score	186	35	45	20	234	57	40	3
Higher score	70	26	50	24	120	57	39	4
Lower ISP								
Lower score	209	51	30	19	275	75	22	3
Higher score	103	45	37	18	147	70	28	2
RIGIDITY								
Age 21–44								
Higher ISP								
Lower score (0–2)	265	20	56	24	302	36	58	6
Higher score (3–4)	69	24	57	19	103	50	44	6

Lower ISP								
Lower score	148	26	43	31	194	61	34	5
Higher score	127	30	53	17	191	62	30	8
Age 45+								
Higher ISP								
Lower score	159	34	45	21	211	54	43	3
Higher score	97	31	48	21	143	61	35	4
Lower ISP								
Lower score	113	49	29	22	145	71	27	2
Higher score	199	49	34	17	277	74	23	3
RELIGIOUS FUNDAMENTALISM								
Age 21–44								
Higher ISP								
Lower score (0–3)	263	18	57	25	274	33	60	7
Higher score (4)	71	34	52	14	131	55	41	4
Lower ISP								
Lower score	170	22	49	29	172	57	34	9
Higher score	105	38	46	16	213	65	30	5
Age 45+								
Higher ISP								
Lower score	172	26	50	24	189	46	51	3
Higher score	84	49	38	13	165	69	28	3

[Continued on next page]

TABLE 93.—*Continued*

	MEN				WOMEN			
	N	Abst. + Infr.	Light + Mod.	Heavy	N	Abst. + Infr.	Light + Mod.	Heavy
Lower ISP								
Lower score	141	41	31	28	143	61	34	5
Higher score	171	56	34	10	279	80	19	1
PROTESTANT ETHIC								
Age 21–44								
Higher ISP								
Lower score (0–2)	188	22	54	24	202	40	54	6
Higher score (3–4)	146	20	59	21	203	40	54	6
Lower ISP								
Lower score	91	25	49	26	123	59	36	5
Higher score	184	29	47	24	262	63	29	8
Age 45+								
Higher ISP								
Lower score	119	33	44	23	132	52	45	3
Higher score	137	33	48	19	222	59	38	3
Lower ISP								
Lower score	83	51	25	24	100	67	32	1
Higher score	229	48	35	17	322	75	22	3

Tendencies scores were not found to be significantly associated with drinking level; among older lower-status men and women, those with high scores were somewhat more likely than others to be abstainers or infrequent drinkers, while among other groups the relationship varied. There were no material differences by men's Alienation scores as to heavy drinking when age and social status were held constant. Among the younger women (of both higher and lower status) there were more heavy drinkers among those with higher Alienation scores. This is consistent with the interpretation that in a society which frowns on heavy drinking, particularly among women, certain atypical personality traits must be operating in order for a woman to be a heavy drinker.

Empathy scores were not found to be related to drinking to any great or consistent extent when sex, age and social status were controlled. Older women with lower scores, however, were somewhat more likely to be abstainers or infrequent drinkers than were those with higher Empathy scores. In general, younger people, both men and women, with higher scores on Impulsivity had a higher proportion of heavy drinkers and a lower proportion of abstainers or infrequent drinkers. Impulsivity scores were less highly related to drinking behavior among older people than younger. Among men of lower social status, those with lower Rigidity scores generally had a higher proportion of heavy drinkers. Differences by Rigidity score among women were negligible as to heavy drinking, but younger women of higher ISP with high Rigidity scores were considerably more likely than those with lower scores to be abstainers or infrequent drinkers.

The differences in drinking between those of higher and lower scores on Religious Fundamentalism were greater than on any of the other scales, consistent with the earlier findings that those belonging to conservative Protestant denominations were quite different from others in their drinking behavior. A low score on Religious Fundamentalism was associated with a higher percentage of heavy drinkers in all but one subgroup. In both sexes, in all age and ISP groups, the percentage of abstainers or infrequent drinkers was much higher among those with high Religious Fundamentalism scores than among those with low scores. The Protestant Ethic scores were not highly related to drinking when age, sex and social status were held constant. There was a slight tendency, however, for men with lower scores to be heavy drinkers, while women with higher scores were more likely than others to be abstainers or infrequent drinkers.

4. *Intercorrelation of Personality Scales* (Table 94). Table 94 shows the intercorrelation of scores on the seven scales: The only intercorrelations of .33 or higher were those between Rigidity, Religious Fundamentalism, and Protestant Ethic. Further combinations or substitutions within these three scales appear to be called for to reduce overlap prior to conducting further studies with these scales.

THE "ESCAPE" DRINKER

Conformity to the societal norm of drinking permits the consumption of large quantities upon occasions when such amounts are considered "reasonable" by members of the group. Those who drink to an extent beyond what is prescribed as reasonable by their own subcultures, however, are not engaging in "social" drinking even if they are drinking in the presence of others. Therefore, it becomes important to distinguish between social and nonsocial drinking, not in terms of circumstances but of reasons.

Reasons for Drinking: "Social" and "Escape" (Table 95)

Other writers (39, 53, 62) have emphasized that the reasons a person advances for drinking can reveal a great deal about whether he is having problems related to his drinking, or might be likely to have problems in the future.[17] It can be hypothesized that rea-

TABLE 94.—*Intercorrelation*[a] *of Scores on Seven Personality Scales*

	Neu- rotic	Alien- ation	Em- pathy	Impul- sivity	Rigid- ity	Relig. Fund.	Prot. Ethic
Neurotic		.21	.12	.16	.03	.06	.03
Alienation			.14	.16	.20	.12	.22
Empathy				.21	.11	.18	.16
Impulsivity					.04	.02	.03
Rigidity						.40	.44
Religious Fundamentalism							.33
Protestant Ethic							

[a] Pearson product-moment coefficient of correlation (rho).

[17] It must be emphasized, however, that the reasons one gives for drinking provide only one aspect of the picture of the individuals' potential problem drinking. More detailed studies on the many types of problem drinking have been reported by Mulford and Miller (53, 54), Park (58), Bailey, Haberman and Alksne (4),

sons for drinking may be rather sharply divided into two types because alcohol has two general functions, one as a social catalyst and the other as a drug. As a social catalyst, alcohol is so interwoven with the fabric of life in America (and many other cultures) that it has acquired a rich body of folklore, connotations, and social usages. Hence many people have socially related reasons for drinking, such as sociability or the celebration of festive occasions. As a drug, alcohol has the power temporarily to alleviate anxieties, lessen tensions and increase self-esteem. Thus we would expect that those who use alcohol regularly as a drug will have need-patterns and tensions which are different from those of persons who use alcohol only in socially related ways.

Previous studies have recognized this twofold function of alcohol. The early study of Riley, Marden and Lifshitz in 1946 (62) classified people's reasons for drinking (given in response to an open-ended question) into "social" and "individual" reasons. They found that social reasons were more likely to be reported by women, younger persons and the less-frequent drinkers, while individual reasons were more often reported by men, older persons and more-frequent drinkers. In their studies in Iowa, Mulford and Miller (53) constructed a "Scale of Definitions of Alcohol" which was based on a list of functions of alcohol given to respondents to check. The Berkeley study (39) adapted some of these functions into a series of items which reflected "social" and "personal involvement" motives for drinking. This series of items was utilized in revised form in the present national survey, as follows:

"People drink wine, beer, whisky or liquor for different reasons. Here are some statements people have made about why they drink. How important would you say that each of the following is to *you* as a reason for drinking—very important, fairly important, or not at all important?"

(*a*) "I drink because it helps me to relax"; (*b*) "I drink to be sociable"; (*c*) "I like the taste"; (*d*) "I drink because the people I know drink"; (*e*) "I drink when I want to forget everything"; (*f*) "I drink to celebrate special occasions"; (*g*) "A drink helps me to forget my worries"; (*h*) "A small drink improves my appetite for food"; (*i*) "I accept a drink

---

Clark (14), Knupfer (43) and Cahalan (10). The latter three writers have used similar concepts, distinguishing between interpersonal problems (e.g., problems with police, friends, spouse or on the job) and personal problems (i.e., subjective or noninterpersonal problems, such as anxiety about one's drinking, drinking for escape reasons, drinking in an addictive fashion). The follow-up national survey will investigate this topic further.

because it is the polite thing to do in certain situations"; (j) "A drink helps cheer me up when I'm in a bad mood"; (k) "I drink because I need it when tense and nervous."

Four of the items constitute "social" reasons for drinking and five can be classified as "personal involvement" or "escape" reasons. The other two items, "like the taste" and "improves appetite," are simple enjoyment-oriented reasons not particularly connected with either social or psychological motivations.

The aggregate results on the individual items are presented in Table 95, which shows that drinkers mentioned social reasons for drinking much more often than they gave personal reasons such as simple enjoyment or dependence upon alcohol to escape from problems: 76% of all drinkers rated two or more of the four social reasons as being either "very important" or "fairly important," whereas only 29% rated two or more of the five escape reasons as being of importance.

The most popular single reason for drinking was "I drink to celebrate special occasions," followed closely by "I drink to be sociable." Only one escape reason ("I drink because it helps me to relax") was chosen more often than the social item of lowest popularity ("I drink because the people I know drink").

Men and women did not differ very much in the reasons for drinking they considered important, except that men were somewhat more likely to say that they liked the taste of alcohol or that it improved their appetites. Thus there is an implication that men tend to get more pleasure out of drinking than women do, and this may help to explain why more men than women drink and why fewer women than men drink alone (see Tables 48 and 49).

More heavy drinkers of both sexes tended to choose each reason as important more often than others did and, relative to social reasons, more chose escape reasons. The only reason not chosen any more often by heavy drinkers was "It's the polite thing to do." The greatest range of difference between infrequent and heavy drinkers (16 vs 76%) was on "helps me to relax" in the case of women. Here again is evidence that the woman heavy drinker, in some respects, differs more from others of her sex than does her male counterpart.

Highlights of subgroup differences[18] in reasons for drinking are

---

[18] Reported in Detail Table A-95; see *Headnote*, p. 229.

Table 95.—*Social, Miscellaneous and Escape Reasons[a] for Drinking, by Sex and Q-F-V Group, in Per Cent[b]*

	N	SOCIAL REASONS				MISCELLANEOUS			ESCAPE REASONS			
		Celebrate Spec. Occ.	Be Sociable	Polite Thing to Do	People I Know Drink	Like Taste	Improves Appetite	Helps to Relax	Need When Tense	Helps Cheer Up	Helps Forget Worries	To Forget Everything
Total drinkers	1848	75	72	59	31	51	36	45	18	25	15	7
Men	909	74	73	59	29	58	46	50	18	30	17	7
Women	939	77	70	58	34	43	26	40	18	21	13	7
Men												
Infrequent drinkers	121	64	57	55	25	25	26	33	11	18	7	4
Light	324	66	71	57	25	50	44	38	14	20	11	6
Moderate	212	79	76	65	30	64	50	61	14	35	16	4
Heavy	252	83	82	59	33	79	56	63	28	43	31	12
Women												
Infrequent	283	74	66	57	26	26	12	16	5	9	6	3
Light	442	75	70	59	33	44	30	40	17	20	12	6
Moderate	142	84	73	54	36	57	29	67	30	30	15	10
Heavy	72	83	82	60	55	71	31	76	51	53	43	22

	Named Two or More Social Reasons	Named Two or More Escape Reasons
Total drinkers	76	29
Men	75	32
Women	76	26

[a] Either "very" or "fairly" important.
[b] The results in other groups are reported in Detail Table A-95; see Headnote, p. 229.

as follows: Younger men and women were more likely than older persons to mention celebrations, sociability and taste as important reasons for drinking; more younger men also said they drank to be polite. Drinking because "the people I know drink" tended to decrease with age, especially among women. A very high proportion (68%) of young men in the highest ISP group said that relaxation was an important reason for their drinking. This group of well-to-do young men had a lower-than-average Neurotic Tendencies score (which includes items reflecting tension or nervousness), and a higher-than-average proportion reporting themselves as well-satisfied with their progress in life. Hence, although they may be subjected to greater pressures than others, because of the pace of their everyday lives, they appear on the whole to be well adjusted to it (perhaps by means of drinking for relaxation). Among men, in general, celebration was chosen as an important reason for drinking by fewer of those in the lower ISP groups than in the upper. The two "forgetting" reasons were generally chosen by more of those in the lower ISP groups.

The Heavy-Escape Drinker. The five escape reasons form a Guttman-type scale which can be scored for the number of individual escape reasons cited. Escape drinkers are here arbitrarily defined for purposes of group analysis as those who rated two or more of the five escape reasons as either "very" or "fairly" important.[19] As noted above, 29% of those who drank at least once a year thus qualified as escape drinkers. Close to a third of this group (9% of drinkers, 6% of the total sample) qualified as both escape drinkers on this scale and as heavy drinkers in the Q–F–V classification. These drinkers, who are perhaps those most likely to be or to become problem drinkers, are analyzed separately as heavy-escape drinkers. Table 96 shows their distribution.

A slightly higher proportion of men drinkers (32%) than of women drinkers (26%) were escape drinkers. Men and women differed less in the proportion of escape drinkers than they did in the proportion of those who were both escape and heavy drinkers; although fewer women drank heavily, relatively more of those who did were classified as escape drinkers (among heavy drinkers, 64%

---

[19] The cutting point on the escape scale (two or more of the five reasons), while arbitrary, permits excluding from the escape drinkers those who checked as important only the most innocuous of the escape reasons ("I drink because it helps me to relax").

TABLE 96.—*Percentage of Escape and Heavy-Escape Drinkers,*[a] *by Sex and Q–F–V Group*[b]

	N	Escape Drinkers[c]	Heavy-Escape Drinkers[c]
Total drinkers	1848	29	9
Men	909	32	13
Women	939	26	5
Men			
Infrequent drinkers	121	17	
Light	324	22	
Moderate	212	37	
Heavy	252	48	48
Women			
Infrequent	283	8	
Light	442	25	
Moderate	142	43	
Heavy	72	64	64

[a] Escape drinkers = those who gave two or more escape reasons. Heavy-escape drinkers = those escape drinkers who were also heavy drinkers by Q–F–V classification.
[b] The results in other groups are reported in Detail Table A-96; see Headnote, p. 229.
[c] Base: total drinkers.

of the women compared to 48% of the men were classified as heavy-escape drinkers).

These findings are consistent with other indications in this national survey and in community surveys (13) that since the American culture is less permissive toward heavy drinking by women than by men, the woman who drinks heavily is relatively more likely to have escape reasons for drinking. The influences operating here may well be some mixture of the following: (1) that the heavy-drinking woman more often has special problems or inner tensions or personality attributes which impel her to flout convention by drinking heavily; (2) that she is less conformist in general and thus relatively more likely to mention less socially acceptable reasons for drinking; or (3) simply that she has problems because of her drinking.

The findings on escape and heavy-escape drinkers among the various demographic groups[20] include the following: No clear-cut difference between ISP groups in escape drinking is evident when sex and age are held constant. Men 60 years and over in the lowest ISP group had the largest proportion giving escape reasons. The

[20] Reported in Detail Table A-96; see *Headnote*, p. 229.

proportions of escape drinkers did not vary much by age. Jews had the lowest percentage of escape reasons, while Protestants of no stated denomination and those giving no religious preference had the highest. Drinkers of Canadian origin had the lowest proportion of escape drinkers, U.S. Nonwhites the highest.

The percentage of heavy-escape drinkers was highest among younger men (age 21 to 39) of the lowest ISP group, but decreased with age in the lowest ISP group but not in the higher groups. Relatively few men over age 60 and women over 50 were heavy-escape drinkers. Relatively high proportions were found among Protestants of no denomination and those with no religious affiliation, among U.S. Nonwhites and Latin Americans and Caribbeans.

Escape Drinkers, by Sex, Age and Social Position. In Table 97, the level of drinking of those who gave two or more escape reasons as important in their drinking and of those who gave fewer is analyzed separately. Even when sex, age and social status are held constant, there is a strong correlation between heavy drinking and selection of escape reasons.

Escape Drinkers, by Alienation Score. Since women heavy drinkers had higher scores on the Alienation scale, it would also be expected that a higher Alienation score would be related to a tendency to drink for escape reasons. Table 98 shows that in nearly all age groups and in both sexes persons with higher Alienation scores tended to be escape drinkers. Among persons aged under 40 and among men of all ages, more of those with higher Alienation scores were heavy-escape drinkers—those who would be expected to contain the highest proportion of problem drinkers.

The Alienation scale is thus demonstrated to be of material assistance as a moderator variable in predicting escape drinking. In other words, with other factors held constant, a higher tendency toward feelings of Alienation is related to a higher likelihood of drinking for reasons of escape from one's personal problems or moods (such as anxiety or depression).

It is evident also that among those aged 40 to 59 and 60 or over, in both men and women, those with high Alienation scores had a higher proportion of abstainers and infrequent drinkers. This finding is interpreted as reflecting the generally more deprived lives of those with high Alienation scores, rather than implying any causal relationship between alienation and abstinence.

TABLE 97.—Percentage of Drinkers in Q–F–V Groups, by Escape and Nonescape Drinkers,[a] Index of Social Position, Age and Sex

	MEN				WOMEN			
	N	Infreq.	Light + Mod.	Heavy	N	Infreq.	Light + Mod.	Heavy
Total drinkers	909	13	59	28	939	30	62	8
Age 21–44								
Higher ISP								
Escape	80	4	59	37	81	6	76	18
Nonescape	212	12	66	22	246	32	64	4
Lower ISP								
Escape	73	6	47	47	74	16	59	25
Nonescape	147	13	66	21	158	43	52	5
Age 45+								
Higher ISP								
Escape	60	3	50	47	56	10	75	15
Nonescape	130	12	69	19	157	36	62	2
Lower ISP								
Escape	71	14	49	37	35	7	75	18
Nonescape	136	28	49	23	129	41	56	3

[a] Escape drinkers gave two or more of the five escape reasons (see Table 95) as being important in their drinking.

TABLE 98.—*Percentage of Escape and Heavy-Escape Drinkers, by Alienation Score*[a] *and Sex*

	N	Abstainers + Infreq. Drinkers	Light, Mod. + Heavy		Heavy-Escape Drinkers[b]
			Nonescape Drinkers	Escape Drinkers	
Total sample	2746	47	35	18	6
Men					
Age 21–39					
Low score	321	25	54	21	9
High score	138	23	46	31	17
Age 40–59					
Low score	331	32	45	23	11
High score	130	36	37	27	13
Age 60+					
Low score	139	42	44	14	4
High score	118	54	20	26	9
Women					
Age 21–39					
Low score	400	52	34	14	2
High score	201	48	25	27	9
Age 40–59					
Low score	382	53	35	12	3
High score	216	65	21	14	3
Age 60+					
Low score	194	68	23	9	c
High score	173	79	11	10	1

[a] High Alienation = agreed with two or more of four statements from Alienation scale.
[b] Base: total sample.
[c] Less than 0.5%.

Escape Drinkers, by Oral Activity Score. Women heavy drinkers were shown to have above-average tendencies to rate the non-drinking "oral" activities (smoking, eating, taking a tranquilizer or other pills or medicines) as being very or fairly helpful when depressed or nervous. This finding leads to the inference that those who rely on nonalcoholic oral resources for relief from anxiety and depression are also likely to drink for escape reasons. Table 99 shows that among both men and women, at nearly all age levels, a higher proportion of those with high Oral Activity scores were escape drinkers. Another way of expressing this relationship is to say that those who rely on nonalcoholic oral activities such as

TABLE 99.—*Percentage of Escape and Heavy-Escape Drinkers, by Oral Activity Score,*[a] *Age and Sex*

| | N | Abstainers + Infreq. Drinkers | Light, Mod. + Heavy | | Heavy-Escape Drinkers[b] |
			Nonescape Drinkers	Escape Drinkers	
Total sample	2746	47	35	18	6
Men					
Age 21–39					
Low Oral activity	342	25	56	19	9
High Oral	117	22	40	38	19
Age 40–59					
Low Oral	323	31	46	23	11
High Oral	138	40	35	25	12
Age 60+					
Low Oral	181	46	39	15	7
High Oral	76	52	20	28	6
Women					
Age 21–39					
Low Oral	389	54	32	14	3
High Oral	212	44	30	26	8
Age 40–59					
Low Oral	392	59	31	10	1
High Oral	206	54	27	19	6
Age 60+					
Low Oral	266	75	18	7	c
High Oral	101	68	17	15	1

a High Oral Activity = mentioned two or more of the nondrinking oral activities (smoking, eating, taking a tranquilizer or other pills or medicines) as being very or fairly helpful when depressed or nervous.
b Base: total sample.
c Less than 0.5%.

smoking, eating and medicines to relieve tension and anxiety also tend to rely on alcohol for relief of stress. The relationship is close enough to warrant continued study of tendencies toward adoption of generalized response patterns—such as reliance on interpersonal resources, diversionary activities or oral activities—in response to stress.[21]

[21] Search for such generalized patterns of response to stress is being continued in the national follow-up study of changes in drinking practices mentioned earlier and in the new studies on patterns of drug acquisition and use being conducted by the Social Research Group and by the Family Research Center, Langley Porter Neuropsychiatric Clinic.

Escape Drinkers, by Cross-Pressures to Drink. Knupfer and her associates, in the principal report on the Berkeley study (39, *pp.* 52–57), analyzed the tendencies toward escape drinking of several kinds of persons "who are not expected to be relatively heavy drinkers": women, persons with strong religious beliefs, persons belonging to the more conservative Protestant denominations (e.g., Baptists, Methodists) as against other Protestants, and those whose parents disapproved of drinking in contrast to those whose parents approved. In each instance, when heavy drinkers from groups which have cultural sanctions against heavy drinking were compared on their reasons for drinking against the reasons given by heavy drinkers from groups without such strong sanctions, it was found that relatively higher proportions of the groups with "cross-pressures" against heavy drinking were escape drinkers. The results thus were consistent with the cross-pressures hypothesis that those who drink heavily in defiance of presumed sanctions against such drinking are more likely than others to drink as a means of escaping (at least temporarily) from personal problems.

Table 100 presents the results of a cross-pressures analysis of the national survey data, conducted on a basis somewhat comparable to the Berkeley analysis. For this analysis, drinkers were divided first by sex, then by heavy drinkers and others, and then into various subgroups which were presumed to differ in their social sanctions against drinking. The major findings were as follows:

(1) *Sex.* Of the small minority of women who were heavy drinkers, a materially higher proportion qualified as escape drinkers than did other women drinkers (64 vs 23%). This is a higher ratio of escape drinking than among heavy-drinking men as against other men drinkers (48 vs 26%). These findings are in keeping with the "cross-pressures" hypothesis and with the Berkeley findings. (2) *Religion.* The Berkeley study found that Baptists and Methodists who were relatively heavy drinkers had a higher proportion of escape drinkers than did other Protestants who drank relatively heavily. The results of the present study are similar, but the subsamples are too small to warrant firm conclusions. (3) *Parental approval.* More of the men heavy drinkers whose fathers disapproved of drinking were escape drinkers than of those whose fathers approved. Concerning mother's approval, there was a similar difference in escape drinking rates among the men and a much larger difference among the women (although the number of cases in

TABLE 100.—*Percentage of Escape Drinkers, by Sex and Cross-Pressures*[a]

	MEN				WOMEN			
	N	Heavy Drinkers	N	Other Drinkers	N	Heavy Drinkers	N	Other Drinkers
Total drinkers	252	48	657	26	72	64	867	23
Catholics	107	43	191	28	34	65	302	24
Liberal Protestants	43	42	123	21	16	c	197	21
Conserv. Protestants	73	48	286	28	19	c	294	23
Father approved of drinking	138	47	279	26	39	62	464	27
Father disapproved of drinking	42	59	181	29	16	c	206	17
Mother approved of drinking	88	47	152	26	27	48	282	23
Mother disapproved of drinking	94	55	343	30	32	79	374	21
Said "Alcohol does more harm than good"	131	41	474	26	43	61	664	20
Did not say so	121	55	183	26	29	69	203	31
Someone[b] tried to get respondent to drink less during last year	41	46	70	23	13	c	29	20
No one tried	211	50	587	29	59	66	838	25

[a] The table should be read as follows: of the 252 men who were heavy drinkers, 48% were escape drinkers; of the 657 other men drinkers (infrequent, light or moderate), 26% were escape drinkers; of the 107 Catholic men who were heavy drinkers, 43% were escape drinkers, etc.

[b] E.g., employers, spouse, friends, people at work, neighbors.

[c] Too few cases for analysis.

these subgroups was quite small). (4) *Attitude on harmfulness of drinking.* Those who felt that alcohol was more harmful than helpful had fewer escape drinkers than did others. (5) *Pressure from others against drinking.* Respondents were divided into those who reported that someone (employer, friends, spouse, co-workers, neighbors) had tried to get them to drink less at some time during the previous year, and those who did not report such pressures. The hypothesis (that the person who is subjected to pressure from other persons to drink less will be more likely to drink for escape reasons) was not borne out by the findings.

Thus these limited cross-pressures analyses indicate that the concept of cross-pressures as contributing to a higher level of escape drinking among those who drink heavily in a milieu which frowns upon heavy drinking is a useful one insofar as the differences between heavy-drinking men and women as a whole are concerned, and evidently as regards some aspects of family upbringing (whether parents disapproved of drinking). But the results of these few cross-tabulations indicate that cross-pressures may not always operate as expected. Further analyses in follow-up studies of the California and national samples are planned to demonstrate whether heavy drinkers who are subjected to other such cross-pressures are more likely than others to drink for escape reasons, and also whether they are more likely to reduce their drinking (because of social pressures or other reasons) over a period of time.

Escape Drinkers, by Effects of Drinking. It has been shown that heavy drinkers mentioned unfavorable rather than favorable effects from their own drinking during the preceding year to a greater extent than did moderate or light drinkers (see Table 73). This is contrary to what would be expected if heavy drinking were primarily accompanied by positive rather than negative reinforcement.

A partial answer to the question as to why heavy drinkers continue to drink if there are more negative than positive effects to be gained from drinking is available through examining the relationship between positive and negative effects experienced by escape drinkers as compared to nonescape drinkers. Our hypothesis is that escape drinking should entail a more powerful operant conditioning than would be true of drinking for primarily social reasons. Drinking behavior should be reinforced more strongly when there is a greater disparity or gradient between the way the drinker feels before and after a few drinks. Since the escape drinker, by definition, is drinking primarily for the purpose of avoidance of personal anxiety or depression while the nonescape drinker is drinking in major part ostensibly to accommodate to someone else's wishes, it is inferred that the escape drinker ordinarily gets a greater immediate positive reinforcing effect from drinking than does the nonescape drinker.

A partial test of this hypothesis is provided by a comparison of the positive and negative effects cited by escape and nonescape drinkers (Table 101). In all six comparisons—light, moderate and heavy drinkers among both men and women—the escape drinkers had a higher proportion who reported having some effects—either positive or negative—from drinking than did nonescape drinkers. Moreover, in every instance the escape drinkers had a higher proportion citing both favorable and unfavorable results from drinking.

TABLE 101.—*Favorable and Unfavorable Effects of Drinking Noted in Past Year by Escape and Nonescape Drinkers, by Sex, in Per Cent*

	N	(1) No Effects	(2) Favorable Only	(3) Unfavorable Only	(4) Both Favorable and Unfavorable	(5) Unclassifiable	(2+4) Total Favorable	(3+4) Total Unfavorable	Ratio 2+4: 3+4
Total drinkers	1848	68	12	15	3	2	15	18	0.83
Men[a]									
Light									
Escape	68	67	19	12	1	1	20	13	1.54
Nonescape	256	78	12	6	2	2	14	8	1.25
Moderate									
Escape	77	52	18	28	1	1	19	29	0.66
Nonescape	135	59	15	20	3	3	18	23	0.78
Heavy									
Escape	118	45	11	35	7	2	18	42	0.43
Nonescape	134	57	6	28	5	4	11	33	0.33
Women[a]									
Light									
Escape	115	64	18	12	3	3	21	15	1.40
Nonescape	327	75	11	10	2	2	13	12	1.08
Moderate									
Escape	60	48	13	28	8	3	21	36	0.58
Nonescape	82	58	14	24	3	1	17	27	0.63
Heavy									
Escape	47	32	25	36	6	1	31	42	0.74
Nonescape	25	38	18	34	4	6	22	38	0.58

[a] Infrequent drinkers are excluded.

The ratios of favorable to unfavorable effects reported were similar in escape and nonescape drinkers in most instances. The ratios were highest among light drinkers, both men and women, and lower among heavier drinkers, whether escape or nonescape drinkers. Thus the findings indicate that more escape drinkers get effects from drinking than do the nonescape drinkers. The issue then arises whether we are warranted in the assumption that escape drinkers obtain more net positive reinforcement than nonescape drinkers and thereby would be more vulnerable to excessive drinking in terms of having problems with others or with their own self-perception. The answer may well lie in the relative strength of the immediate positive reinforcement as against the later negative reinforcement. As stated by Conger (16, *p. 320*):

"If we assume that drinking is learned because it is reinforced, one apparent exception is offered by the man whose drinking is, at least socially, more punishing than rewarding. The man who is alienating his boss, his wife and his friends hardly seems to be socially rewarded for drinking. However, two factors should be considered here. One is the immediacy of reinforcement. Immediate reinforcements are more effective than delayed ones. This learning principle is called the gradient of reinforcement. It may be that, according to this principle, the immediate reduction in anxiety more than compensates for the punitive attitude of the man's wife the next morning. The other factor is the amount of drive and conflict. The personal anxiety-reducing effects of alcohol may, if the anxiety is great enough, constitute greater reinforcement than the competing social punishment."[22]

Those who are escape drinkers report a higher level of anxiety and depression than do nonescape drinkers. If drinking temporarily alleviates these handicaps, the escape drinker would have more incentive to drink. Further, it is possible that the anxiety-ridden drinker may continue or resume drinking in order to forestall as long as possible the recurrence of both the anxieties and the guilt feelings which stem from socially disapproved drinking. Thus, up to a point, social disapproval of drinking may serve to increase the compulsion toward continued drinking on the part of the anxious escape drinker.

---

[22] The same principle of the gradient of reinforcement has also been invoked with respect to eating, by Ferster, Nurnberger and Levitt (18), who say that, "The long-term aversive consequences of overeating are so postponed as to be ineffective compared to the immediate reinforcement of food in the mouth."

On the basis of the evidence available, it is believed that those who drink for escape reasons will be more likely to become problem drinkers in the future than will nonescape drinkers. This prediction, however, is contingent upon the ways in which the drinker's personality resources and environmental forces operate in the future. When the liabilities of alcohol become more immediately negatively reinforcing than its assets are positively reinforcing, it is assumed that the escape drinker will reduce his drinking. Unless positively reinforcing substitutes for alcohol are found by the escape drinker, however, he is likely to yield to the strength of habit and resume drinking under conditions of stress.

Summary of Differences between Escape and Nonescape Heavy Drinkers (Table 102)

A special analysis of the characteristics of the escape and nonescape groups among the heavy drinkers revealed the following differences (Table 102):[23]

Background Characteristics: The heavy-escape drinkers were relatively older and of lower social status and income than other heavy drinkers and they included an above-average percentage of Nonwhites. They tended to be less well integrated into social activities, as indicated by their lower rate of participation in such interpersonal activities as visiting or going out. Somewhat more of them had parents or spouses who drank; and more said their fathers or mothers had not approved of people who drank.

Opinions about Drinking: Much higher proportions of the heavy-escape drinkers than of other heavy drinkers said they worried about their drinking (men, 29 vs 14%; women, 30 vs 6%). Similarly, higher proportions of heavy-escape drinkers considered themselves at least fairly heavy drinkers or would miss drinking if they had to give it up. Heavy-escape drinkers appeared to be more apprehensive than other heavy drinkers about the role of alcohol in their lives. More frequently than other heavy drinkers, they reported both favorable and unfavorable effects from drinking—although, as discussed above, it is likely that the immediate positively reinforcing effects of alcohol often may outweigh the less im-

---

[23] Further subgroup analyses are reported in Detail Table A-102; see *Headnote*, p. 229.

TABLE 102.—*Summary of Differences between Nonescape- and Escape-Heavy Drinkers, in Per Cent*[a]

	Men Heavy Drinkers Nonescape	Men Heavy Drinkers Escape	Women Heavy Drinkers Nonescape	Women Heavy Drinkers Escape
N	134	118	25	47
Background Characteristics				
Age 50 or older	26	32	6	12
Lowest ISP group	21	23	20	32
Under $6000 family income	28	34	24	48
Single, divorced, separated or widowed	16	19	22	35
U.S. Nonwhite	2	11	12	19
Go to church less than once a week	57	66	44	67
Social Activities				
Watches TV often in evening	49	57	50	69
Goes out for entertainment often	26	35	40	22
Participates in none of three interpersonal activities (visiting, having visitors, going out for entertainment)	39	43	28	40
Has close friends from work	63	72	58	58
Drinking Habits, Attitudes of Parents, Spouse				
Father drank at least twice a month	55	60	42	53
Mother drank at least twice a month	19	26	22	21
Spouse drinks at least twice a month	58	70	92	97
Father disapproved of drinking	13	20	8	29
Mother disapproved of drinking	33	45	26	55
Usual Circumstances of Drinking				
Drinks more when with:				
People from work[b]	19	24	18	18
Close friends	42	55	46	61
Members of immediate family	11	17	14	38
More than half of following drink quite a bit:				
People from work[b]	30	40	34	41
Close friends	21	38	36	38
Drinks wine or beer fairly often when with:[b]				
Friends	42	48	41	51
Self	25	31	10	21
Drinks spirits fairly often when with:[b]				
Friends	46	48	37	64
Self	9	20	2	6
Drinks spirits fairly often on weekends[c]	46	72	60	68

TABLE 102.—*continued*

	Men Heavy Drinkers		Women Heavy Drinkers	
	Nonescape	Escape	Nonescape	Escape
Effects of Drinking Noted in Past Year				
Hangover, headache	12	23	10	24
Nauseated	5	12	22	8
Relaxed	3	4	0	13
Age at Start of Drinking				
Started drinking when under age 18	28	34	20	15
Started drinking when 25 or older	10	10	14	26
Opinions About Drinking				
Worries at least a little about own drinking	14	29	6	30
Considers self at least a fairly heavy drinker	11	22	4	22
Would miss drinking a lot if had to give it up	11	23	8	35
Others tried to get respondent to drink less during past year	8	30	20	26
Did not agree that drinking does more harm than good	41	55	34	43
Had close relative with serious drinking problem	38	41	36	48
Good things to be said about drinking: Helps people to relax	23	58	32	58
Bad things to be said about drinking: Bad for health, long-term	37	30	20	30
Bad for family life	27	23	12	29
Outlook on Own Fortunes and Values				
Good things during past year:				
Own health good	25	38	24	33
Family's health good	16	19	4	10
Financial improvement	24	33	38	25
Respondent or spouse had steady work	13	20	10	20
Bad things during past year:				
Respondent's health, aging	7	13	4	16
Illness, accidents in immediate family	9	8	4	19
Last year not a good year	32	31	24	42
Childhood not mostly happy	20	18	18	37
Had more than one's share of problems	21	37	14	44
Main things wanted out of life:				
Financial or job security	61	60	30	45
Material things	20	26	26	42

[Continued on next page]

TABLE 102.—*continued*

	Men Heavy Drinkers		Women Heavy Drinkers	
	Nonescape	*Escape*	*Nonescape*	*Escape*
Not very satisfied in attaining goals	13	17	16	20
Would prefer different occupation for self or spouse	34	38	26	39
Health not excellent or good	12	24	14	29
Activities Helpful in Relieving Depression				
Activities very or fairly helpful when depressed or nervous:				
Having a drink	59	84	50	83
Smoking	45	56	50	64
Eating	26	38	32	60
Taking a tranquilizer	3	9	10	24
Taking other kind of pill or medicine	9	16	14	36
Working harder around the house or on job	60	70	72	71
Going to church or saying a prayer	46	55	64	84
Talking it over with a friend or relative	64	67	52	66
Just trying to forget about it	41	53	42	51
Personality Measures				
Keep it to oneself when one gets angry	28	35	14	27
Higher scores on personality scales:				
Neurotic Tendencies (4 or 5 symptoms)	16	33	42	56
Alienation (2–4 out of 4)	22	41	24	53
Empathy (3–4 out of 4)	51	57	54	73
Impulsivity (3–4 out of 4)	27	42	46	47
Rigidity (3–4 out of 4)	30	39	40	53
Religious Fundamentalism (4 out of 4)	16	27	28	35
Protestant Ethic (3–4 out of 4)	50	60	56	74

[a] Results in other groups are fully reported in Detail Table A-102; see Headnote, p. 229.
[b] Based on total who meet socially with such people.
[c] Based on total drinking these beverages.

mediate negative aftereffects (both physiological and social) of heavy drinking in inducing the heavy-escape drinker to become an alcoholic.

General Outlook: More of the heavy-escape drinkers than of other heavy drinkers said they had "more than my share of problems," rated the previous year as not a good year, and said their childhoods were not "mostly happy." They also expressed greater dissatisfaction about attaining their life goals, their occupations and the state of their health. In talking about the good and bad things that had happened to them during the preceding year, they were more likely to emphasize matters of health and having steady work.

Activities Helpful in Relieving Depression or Nervousness: The heavy-escape drinkers were found to have a higher incidence than other heavy drinkers of dependence upon both drinking and other activities to allay depression or nervousness, whether oral activities (such as eating, smoking, or taking tranquilizers or other medicines) or nonoral activities (such as going to church or praying, talking problems over with a friend or relative, or just trying to forget about it). More of the heavy-escape drinkers also had high scores on the scales of Neurotic Tendencies and Alienation. In sum, the heavy-escape drinkers were found to be more reactive in general than other heavy drinkers.

Finally, as a result of these findings, it is expected that the escape scale will be useful in identifying in advance those who will be more likely to increase their drinking, and to be problem drinkers in the future.

Chapter 7

Summary, Conclusions and Research Implications

T HE national survey of drinking practices, which was conducted throughout the United States (exclusive of Alaska and Hawaii) in late 1964 and early 1965, was based on 2746 personal interviews with a random sample of adults, representative of the population aged 21 and older, living in households. The sample was drawn in accordance with probability procedures, and interviews were completed with 90% of the 3043 selected eligible persons.

Summary of Principal Findings

1. Amount and Variability of Drinking (Chapter 1)

A Q–F–V Index was developed based on the quantity, frequency and variability of drinking of alcoholic beverages. The classification system takes into account, first, the over-all frequency of drinking and, second, a combination of the quantity and variability (of the most frequently drunk beverage) utilizing the principle that those who drink large amounts per occasion should be classified as heavier drinkers than others who consume about the same volume in a given period of time but do so in smaller quantities per drinking occasion. This classification resulted in a division of respondents into the following five Q–F–V groups:

1. Abstainers (32%): drink less than once a year or not at all.
2. Infrequent drinkers (15%): drink at least once a year but less than once a month.
3. Light drinkers (28%): drink at least once a month but with a low quantity–variability rating.
4. Moderate drinkers (13%): drink at least once a month, with a medium quantity–variability rating.
5. Heavy drinkers (12%): drink at least once a month, with a high quantity–variability rating (a typical heavy drinker would be one who drinks nearly every day with five or more drinks at a time at least occasionally, or drinks at least weekly with usually five or more drinks on most occasions.)

184

The survey confirmed that the use of alcohol is typical rather than unusual behavior for both men and women in the United States: 68% of the respondents said they drink at least once a year and so were classified as drinkers; 10% used to but no longer drink; and 22% had never drunk alcoholic beverages.

Of the 12% who were classified as heavy drinkers, half (6% of the total sample) were further classified as heavy-escape drinkers in that they chose, as factors which were important in their own drinking, two or more of five reasons which implied a desire to escape from the problems of everyday living (Chapter 6). The heavy-escape drinkers are not necessarily alcoholics, since many of them may have had no other signs of alcohol-related problems. However, the group undoubtedly includes many if not most of those who would be defined as alcoholics by most criteria.[1] A follow-up study of the same respondents, conducted in 1967, will help to establish the proportions of heavy-escape drinkers who do have special problems related to alcohol.

2. Demographic Variations in Drinking Patterns (Chapter 2)

Sex and Age: 77% of the men and 60% of the women reported drinking at least once a year; 21% of the men and 5% of the women were classified as heavy drinkers.

Among men, abstainers were in the minority at all age levels; a majority in each age group up to 65 drank at least once a month. The highest proportions of heavy drinkers were found among men aged 30 to 34 and 45 to 49 (30% of both groups).

Among women, however, half or more of each age group either did not drink at all or drank less than once a month. The highest proportions of heavy drinkers among women were only about 10% and were found at ages 45 to 49 and 21 to 24.

The findings of the survey are consistent with Gallup Poll trend estimates which indicate (*a*) that the proportion of persons who drink has increased since World War II, and (*b*) that the pro-

---

[1] The number of alcoholics in the United States has been estimated by Keller (35) as about 4.5 million. The absence of a reliable base figure for the noninstitutionalized household population aged 21 years and over sampled in this survey, in the contiguous states, makes it unwise to project our percentages directly, but it is evident that the number of heavy-escape drinkers in the country is in the neighborhood of 6.5 million. Thus it seems likely that the group includes many if not most of the people who by one criterion or another would be considered alcoholics, as well as considerable numbers who would not be so classified.

portion of drinkers is much lower among both men and women aged 50 and over than among younger persons.

Social Position: As an indicator of socioeconomic status the survey utilized a four-way grouping based on the Hollingshead Index of Social Position (ISP), 'which combines the individual's education and the occupation of the family breadwinner, taking into account the status or power position associated with the occupation (28). With differences in age and sex allowed for, the proportion of drinkers (nonabstainers) was consistently lower at the lower social levels. The proportion of drinkers was lowest among older women (60 years and over) in the lowest ISP group (34%) and was highest among young men aged 21 to 39 of the highest ISP (88%). Lower proportions of light and moderate drinkers were in the lower ISP groups than in the higher, while the proportion of heavy drinkers in the total sample was about the same at all social levels. Among drinkers, however, the proportion of heavy drinkers tended to be a little higher at the lower social levels. These findings should modify perspectives on the "abstemious middle classes": relatively more of the well-to-do and middle-class people report drinking at least occasionally, but fewer of those who do drink, drink heavily.

Occupation: Farm owners and operators, both men and women, showed the highest proportions of abstainers (40 and 74%, respectively); they were also lowest in the proportion of heavy drinkers (12% of the men, none of the women). While men whose family's main earners were in the professional and business fields each reported about 80% drinkers, the businessmen (managers, proprietors, officials) had a higher proportion of heavy drinkers than did the professionals (24 vs 15%). Operatives (semiskilled workers) and service workers (including domestics), especially men, appeared to be slightly above average in the proportions of heavy drinkers (about 25%).

Education: Both men and women with less than a high-school education were much more likely than others to be abstainers, while majorities of all college graduates were light or moderate drinkers. Most likely to be heavy drinkers were men who had completed high school and men who did not finish college.

Marital Status and Parental Rearing: Single and divorced or separated persons were more likely than those who were married to be heavy drinkers; the difference was particularly marked in persons aged under 45 of lower social status (38 vs 21% in men,

17 vs 4% in women). Widows and widowers (generally older people) were much less likely than others to be either drinkers or heavy drinkers.

Among men and women aged under 45 years, there was very little difference in the incidence of heavy drinking according to whether or not respondents had been raised by both parents until they were 16. But among men over 45, those who had not been raised by both parents showed almost twice the proportion of heavy drinkers as those who had been. Whether this difference stems primarily from greater childhood deprivations or inconsistencies in social controls among men now aged over 45 than among men of a younger generation, or from other variables, cannot be established from a survey conducted at a single point in time.

Region and Degree of Urbanization: The highest percentages of drinkers were found in the Middle Atlantic states (83%) and in New England (79%). Both areas are relatively urban in character. The lowest percentage of drinkers was in the less urbanized East South Central states (35%); however, this area had about an average proportion of heavy drinkers among those who drink. These results are consistent with other findings showing a higher incidence of drinking in the more urbanized areas. Another factor is religion: the conservative Protestant denominations which preach against the use of alcohol are better represented in the South than in other regions.

Sharp differences in proportions of drinkers were noted by size of community: the proportion who said they drink at least once a year ranged from only 43% among farm residents to 87% among those living in the largest suburbs. Farm residents also had the lowest proportion of heavy drinkers (5%). The tendency for those living in the more highly urbanized areas to include higher proportions of heavy drinkers held for all age and sex groups; it was most pronounced at the lower ISP levels.

Race: White and Nonwhite men did not differ much in rates of drinking. Negro women, however, differed quite a bit from their White counterparts: they had higher proportions both of abstainers (51 vs 39%) and of heavy drinkers (11 vs 4%).

Country of Origin and National Identity: Respondents who were born outside the U. S. A. included a materially higher than average percentage of drinkers than did native-born respondents—but of moderate rather than of heavy drinkers. Of the larger group whose fathers were born outside the United States, 80% were drinkers, compared to only 64% of those whose fathers were native born. When findings are adjusted for age level (to control for the fact that respondents whose fathers were born in some countries were older on the average than those whose fathers were born in other countries), those with fathers born in Ireland had the highest adjusted proportions of both drinkers and heavy drinkers. Those whose fathers came from Latin America or the Caribbean had the highest adjusted proportion of abstainers; but among those who drank, they had a relatively high proportion of heavy drinkers.

When respondents were classified according to their national identity (father's country of birth or country of origin of most of their ancestors), those identifying themselves as primarily Italian in origin had the highest proportion of drinkers (91%), followed closely by those of Russian, Polish or Baltic origin (86%). Among those with any national affiliation the highest proportions of abstainers were found in the Scotch-Irish (50%) and in the Scotch and English (40%) groups.

Religion and Church Attendance: Jews and Episcopalians had the lowest proportions of abstainers of any religious groups (less than 10% each). Jewish women were very unlikely to be heavy drinkers. Those who belonged to the more conservative Protestant denominations had relatively high proportions of abstainers (48%) and relatively few heavy drinkers (7%).

Catholics had above-average proportions both of drinkers (83%) and heavy drinkers (19%). Catholic men had the highest proportion of heavy drinkers among any of the religious groupings (33%). A special cross-tabulation of drinking by various religious and national identity groups showed that Catholics had generally higher proportions of heavy drinkers even when ethnic affiliation was held constant—except that Irish "liberal" Protestants were more likely to be heavy drinkers than were Irish Catholics.

Twice as high a proportion of those who said they never went to church (22%) were heavy drinkers as of those who said they went every week (10%). The proportions of abstainers were relatively high both among those who went most frequently and those who went least frequently. When churchgoing was held constant, the proportion of heavy drinkers was higher among Catholics than among liberal Protestants, and higher among liberal Protestants than among conservative Protestants.

To illustrate the major demographic differences in drinking patterns, Chart 3 shows those groups in the general population who are most likely to be drinkers; and among drinkers, those most likely to be classified as heavy drinkers:

CHART 3.—*Demographic Characteristics of Drinkers and Heavy Drinkers*

Most Likely to be Drinkers:	*Among Drinkers, Most Likely to Be Heavy Drinkers:*
Men aged under 55, women under 50	Men aged 45 to 49
Men and women of higher social status	
Professional people; semiprofessionals; technical workers; sales workers; managers; officials	Operatives; service workers
College graduates	Men who completed high school and men who did not finish college
Single men	Single, divorced, or separated men and women
Residents of Middle Atlantic, New England, East North Central, and Pacific areas	Residents of Middle Atlantic, New England, and Pacific areas
Residents of suburban cities, towns	Residents of largest cities
Those whose fathers were foreign-born, especially of Italian origin	Those whose fathers were Latin American/Caribbean, Italian, or British in origin (Irish, when adjusted for age levels)
Jews, Episcopalians	Protestants of no specific denomination; Catholics; those without religious affiliation
	White men; Negro women

3. Drinking of Specific Beverages (Chapter 3)

Four out of 10 respondents said they drank wine as often as once a year; only 1% were heavy wine drinkers. Half of the respondents reported drinking beer at least once a year; 7% of the total sample were heavy beer drinkers. Distilled spirits (or drinks containing spirits) were drunk by 57% at least once a year; 6% were heavy drinkers of spirits. One-quarter of the respondents said they drank all 3 beverages at least once a year.

Compared to the other two beverages, wine was drunk relatively more often by women than by men; by moderate rather than heavy

drinkers; by persons of upper social status; by residents of the
Pacific and Middle Atlantic states (which include wine-producing
areas); and by those living in the larger suburbs. Beer was drunk
by above-average proportions of the heavier drinkers, men, and
younger persons. Spirits (including mixed drinks) were drunk by
relatively more of the heavier drinkers, persons of upper social
status, men in their 30s and 40s, and women in their 20s.

4. Behavioral Correlates of Drinking (Chapter 4)

Drinking by Parents and Spouse: Larger proportions of younger
persons and those of higher social status had both frequent-drink-
ing parents and parental approval of drinking. Permissiveness
of parents about drinking was generally correlated with a higher
proportion of drinkers. Heavy drinking by women was closely
correlated with heavy drinking by their husbands, and vice versa.

Usual Circumstances of Drinking: In general, alcoholic beverages
were served relatively more often when meeting socially with people from work than even when with close friends.

People said they drink most often with friends (including those
from work), next most often with members of their families, and
least often by themselves. Heavy drinkers were more likely than
others to say they drink alone, but less than a quarter do so "fairly
often." Moreover, small minorities of up to 13% of both light and
moderate drinkers also reported drinking fairly often alone.

5. Retrospective Reports of Changes in Drinking (Chapter 5)

A rather high variability in individuals' drinking practices over
time is indicated by the fact that half (51%) of the total sample
reported they had changed their drinking habits since starting to
drink, either by quitting drinking or by having drunk more or less
in the past than they did at the time of interview. More of the men
(67%) than of the women (38%) said they had changed—the difference resulting primarily from the larger percentage of women
than men who said they had never drunk (32 vs 9%). The existence
of substantial changes in drinking patterns over time is confirmed
both by national Gallup Poll trend data and by longitudinal community studies.

A relatively larger proportion of those of highest social status
started drinking later in life and also continued drinking to a more

advanced age than did those of lower status. This finding is consistent with the general differential in the phasing of various activities, remarked on by Kinsey and others (36), whereby upper-status persons generally begin certain activities associated with adulthood (e.g., sex, smoking, drinking) at a relatively later age than do those of lower status, but tend to continue to an older age.

The principal reasons for drinking less than in the past centered around having more responsibilities or problems, financial considerations, or going out for entertainment less often; relatively few mentioned guilt-related or moral or religious reasons for reducing their drinking. Reasons cited for drinking more were primarily social—more visiting, more entertaining or the influence or example of one's spouse or associates.

Past Drinking by Abstainers: One-third of the nondrinkers said they used to drink once a year or more. Since large proportions of former drinkers in all age groups up to 45 said they had stopped drinking within the last 10 years, the results suggest that many of those now classified as abstainers may move in and out of the drinker group at intervals. The turnover in drinking habits is being checked in detail in later longitudinal studies of the respondents interviewed in this survey.

The leading reasons given by abstainers for not drinking were religious or moral grounds (31%), lack of need or desire for alcohol (26%), and bad effect on health (20%). Men abstainers put relatively more emphasis than women upon health and financial reasons, while women abstainers were more likely than were men to mention religious or moral reasons, need or desire, upbringing, and past examples.

6. Psychological Aspects of Drinking (Chapter 6)

Perception of Effects and Implications of One's Drinking: Favorable and unfavorable effects of one's own drinking were mentioned by approximately equal proportions of drinkers; but two-thirds said they did not recall having any particular effects from drinking during the last year.

Only 9% of all drinkers said they worried at all about their own drinking, and 12% said that other people (wife or husband, friends, neighbors, employer or co-workers) had tried to get them to drink less at some time during the past year. Only 3% of all drinkers and

16% of the heavy drinkers rated themselves as at least "fairly heavy" drinkers.

Opinions about Drinking: Although most drinkers do not appear to consider their own drinking a problem, a pronounced general ambivalence toward alcohol is seen in the finding that three-fourths of all respondents (and a majority of even men heavy drinkers) said they thought drinking does more harm than good. Three-fourths also said they regarded alcoholism as either a very serious or a fairly serious public health problem in America. The lower social status groups were consistently more negative than others toward drinking.

The leading good thing said about drinking was that it helps people mix socially. The leading bad things said about drinking were concerned with health, family life, accidents, and economic and psychological consequences.

Personality Correlates of Drinking: The heavy drinkers voiced only a slightly lower level of satisfaction in meeting their life goals than did the lighter drinkers or nondrinkers. Relative to other persons, heavy drinkers laid slightly greater stress upon the goals of family life and friends and on their desire for emotional security and happiness. Women heavy drinkers were more likely to express dissatisfaction with their (or their husbands') occupations, their neighborhoods and their educational attainments than were other women.

The lowest proportion considering themselves to be in excellent or good health was found among abstainers (who are more likely than drinkers to be older people). Among those who drank, heavy drinkers did not materially differ from others in rating their health. Above-average proportions of men heavy drinkers and women abstainers were overweight; but there was little difference on this factor according to type of beverage drunk.

There was a strong relationship between drinking and cigarette smoking. The correlation was specially evident among women: 81% of the heavy-drinking women smoked cigarettes, compared to only 19% of nondrinking women.

More heavy drinkers than others relied on smoking and, in the case of women, on eating to relieve nervous tension; among men, heavy drinkers were less likely than others to rely on eating or taking tranquilizers or other pills.

Seven brief Guttman-type scales generally showed relatively

little relation to classifications on the q–f–v index of drinking. However, certain scales (particularly those measuring Alienation, Impulsivity and Religious Fundamentalism) were found to be related to heavy drinking within certain sex–age–isp groupings. Combinations of such scales may prove useful in predicting changes in drinking in the future.

The Escape Drinker: The reasons for drinking given by the majority of drinkers were primarily social. In order to study the factor of personal involvement or escape through alcohol, respondents were also scored on an "escape" scale consisting of the following 5 reasons for drinking (included in a longer list of 11 reasons): "I drink because it helps me to relax"; "I drink because I need it when tense or nervous"; "A drink helps to cheer me up when I'm in a bad mood"; "A drink helps me to forget my worries"; "I drink when I want to forget everything."

Of all respondents, 20% were classified as escape drinkers (29% of all drinkers), because they rated two or more of these five reasons as "very" or "fairly" important in their drinking; 6% of respondents (9% of drinkers) were classified as both escape drinkers and heavy drinkers. This group of heavy-escape drinkers is expected to show an especially high incidence of problems related to drinking in the forthcoming longitudinal study.

Heavy drinkers who drank for escape reasons were found to be different from other heavy drinkers in a number of respects: they were relatively older, more likely to be of lower isp, and more pessimistic and alienated in their outlook toward their lives and their futures.

7. Implications of Drinking, by Social Status

Sex, age and social position interact to make for large group differences in proportions of drinkers, ranging from 88% among young men in the highest isp group down to 34% among older women in the lowest group. On the other hand, the proportion of heavy drinkers was about the same in all isp groups within any sex–age group. Thus the lower social status groups have a lower proportion of drinkers but relatively more heavy drinkers. Drinking therefore seems to serve different functions for people in lower and upper status groups.

There are many other indications that the implications of alcohol vary considerably for persons of different status. Some of the key findings which bear upon this point are presented in Table 103, a compilation of sex–age–ISP data from earlier tables in which comparisons are focused on the top and bottom quartiles of the ISP index. The differences in implications between those of high or low status may be summarized as follows:

Escape Drinking: The men show no contrast between those of high and low status in the 21–39 age group, but in the two older age groups, a higher proportion of the men of low status than of high status were escape drinkers. Heavy-escape drinking was more prevalent among the low than the high status groups at the youngest age level (21–39).

Drinking as Part of a Life-Style: In all sex–age comparisons, except women aged 21 to 29, a significantly higher proportion of those of high social status than of low status said they "would miss drinking" if they had to give it up.

Others' Disapproval of One's Drinking: On every sex–age group comparison, a higher percentage of drinkers of low than of high status reported that other persons (family, spouse, friends, neighbors, or people at work) had tried to get them to drink less at some time during the last year.

Negativism toward Drinking: Respondents of low status were consistently more negative in their attitude toward drinking than were those of high status, with higher proportions of nearly all the low-status groups saying that "drinking does more harm than good."

Different Perceptions of Effects of Drinking: The attitudes of those of low and high status also differed with respect to the effects of drinking. Those of low status were more likely than the corresponding high-status groups to report as bad effects "fights resulting from drinking," while those of high status mentioned relatively more often as bad effects the health problems caused by drinking.

Additional evidence of different views of effects of drinking appears in the responses on what kinds of activities are helpful when depressed or nervous: a higher proportion of high-status people at most age levels mentioned drinking as a means of relief for such conditions, while those of low status were relatively more likely to mention other oral means of relief (eating, smoking, tranquilizers, or other pills or medicines). This finding is in line with the greater proportion of drinkers found among those of high status.

TABLE 103.—*Implications of Drinking for Persons of High and Low Social Status (ISP),[a] by Sex and Age, in Per Cent*

	MEN						WOMEN					
	Age 21–39		Age 40–59		Age 60+		Age 21–39		Age 40–59		Age 60+	
	High ISP	Low ISP	High ISP	Low ISP	High ISP	Low ISP	High ISP	Low ISP	High ISP	Low ISP	High ISP	Low ISP
Total sample (N)	132	81	137	93	39	91	171	132	128	167	62	118
Total drinkers (N)	116	62	111	68	30	57	147	79	98	70	36	35
Drinkers (of total sample)	88	75	80	73	79	64	86	59	77	41	59	34
Heavy drinkers (of total sample)	24	25	23	23	13	14	5	9	4	5	1	0
Heavy drinkers (of drinkers)	27	33	28	31	16	22	6	16	6	12	2	0
Escape drinkers (of drinkers)	37	36	24	34	38	44	26	33	29	30	14	14
Heavy-escape drinkers (of drinkers)	11	22	12	13	13	8	3	12	4	8	2	0
Drinkers saying they would miss drinking	59	41	49	34	43	31	29	29	40	7	27	9
Drinkers saying others have advised them to reduce drinking	14	23	10	28	3	18	5	12	10	12	0	5
Respondents saying that drinking:												
Does more harm than good	65	79	62	75	61	76	82	90	68	94	82	78
Bad for health	42	31	32	24	26	29	37	30	42	31	32	26
Causes fights	14	33	14	22	15	26	13	26	18	30	21	25
Helpful when depressed or nervous	45	38	45	38	34	34	29	16	39	11	15	12
Other oral activity helpful[b]	67	69	59	78	55	75	69	76	64	77	60	71

[a] High = highest scores on Index of Social Position (11 to 36). Low = lowest scores (60 to 77).
[b] Oral activity other than drinking—one or more of following helpful when depressed or nervous: eating, smoking, tranquilizers, other pills or medicines.

In sum, proportionately more of those of high than of low social status tend to drink, but to drink moderately, and to see alcoholic beverages as part of their life style and as not particularly harmful. On the other hand, there is apparently a greater tendency on the part of those of low social status to see alcohol as harmful and to have been taken to task by significant others for their drinking.

A case could be made for the plausibility of the hypothesis that alcohol constitutes a greater threat to those of low social status than to those of high status, on the grounds that the well-being and livelihood of the lower-status person is much more easily jeopardized by any untoward event. As Knupfer et al. have noted (39), those of upper status enjoy a much greater range of options in life, including less threat of being dismissed for having hangovers or showing the effects of drinking. The data cited here substantiate the hypothesis and provide some evidence that alcohol does indeed have more negative aspects for the lower status groups than for the upper.

8. Profile Analysis of Drinker Types

The major contrasts and similarities among population groups with different drinking patterns are summarized in Table 104.[2] Most of the data shown were presented in earlier tables in this monograph.

Profitable analyses can be made by comparing the two extreme groups, abstainers and heavy drinkers, with the light drinkers. Such a comparative profile analysis of abstainers compared to light drinkers yields results consistent with those of Knupfer in a Berkeley survey (38). Abstainers were more likely to be older people. They tended to include a larger proportion of deprived persons, being generally of lower social status and income. Relatively more of them lived in the South and in rural areas. More had native-born fathers, belonged to conservative Protestant denominations, and took part in religious activities frequently. Fewer parents of abstainers drank than did the parents of drinkers.

Abstainers were consistently more negative toward drink: relatively more abstainers said that drinking does more harm than good, that alcoholism is a serious problem, and that there is nothing

[2] Further subgroup analyses are reported in Detail Tables A-104 and A-105; see *Headnote*, p. 229.

TABLE 104.—*Summary of Differences between Q–F–V Groups, by Sex, in Per Cent*[a]

	MEN			WOMEN		
	Abst.	Light	Heavy	Abst.	Light	Heavy
N	268	324	252	630	442	72
Age 50 or older	52	38	29	51	30	9
Lowest ISP group	29	21	22	36	18	28
Main earner blue-collar worker	51	43	50	61	41	55
Under $6000 family income	54	41	30	68	35	40
South Atlantic region	19	15	7	17	9	18
East South Central region	17	6	4	19	3	5
Central cities over 50,000	24	25	38	22	35	45
Farms	13	8	3	13	1	1
Father born in U.S.A.	84	72	67	84	64	74
Catholic	12	29	44	16	37	48
Baptist	30	18	11	30	10	10
Participate often in church activities	35	17	11	35	15	9
Father drank twice a month	30	44	58	22	46	49
Mother drank twice a month	3	11	22	3	19	22
Drinks served more than ½ time with close friends	4	23	66	2	27	64
Drinking does more harm than good	92	71	53	93	75	60
Alcoholism a serious problem	84	67	58	83	80	76
Nothing good about drinking	60	22	12	64	21	14
Drink helpful to relieve depression	5	40	71	1	36	71
Last year not a good year	39	32	31	39	29	35
Had more than my share of problems	28	24	29	32	20	33
Health not excellent or good	34	18	18	36	18	24
Higher scores on personality scales:						
Neurotic tendencies	26	24	24	43	38	51
Alienation	36	29	31	45	32	42
Rigidity	48	44	35	54	39	48
Religious Fundamentalism	55	37	21	68	39	32

[a] Further results are reported in Detail Tables A-104 and A-105; see Headnote, p. 229.

good to be said about drinking. Abstainers also had a somewhat gloomier perspective than others on life in general: more of them said that last year had not been a good year for them, that they had had more than their share of problems, and that they were not in good health (some of this difference may stem from the fact that abstainers are generally older than drinkers). Relatively more

of them had higher scores on the brief psychological scales measuring tendencies toward alienation from society and toward rigidity
or absolutism in social and religious philosophy.

Table 104 also permits profile comparisons of heavy drinkers of
both sexes with other types. The characteristics of abstainers and
of heavy drinkers were found not always to be poles apart, because
members of both these groups tended to be somewhat more alienated from society and more unhappy with their lot in life than
were persons in the middle drinking groups. In particular, heavy
drinkers resembled abstainers more than other drinkers in the
following respects: half or more of both groups were from blue-
collar families; relatively larger proportions of both felt they had
had more than their share of problems; and both scored higher
than light drinkers on the Alienation scale.

On the other hand, heavy drinkers contrasted with abstainers
in being younger, having larger incomes, living in more urbanized
areas, having a larger proportion of Catholics but fewer churchgoers, reporting more drinking by parents and friends, finding good
things to say about drinking, and finding drinking helpful to relieve depression. Similarly, the major respects in which heavy
drinkers differed from light drinkers were in being more likely to
be aged under 50, to live in cities over 50,000, to be Catholic, to
serve drinks with friends, and to find drinking helpful when depressed or nervous. However, it should be noted that, in many
respects, heavy drinkers did not differ as much in their characteristics and attitudes from other drinkers as did heavy drinkers who
gave escape reasons for drinking in comparison to other heavy
drinkers who did not give escape reasons (see Table 102). Thus
it appears that it is not necessarily heavy drinking as such, but
heavy drinking coupled with nonsocially-oriented reasons for drinking which is most likely to lead to drinking problems and their
attendant alienation from society and difficulties of adjustment
vis-à-vis families, communities and work environment.

9. *Analysis of Massed vs Spaced Drinking* (Appendix I)

A new Volume–Variability (v–v) index was developed in an attempt to overcome the shortcomings of other indices by eliminating
the misleading practice of lumping together those who drink relatively small amounts frequently and those who drink relatively

large amounts sporadically. The v–v index divides the population into eight groups: abstainers and infrequent drinkers as defined by the Q–F–V method, plus three volume-per-month groups, each subdivided into those who tend to mass their drinks (by having five or more on at least some occasions) and those who space out their drinking (by never taking as many as five drinks on any occasion).

When volume is thus held constant, the "massed" or high-maximum drinkers are found to be (in comparison to the "spaced" or low-maximum drinkers) younger; more gregarious; more likely to drink more than usual when with people other than members of their immediate families; less settled or satisfied with their achieving of life goals; and, among the women, more likely to show tendencies toward neuroticism and alienation from society.

These findings are consistent with those obtained by Knupfer (42) in a San Francisco study in which she compared "daily light" drinkers to "weekly heavy" drinkers who drank approximately the same volume.

On the basis of the analysis described in Appendix I, it is believed that indices of drinking behavior which utilize the same principles as the v–v index will be found more useful for most purposes of description and analysis of the correlates of drinking behavior than earlier indices based on total intake over time (as determined by multiplying usual quantity and frequency).

Conclusions

1. In the U. S. A. as a whole, drinking is typical behavior; both abstinence and heavy drinking (especially for escape from life's problems) are atypical.

2. The level of drinking (as distinct from heavy drinking or problem drinking) varies according to the position of the individual in society; but in most social-status groups a much higher proportion of men and younger persons drink than do women and older people.

3. Several kinds of evidence indicate that the proportion of women who drink is increasing. Further, if there is merit in the idea of the diffusion of customs, the higher prevalence of drinking among women in the upper social levels and in areas of high ur-

banization should be followed by an increase in the proportion of drinkers among women of lower status and in the smaller towns and rural areas.

4. Whether a person drinks at all is primarily a sociological and anthropological variable rather than a psychological one. This is evident from the great differences in the incidence of drinking by sex, age, social status, region, degree of urbanization and religion —all of which are primarily sociological variables—and the relatively small relationships between drinking and several psychological measures. However, among the limited psychological scales employed in this survey, certain measures of individual personality were found useful in explaining some of the variations in heavy drinking (and thus, presumably, problem drinking). These include measures of alienation, neurotic tendencies and psychological involvement with alcohol ("escape" drinking).

5. The combination of heavy drinking and escape drinking appears to be related to what Fromm (23) has called "the process of alienation": the heavy-escape drinker was found to be relatively more unhappy than others with his progress in life, more likely to exhibit neurotic tendencies, and more dependent upon external aids to alleviate depression or nervousness.

6. Drinkers who mass their drinks (e.g., as many as five or six or more drinks on an occasion at least once in a while) appear to have more alcohol-related problems than do drinkers of equivalent over-all volume who space their drinks out over more occasions. Therefore, in analyzing drinking patterns, it is desirable to use an index (such as the Volume–Variability index described in Appendix I) which distinguishes between massed versus spaced drinking within various aggregate volume groups, rather than the more common groupings based on total consumption alone.

7. There is a high turnover in the drinker or nondrinker status of many individuals, in addition to the general tendency for older persons to drop out of the drinking and heavy-drinking classes.

8. It is not possible to establish from a single study whether the proportion of heavy drinkers is increasing or decreasing. The fact that the per capita consumption of alcohol has been holding fairly constant in the face of an apparently increased proportion of persons drinking (especially among women) suggests that the rise in the number of drinkers must be balanced to some extent by a lower average rate of consumption. This could be accounted for, however,

by the usual cutting-down or quitting by older people and the fact that the newer drinkers are likely to drink relatively little, and does not necessarily imply any reduction in heavy drinking by the continuing drinking population. Continued research on the correlates of changes in drinking habits should clarify the ways in which the society operates, formally and informally, to bring about increases and decreases in the amount and kind of drinking.

RESEARCH IMPLICATIONS OF THE STUDY

The survey presented in this monograph has been concerned with the who, what, when, how much and why of drinking in the United States at a particular period of time (winter 1964–65). It is believed that the findings have helped to clarify a number of points about the correlates of drinking behavior as well as to confirm many piecemeal findings from earlier small-scale studies. The chief usefulness of a descriptive study of this kind is not the immediate solution of practical problems of prediction and social control, but the establishment of a baseline from which an expanded program of analytic studies can be set up to predict and perhaps influence human actions in the future.

Several programs of further research are suggested by the questions which the present survey raises or highlights but cannot answer. Special efforts will be needed to ensure that such studies are sufficiently interdisciplinary to meet the need for a concerted attack on research problems concerning alcohol. As we look back over the findings in this national survey, we are struck by the need for study on single sets of individuals of the interactions of physical, cultural and psychological correlates of various types of alcohol consumption. Study of these interactions will require the concerted efforts of a number of disciplines, particularly biochemistry, neurophysiology, internal medicine and psychiatry, in addition to the social sciences of sociology, psychology and anthropology. A good general model for such studies is the Hunterdon County (N. J.) study reported by Trussell and Elinson (70), in which sampling surveys of attitudes and behavior were supplemented by clinical tests and physical examinations of many of the same individuals. This kind of design not only makes it easier to carry out a more intensive study of psychosocial correlates than can be attempted in an initial interview (which must be limited to an hour or two), but also makes it possible to measure the rarely obtained correlations between psychosocial information and neurophysiological and other clinical data which can be crucial in the study of alcohol use and problems.

Combinations of neurophysiological, psychosocial and demographic information can and should be obtained on the same individuals from probability samplings of target segments of the population. In the past, the few studies which have combined these types of information have usually been conducted on captive populations of clinic patients. Consequently, their general applicability has been questionable, both because of the unrepresentativeness of the individuals and the institutional influences upon their outlook and motivations.

The experience gained in the survey reported on in this monograph suggests many fruitful avenues for further research. The inevitable lag in analysis and publication of this study means that many of these avenues have already been partly explored, by other researchers as well as ourselves. But for those who would like to make new pathways—or even just to pave roads already laid out in rough form—here are some paving stones and direction signs from the findings of our national study, which may serve to stimulate further thinking in various areas:

Amount of Drinking

1. The minimum levels of drinking included in the definition of our heavy drinker category are still far below the patterns given in traditional clinical descriptions of the institutionalized alcoholic. Investigation is needed, in further single-shot surveys, of the prevalence of such extreme amounts of drinking in the noninstitutionalized general population.

2. A survey designed primarily to study the correlates of drinking at various levels of consumption can yield only a very limited description of the social contexts of drinking. Short-term panel surveys or diary studies asking about the context and content of all drinking occasions over the course of a certain period, such as 6 months or a year, would be very useful. Such a drinking and dietary diary study was done by Lolli and associates (46) with Italian and Italian American volunteers in New Haven: Each subject maintained a diary record for several weeks or months and

also underwent a sociological examination, a physical examination, a sugar tolerance test and several psychological examinations.

3. One would suppose, as Jellinek (33) seems to imply, that heavy drinking is a cumulative process, in which the individual gradually increases his consumption over the years up to a peak, at which time either serious consequences or the process of aging results in a cessation or reduction of heavy drinking. However, the data in the national survey showed bimodal humps in heavy drinking among men at ages 30–34 and 45–49 and among women at ages 21–24 and 45–49 (see Table 1). These findings might be shrugged off as chance fluctuations in small-sized samples (100 to 150 per age group), except that the Washington Heights (N.Y.) studies of Bailey, Haberman and Alksne (4) found three similar humps in "probable alcoholics," at ages 25–34, 45–54 and again at 65–74 (the latter being attributed largely to the number of elderly widowers who acknowledged a drinking problem). Will a replication of the national study, with larger samples in the crucial 30 to 50 year group, find the same humps in heavy drinking (and, presumably, problem drinking) at two or more points along the life cycle? And if the humps are real, to what can they be attributed—to sociopsychological pressures and deprivations peculiar to certain stages in the life-cycle in our culture; or to neurophysiological (including glandular and nutritional) factors; or to an interaction of sociopsychological, cultural and physical factors? Findings on this question would have implications for individual therapy and mental health programs.

Problem Drinking

1. It is necessary to warn against equating our heavy-escape drinkers with alcoholics or even problem drinkers as usually described. All our heavy-escape drinkers drink enough so that alcohol plays a significant part in their patterns of living, and they have further admitted to some psychological dependence on alcohol. Hence, as previously mentioned, it is not unreasonable to assume that most so-called alcoholics are included in our heavy-escape group. But the test of this assumption in individual cases remains to be investigated.

2. We would hypothesize that heavy-escape drinkers who show no present extrinsic consequences of their drinking would be the

most likely candidates to show such consequences in the future. This kind of hypothesis can only be tested with a longitudinal study.

3. There are many indications that those who drink for escape reasons tend to be more "reactive" or emotionally labile than others.[3] To what extent will this reactiveness of the escape drinker, based on respondents' own reports in a survey, hold up under independent clinical tests? And if it is borne out, does this characteristic precede or follow the drinking behavior? What implications does it have for experimental programs of drug therapy, individual psychotherapy, or broad programs of mental health and public education?

Changes in Drinking

1. All surveys show clear relationships between age and amount of drinking. Whether these differences result from aging processes and progression through life-stages of the individual, or represent generational differences in relation to drinking behavior (e.g., whether those over age 60 "set" their adult social patterns during Prohibition), or both, is a matter best investigated by longitudinal studies.

2. Preliminary results from short-term longitudinal studies in Connecticut and California indicate that there is a substantial turn-over in the drinking and heavy-drinking population, with about one-fourth showing changes in drinking habits or reasons for drinking within a span of only 3 years (10, 72). The Hartford study also found that problem drinking appears to increase or diminish in response to even short-term changes in a person's status on certain sociocultural or personality variables. These preliminary findings lend encouragement to the prospect that further studies in this series will yield conclusive information on some of the influences which are most likely to have an effect on changes in drinking habits.

3. A useful technique for testing hypotheses about net effects of a number of variables in longitudinal studies is the cumulative

---

[3] This is deduced both from the responses in this survey and those reported by Knupfer and associates (39) as well as the results of the Washington Heights studies mentioned earlier (4), where it was found that "presumed alcoholics" (problem drinkers) had a higher rate of psychophysiological impairment, frequent anger, guilt feelings, fears and periods of depression or manic behavior.

scoring of independent variables to predict change in drinking behavior (e.g., change in problem drinking, or change in or out of
the drinker population, or change in the type of beverage drunk).
One illustration of the utility of cumulative scoring is provided by
the recent Hartford 3-year longitudinal study (although the use
there was for the prediction of level of problem drinking rather
than of change). Application of combined sociological and psychological variables, adapted after the work of Jessor and associates in
their Tri-Ethnic study (34), yielded the finding that among those
showing the lowest risk of problem drinking only 12% were found
to have been problem drinkers within the previous 3 years, while
72% of those of the highest risk on the combined sociological and
psychological scores were problem drinkers (10, *Table 103*). These
and other findings from the Hartford longitudinal study showed
that (*a*) the combinations of sociological and psychological variables helped to explain more of the variance in problem drinking
than any of the variables taken singly, and (*b*) the relationship
between sociological and psychological variables is not necessarily
an additive one, since those who had a high psychological score
combined with a low sociological score had a higher rate of problem drinking than did those with the converse combination of
scores.

Attitudes and Values

1. The present survey has just begun to scratch the surface of
this topic in relation to drinking patterns. Other areas which might
be systematically explored include the relative importance of social versus moral reasons for drinking (or not drinking) within
various subgroups; the expectations and tolerance of others' behavior (to define more clearly the group mores and sanctions that
determine the pressures against drinking and heavy drinking by
different types of people); opinions on desirability and effectiveness of early education for moderation in drinking versus that for
abstinence; comparative attitudes on the use of alcohol, drugs and
narcotics.

2. There is a need for still more descriptive studies—again, combining the approaches of all the relevant disciplines such as biology,
neurophysiology, clinical medicine, psychology, sociology and social anthropology. Such single-shot surveys should not only be

concerned with the use and abuse of alcohol, but should also focus on life-adjustment processes, explore the interactions of early experiences, the development of life styles and values, and the operations of various kinds of stress in the evolution of healthy and unhealthy patterns of alcohol use as one aspect of general mental health.

3. This and other studies have clearly indicated that there are basic differences in individual mechanisms for coping with stress. For example, a larger proportion of men and younger people and those of upper social status said they found drinking or "working harder" helpful when depressed or nervous, while a larger proportion of women, older persons and those of lower status found more passive resources helpful (e.g., other oral resources such as eating or taking pills or medicines or repression in the form of "trying to forget it"). These differences in reactions to stress may stem from early training, nutritional and genetic factors or environmental conditioning; they may become reinforced and crystallized or remain fluid and shift according to circumstances or time period. It may be that further research can isolate basic types of coping syndromes, of which the following three might be hypothesized:

(a) People who rely most on other persons in times of stress; such a person would depend on members of his family, friends, minister or priest, physician, or other professional or empathic persons for support when needed. It can be predicted that such persons will be most adversely affected by the loss or defection of significant others in time of need. In such situations, while the excessive use of alcohol will depend upon the immediate environmental and cultural influences, resort to such noninterpersonal props would tend to give way to human props whenever the latter are available.

(b) People who rely most on things or substances (alcohol, tobacco, food, medications) to cope with stress; such a person would tend to be more cynical or unsure of human relationships than the other-dependent persons. Their dependence on alcohol or other substances, once well-developed, would tend to be consistent and chronic, because their nonreliance on personal relationships will make them unreceptive to personal appeals.

(c) Self-reliant people; such persons are not necessarily lacking in interpersonal resources, but they have learned through experience how to organize their environment so as to cope with stress through their own resources. Such a person will tend either to counteract stress by direct action if within his abilities, or else to detour around obstacles by redefining his goals or modifying his tactics in pursuit of them. In such individuals, use of alcohol for escape from stress will tend to be relatively rare, although in the American culture the "autonomous" individual may drink heavily upon occasion (particularly when young) as a means of experimentation or temporary heightening of mood.

It is recognized that these three hypothesized types of people are abstractions, and that mixed types will be frequent in real life. However, the considerable differences in the coping mechanisms of individuals that we have documented suggest that powerful latent patterns of values and expectations underlie these differences in coping behavior, and that isolating such patterns can be fruitful in predicting and controlling excessive use of alcohol or other drugs.

Of particular interest would be the possible physiological (glandular, etc.) concomitants of adjustment at various life stages. Again, only a concerted study which pooled clinical and sociopsychological survey data as well as information on many relevant aspects of life adjustment and coping resources (e.g., drugs, diversions, and various interpersonal and noninterpersonal resources in addition to alcohol) would provide a clear picture of the adjustment process. Certainly future studies should cover a much wider compass than merely behavior related to use of alcohol, even if the primary interest is in the use of alcohol.

4. The need for a concerted approach which integrates the contributions of sociology, social anthropology, psychology and medicine can be illustrated by the possibility that there exists a "neurophysiological susceptibility" to alcohol. If such a susceptibility exists, we believe that it will be found to have evolved out of the early interaction of a number of hereditary and environmental processes rather than springing full-blown from hereditary sources alone. Following the cognitive approach to learning of such psychologists as Bruner, Goodnow and Austin (7) and Hebb (27), the study of motivation and learning should prove useful in trying to understand such a phenomenon as neurophysiological susceptibility to alcohol.

5. There is need for further study of aspirations in relation to achievements and life satisfactions, to determine the correlates of

anxiety and depression, especially at different age levels. Noteworthy is the paradox pointed out by Gurin, Veroff and Feld (25) in their national study of mental health and adjustment, in which older people (despite having more physical infirmities) generally reported "worrying less often, fewer feelings of inadequacies in marriage, fewer problems in marriage, in raising children, and on the job, and a more positive self-image coupled with fewer perceived shortcomings in the self" (pp. 212-214).

Certainly a more concerted multidisciplinary focus on the apparent increase in life adjustment with advancing years would not only be of value in its own right in providing a better basis for comprehending such mental-health phenomena, but the findings could have considerable implication for the study of alcohol and drug use, since there is a definite pattern for use of both to taper off in advanced years. This study has also shown that drinking patterns differ by social level, with those of lower status tending to start drinking younger and either to quit or drift into escape drinking at an earlier age than those of upper status. Future studies should focus on the correlates of adjustment at various age levels in both men and women, and at different social levels, studying the same individuals over time.

In pursuing the avenues of research just discussed, various types of studies would be useful. Some could be explored effectively with single-shot, fresh probability samples. The short-term panel approach could be highly useful in measuring fluctuations in amounts and kinds of alcoholic beverages drunk, and under what circumstances, and in association with what activities—eating, driving, working, recreation, etc. Still other research objectives can be met best by longitudinal surveys, with repeated interviews of the same respondents. Such longitudinal studies represent the only known means of establishing conclusively the temporal sequences involved in the process of development of heavy drinking habits or of tapering off into moderate drinking or abstinence. The longitudinal approach requires that fresh samples be taken from time to time to replenish the youngest age group and permit projection of the findings against the total population. It also requires that sufficient independent samples be taken from time to time to estimate the possible introduction of biases through such phenomena as increased respondent sophistication with repeated interviews or the effects of cumulative attrition of the original sample over the years. Among the advantages of the longitudinal approach is that not only are trend data thus obtained, but the accumulation of a "data bank" of information on the same set of individuals makes it possible to do a much more detailed study of single cases than can be done with information limited to that obtained during the span of a single interview at one time.

Still another approach that might be fruitfully explored is cross-cultural. Other than the statistical approaches of Field (19) and Horton (30), most of the past studies reported in the literature have been highly anecdotal in nature and subject to the usual potential biases of such narrative accounts. There appears to be a genuine need for a new type of cross-cultural study which would be conducted with reasonable comparability of method, would be interdisciplinary in nature (physiological and clinical as well as anthropological, sociological and psychological), and would focus on cultures selected so as to control for such key variables as presumed style of drinking, level of acculturation and dietary habits. Such studies are needed in order to test whether drinking behavior in contemporary America operates according to the same or different principles as drinking behavior in other types of cultures.

Many cross-cultural studies can be conducted within the United States itself. One excellent illustration is the Tri-Ethnic study of Jessor and associates (34), in which Ute Indians, Mexican Americans, and Anglo-Americans living in the same isolated Colorado community were studied in relation to drunkenness and certain other types of delinquency. Here the fact that the three ethnic groups exhibited quite dissimilar behavior even though they lived in fairly close physical proximity to each other emphasizes the importance of one's immediate reference group in reinforcing certain behavior and attitudes.

Yet another productive line of inquiry might be a comparative study of two or more communities, matched as far as possible on certain key characteristics but with very different rates of alcoholism. Such a study, basically descriptive in nature, should throw considerable light on the factors that make for social maladjustments related to alcohol. A variant of this approach would be the use of similar communities with equivalent alcoholism rates as testing grounds for various mental-health information or action programs, using before-and-after surveys to compare results. The findings of such a study could have obvious implications for the planning and evaluation of future communication programs in the alcohol field.

In developing such research plans as these, it is hoped that the techniques and findings presented in the present monograph will be of some material use.

Appendix I

Measuring Massed versus Spaced Drinking*

IN the construction of indices of amount of drinking, studies of drinking practices have tended to emphasize the aggregate volume of alcoholic beverages consumed, without taking into consideration the ways in which the drinking is spaced. As Knupfer (42) has said:

"In drinking alcoholic beverages it seems obvious that the effect of a given amount of intake depends upon the time period over which the intake occurs. Yet this factor is usually neglected in surveys of drinking patterns. . . . The same weekly total could be obtained for the person who takes 2 drinks every day, the one who takes 14 drinks every Saturday night, and the one who takes 7 drinks twice a week. It is reasonable to assume that these 3 types represent different kinds of living and drinking patterns. . . . Now, obviously, in a survey we cannot achieve the accuracy of an actual blood alcohol determination in terms of effective amount of alcohol delivered to the brain. The question is, what sorts of compromises can be made between this and such gross figures as yearly consumption per capita?"

The most familiar type of index of drinking behavior is the Quantity–Frequency (Q–F) Index of Straus and Bacon (68), which was adapted by Mulford and Miller for application in their Iowa studies (52), by Mulford in a 1963 national quota sample (56), and by Maxwell for a Washington State study of drinking (48). These variants of the Q–F use the average amount per drinking occasion as the measure of quantity, thus making no distinction between the person who achieves a certain average quantity by drinking extremely large amounts on some occasions and very small amounts on others and the one who achieves the same average quantity through drinking about the same amount on each occasion.

Knupfer's article clearly demonstrates the usefulness of an index which would distinguish between these different kinds of drinkers. In analyzing her data from a San Francisco survey, she isolated 2 groups with approximately the same weekly intake—91 "daily light" drinkers and 54 "weekly heavy" drinkers—finding them different

* Reprinted from Quart. J. Stud. Alc. 29: 642–656, 1968.

211

in many respects.[1] The results supported Knupfer's position. What is needed, however, is a means of comparing the behavior and attitudes of those who mass their drinks as against those who space them out, on several equated levels of aggregate consumption, in order to be able to draw conclusions about the correlates of massed versus spaced drinking over the whole range of drinkers, rather than just such groups as daily-light and weekly-heavy drinkers.

In this Appendix we describe the development of a Volume–Variability (v–v) Index of massed versus spaced drinking which holds volume constant, and shows how findings using such an index contrast with results obtained with a variant of the more traditional Q–F, the Quantity–Frequency–Variability (Q–F–v) Index.

COMPARISON OF THE V–V AND Q–F–V INDICES

The Q–F–V Index

The Q–F–v Index took the following factors into account: The type of beverage drunk most often—whether beer, wine or spirits; the amount of this beverage consumed on an occasion—how often the person had as many as five or six, or three or four, or one or two drinks; the variability of drinking, as shown by the modal (most usual) amount consumed and the highest amount drunk at least occasionally. The quantity and variability components were combined to arrive at the following 11 classes:

Quantity–Variability Classification	Modal Quantity (Amount drunk "Nearly every time" or "More than half the time")	Maximum Quantity	
1	5–6+	5–6+	
2	3–4	5–6+	"less than ½ time"
3	3–4	5–6+	"once in a while"
4	Not specified	5–6+	"less than ½ time"
5	3–4	3–4	
6	1–2	5–6	"less than ½ time"
7	Not specified	5–6+	"once in a while"
8	1–2	5–6+	"once in a while"
9	1–2	3–4	"less than ½ time"
10	1–2	3–4	"once in a while"
11	1–2	1–2	

[1] For example, daily-light drinkers, in contrast to weekly-heavy drinkers, were found to fit significantly better into the European wine culture (Catholic, usual beverage being wine, drinking most often at home and with the family); they were more likely to be aged 40 or over, white-collar, reared in smaller towns or rural areas, and less sociable in terms of visiting others, going to parties and frequenting taverns.

This Quantity–Variability classification for the beverage drunk most often was then combined with the frequency of drinking of any alcoholic beverage to yield the combined Q–F–V Index.

While the Q–F–V, like similar indices, has been highly useful in the past in describing differences in drinking behavior and attitudes of the five Q–F–V groups, its shortcomings are rather obvious. One is the necessarily arbitrary nature of the classifications of "heavy," "infrequent" and "light" drinkers, evident from a casual inspection of Figure 1 in Chapter 1. It would be difficult to persuade any two analysts to agree completely on the classification of persons in certain cells: for example, should the person who drinks three times a day (perhaps wine) but never has more than one or two drinks on an occasion—and who therefore is unlikely ever to become intoxicated—be classified as a "heavy" drinker? And should a person who drinks only about once a month but who drinks five or six or more drinks every time he does drink be classified as a "moderate" drinker? Another, and more serious, shortcoming is the one Knupfer points out: that such a drinking typology mixes together persons of quite dissimilar life styles. A third defect is that the use of evaluative terms such as "heavy," "moderate" and "light" helps to reinforce the already-too-prevalent tendency toward branding groups of people with labels which may be considered invidious.

In short, there is need for an index of drinking behavior which is relatively uncomplicated, is determined objectively and avoids emotion-laden labeling connotations. We believe that the new V–V Index, described below, meets these qualifications.

The Volume–Variability Index

The basic method of the Index entails a two-step operation: (1) to classify each respondent according to his average daily volume, and (2) to divide each of several daily-volume groups into subgroups according to how variable the person is in his intake from day to day.

1. The average daily volume was estimated by multiplying the frequency of consumption of each beverage (expressed in terms of numbers of drinking occasions per 30 days) by the estimated quantity of the beverage consumed per occasion, as follows:

(a) Frequency of consumption was estimated by converting the reported frequency into the number of times in an average month the person drank each beverage, using the following values:

	No. of Drinking Occasions per Month
Three or more times a day	90
Two times a day	60
Once a day	30
Nearly every day	22
Three or four times a week	15
Once or twice a week	7
Two or three times a month	2.5
About once a month	1
Less than once a month but at least once a year	°
Less than once a year or Never	0

° No value was assigned to this category, since such persons were not asked amount and variability of consumption. This shortcoming is being rectified in subsequent studies now in progress.

(b) The quantity–variability data were converted to an estimate of the average number of drinks consumed per occasion. Each drinking level was assigned a fraction of the respondent's total drinking occasions for the beverage, based on his responses to all 3 levels, the fraction was multiplied by the average number of drinks at that level (6.0 for 5 or more, 3.5 for 3 or 4, 1.5 for 1 or 2), and the products were summed. The average drinks per occasion were multiplied by the number of occasions per month, and divided by 30 to yield an average daily volume for each beverage. For example, a respondent drinking beer once a day, 5 or 6 drinks "once in a while" and 3 or 4 "nearly every time" was estimated to have an average daily beer volume of 4.0. The average daily volumes of the 3 beverages were summed to yield a total average daily volume.[2]

(c) "Abstainers" and "infrequent drinkers" were defined in the same way as for the earlier Q–F–V Index: respectively, those who drank less than once a year, and those who drank at least once a year but less often than once a month. Those drinking at least once a month were then divided into three groups on the basis of their average daily volume: "low" (0.05 to 0.58 drinks per day), "medium" (0.59 to 1.49 drinks per day) and "high" (1.5 or more drinks per day).[3]

2. Variability was established for each of these three volume groups by subdividing them according to whether the respondents drank a "high maximum" (five or six or more drinks on an occasion at least once in a while) or a "low maximum" (never drank as many as five on an occa-

[2] In addition to computing each person's mean daily consumption on the basis of steps a and b, each person's variance across days was also computed to serve as a measure of within-person variability in drinking. This variance will be useful in other analyses; but since it was found to correlate highly with a simpler measure of "higher maximum" versus "lower maximum," the latter dichotomy was used instead of the variance measure in the drinking typology presented below.

[3] These unequal intervals were chosen on an empirical basis so as to provide sufficient numbers in each of the six volume/maximum-per-occasion subgroups for statistical adequacy in analyzing the characteristics of persons in each group.

sion) of any beverage. Thus the v–v Index divides the population into eight rather than five groups: "higher maximum" and "lower maximum" within each of three daily-volume groups, plus the infrequent drinkers and abstainers.

Table 105 shows the distribution of the total national sample on the v–v and q–f–v indices: (1) Abstainers and infrequent drinkers are the same in the two systems (and hence are lumped together in subsequent tables). (2) The high-volume–high-maximum group contains most of the persons in the q–f–v "heavy" group. Therefore, insofar as the heaviest-drinking group is concerned, it makes very little difference which index is used—for both classify most of the people in the top group in the same way. (3) The same can be said of the low-volume–low-maximum group—19 of the 20% in this group also fall in the "light" q–f–v group.

There is, however, considerable difference in classification in the two systems when it comes to respondents of medium volume or light or moderate q–f–v classification. It will be shown later that the v–v classification system enables us to bring to light rather material differences among people who drink only medium amounts of alcoholic beverages in terms of total consumption, depending upon whether they drink on a massed or a spaced-out schedule.

TABLE 105.—*Interrelationship of the Volume–Variability and Quantity–Frequency–Variability Classification Systems, in Per Cent*

V–V Classification[a]	Q–F–V CLASSIFICATION					Totals
	Abst.	Infreq.	Light	Mod.	Heavy	
Abstainer	32					32
Infrequent		15				15
Low volume, low maximum			19	1		20
Low volume, high maximum			2	5	[b]	7
Medium volume, low maximum			5	1	[b]	6
Medium volume, high maximum			[b]	4	2	6
High volume, low maximum			2	1	1	4
High volume, high maximum			[b]	1	9	10
Totals	32	15	28	13	12	100
N[c]						2733

[a] Abstainers are those who said they usually drink less than once a year or not at all. Infrequent drinkers are those who said they usually drink at least once a year but less than once a month. The other volume and variability definitions used are as follows: Low Volume, 0.05–0.58 drinks per day; Medium Volume, 0.59–1.49; High Volume, 1.5 or more; Low Maximum, less than 5 drinks per occasion; High Maximum, 5 or more.

[b] Less than 0.5%.

[c] The table excludes 13 persons who were not classifiable on volume or maximum number of drinks per occasion. N = unweighted number of interviews. All percentages in this article are based on responses which are weighted to give appropriate representation to the number of adults in the household.

CORRELATES OF MASSED VS SPACED DRINKING

Illustrative differences in the proportions which fell into the various v–v groups are summarized in Tables 106 to 110.

Sex and Age

As can be seen in Table 106, men were much more likely than women both to drink more often than once a month and to have a high-maximum (five or six or more drinks at least some of the time).

In both men and women, those in the youngest age group (21 to 29) had a slightly lower proportion of persons drinking a high volume (combining low- and high-maximum) than those in other age groups up to 60. However, younger people also had a higher proportion of high-maximum drinkers than did older people. Thus, paradoxically, while those in their 20s had a lower percentage in the highest-volume groups than those in their 50s, relatively more of them would appear to be subject to at least occasional intoxica-

TABLE 106.—*Volume–Variability Drinking Classification by Sex and Age, in Per Cent*

| | | LOW VOL. | | | MED. VOL. | | HIGH VOL. | | |
	N	Abst. + Infreq.	Low Max.	High Max.	Low Max.	High Max.	Low Max.	High Max.	Total High Max.[a]
Total sample	2733	47	21	6	6	6	4	10	22
Sex									
Men	1171	33	18	9	7	9	5	19	37
Women	1562	58	23	4	5	3	3	3	10
Sex by Age									
Men, 21–29	214	25	17	17	7	15	3	17	49
30–39	242	24	21	12	7	13	2	20	45
40–49	263	28	16	7	8	12	5	24	43
50–59	196	41	17	7	4	4	7	20	31
60+	256	47	20	4	7	2	7	12	18
Women, 21–29	253	52	26	9	5	5	1	3	17
30–39	344	51	24	6	7	5	2	5	16
40–49	332	50	29	3	3	5	4	5	13
50–59	263	66	17	3	7	1	5	1	5
60+	367	73	16	1	3	b	6	1	2
No age given	3								

[a] Base: total respondents.
b Less than 0.5%.

tion—in terms of having a higher proportion of persons who drink five or six or more drinks at least occasionally. This finding is consistent with the popular impression that younger persons tend more often to be sporadic drinkers who are "testing their limits." It also illustrates how mere measures of volume would be inadequate to describe drinking behavior unless accompanied by some measure to indicate whether the volume was massed into a few occasions or spaced out over many occasions.

Social Position

The analysis by social position, given in Table 107, shows results in 24 groups, divided according to the Hollingshead two-factor Index of Social Position, with age and sex controlled. It shows that there is a slightly higher proportion of drinkers with a high-maximum (regardless of volume) among younger men (21 to 39) of upper socioeconomic status than among younger men of lower status. However, the reverse is true among men aged 60 and over, in whom a high-maximum is more common among the men of lowest status—even though a much higher proportion of older men at the lower socioeconomic levels are abstainers or infrequent drinkers, leaving fewer regular drinkers at the lower levels. In other words, while a higher proportion of the well-to-do men aged over 60 drink a higher volume than less well-to-do men of the same age, over the long run the well-to-do older men tend to manage that volume rather differently by spacing their drinks out to a greater degree.

Region and Urbanization

Comparing drinker types in the various regions (Table 108), the highest percentages of those drinking more than infrequently were found in the Middle Atlantic, New England and Pacific states, while the highest proportion of abstainers or infrequent drinkers was found in the East South Central region. The proportions with high-maximum tended to follow the same regional pattern, except that the heavily industrial East North Central region, like the coastal areas, had an above-average proportion of high-maximum drinkers.[4]

[4] The data from the Mountain states are not considered to be very reliable, since they are based on a small subsample and include an unusual number of interviews in heavily Mormon Utah.

TABLE 107.—*Volume–Variability Drinking Classification by Index of Social Position, Sex and Age, in Per Cent*

	N	Abst. + Infreq.	Low Vol. Low Max.	Low Vol. High Max.	Med. Vol. Low Max.	Med. Vol. High Max.	High Vol. Low Max.	High Vol. High Max.	Total High Max.[b]
Men									
Age 21–39									
Highest ISP[a]	131	17	20	13	9	20	2	19	52
Upper Middle	117	26	20	14	6	13	2	20	47
Lower Middle	127	25	19	16	6	13	4	18	47
Lowest	81	31	15	16	7	8	3	20	44
Age 40–59									
Highest ISP	137	27	15	5	13	8	9	24	37
Upper Middle	110	29	16	10	5	13	7	20	43
Lower Middle	120	42	17	7	3	6	2	23	36
Lowest	92	39	19	7	3	7	3	21	35
Age 60+									
Highest ISP	39	35	24		10		20	11	11
Upper Middle	52	41	15	6	16	2	10	10	18
Lower Middle	74	58	17	2	2	3	4	14	19
Lowest	91	50	24	5	4	4	1	12	21
Women									
Age 21–39									
Highest ISP	169	37	31	5	14	5	4	3	13
Upper Middle	147	48	24	11	3	7	1	6	24
Lower Middle	149	61	23	6	2	3	2	4	13
Lowest	132	59	20	6	5	6		5	17
Age 40–59									
Highest ISP	127	35	38	4	6	4	9	4	12
Upper Middle	153	49	24	5	5	4	5	7	16
Lower Middle	150	68	20	1	5	2	2	3	6
Lowest	165	75	14	2	3	4	2	1	7
Age 60+									
Highest ISP	62	63	20				15	1	1
Upper Middle	98	75	12		7		5		
Lower Middle	89	68	20	1	3	1	4	3	5
Lowest	118	79	14	2	2			3	2
No age given	3								

[a] Hollingshead Index of Social Position, with ISP scores grouped as follows: 11–36, Highest; 37–48, Upper Middle; 49–59, Lower Middle; 60–77, Lowest.
[b] Base: total respondents.

TABLE 108.—*Volume–Variability Drinking Classification by Region and Urbanization, in Per Cent*

	N	Abst. + Infreq.	Low Max.	High Max.	Low Max.	High Max.	Low Max.	High Max.	Total High Max.[a]
			Low Vol.		**Med. Vol.**		**High Vol.**		
Region									
New England	154	37	25	9	7	6	3	13	28
Middle Atlantic	491	32	23	7	8	7	8	16	30
South Atlantic	349	57	18	5	4	4	4	7	16
East South Central	245	74	12	3	3	2	2	4	9
East North Central	595	43	21	8	7	7	3	12	27
West South Central	246	53	24	4	4	6	3	6	16
West North Central	236	53	23	8	3	5	2	6	19
Mountain	87	59	12	9	3	8		8	25
Pacific	330	38	19	7	7	9	7	12	28
Urbanization									
SMSA[b]									
CC[c] over 1 million	259	38	22	7	9	6	5	13	26
CC 50,000– 1 million	551	40	20	8	6	8	4	13	29
Outside CC 50,000– 1 million	186	29	25	8	6	11	8	12	31
2500–49,999	419	33	25	7	7	5	6	16	28
Outside CC non- farm under 2500	297	49	23	6	4	7	4	7	20
NON-SMSA									
2500–49,999	372	49	20	6	8	5	4	9	20
Nonfarm under 2500	463	65	15	5	3	5	2	6	16
Farm	186	72	14	4	3	2	2	3	9

[a] Base: total respondents.
[b] Standard Metropolitan Statistical Area.
[c] Central City.

There were marked differences by urbanization or size of community: the highest percentages of more-than-infrequent drinkers were found in the larger suburbs and the central cities, as were the highest proportions of those drinking a high-maximum amount. Such differences may well be attributable to higher incomes in the suburbs and perhaps also to a higher incidence of alienation in the cities. Certainly there is no clear-cut evidence here of a markedly higher degree of "spree" drinking (low or medium volume, but a high-maximum amount per occasion) in any one community-size group as against the others.

Religion and National Identity

Episcopalians, Catholics, Lutherans and Jews had the highest proportions among religious groups of those drinking once a month or more (Table 109). Jews also had a below-average proportion who ever drank as many as five drinks per occasion, while Catholics, Episcopalians, and Protestants of no specific denomination, as well

TABLE 109.—*Volume–Variability Drinking Classification by Religion and National Identity, in Per Cent*

	N	LOW VOL. Abst. + Infreq.	LOW VOL. Low Max.	LOW VOL. High Max.	MED. VOL. Low Max.	MED. VOL. High Max.	HIGH VOL. Low Max.	HIGH VOL. High Max.	Total High Max.[a]
Religion									
Presbyterian	159	40	22	5	8	5	8	11	21
Episcopalian	80	22	23	13	15	7	7	12	32
Lutheran	204	34	24	9	9	7	4	13	29
Methodist, etc.[b]	513	51	22	5	4	5	3	9	19
Baptist	519	64	17	5	3	4	1	5	14
Other Conservative Protestants[c]	269	76	12	3	3	3	1	2	8
Protestant, no denomination	46	45	12	10	6		6	21	31
Catholic	761	32	23	8	6	10	6	15	33
Jewish	71	36	33	6	14	2	2	7	15
No religion; No answer	68	34	12	16	6	7	3	22	45
Misc., not tabulated	43								
National Identity[d]									
U. S. A., White	137	69	15	6	1	3	2	4	13
U. S. A., Nonwhite	216	50	21	4	6	5	2	11	20
English, Scotch	583	55	15	6	5	5	5	10	21
Irish	420	46	21	8	4	7	4	11	26
Scotch–Irish	72	61	18	3	9	1	1	8	12
Canadian	42	40	26	8	3	5	3	16	29
Italian	118	24	30	5	7	10	10	14	29
Latin-American & Caribbean	58	37	20	8	10	9	3	13	30
Russian, Polish & Baltic	148	49	7	10	9	7	2	15	32
German	490	41	23	9	7	6	4	10	25
Other European	423	42	25	5	6	8	5	10	23
Misc., not tabulated	26								

[a] Base: total respondents.

[b] Including United Church of Christ, Congregationalist, Disciples of Christ, Evangelical, United Brethren.

[c] Belonging to a denomination other than Methodist or Baptist which officially disapproves of use of alcohol.

[d] National Identity: Father's country of birth, or country from which most ancestors came.

as those of no religion, were above average in the percentage having five or more drinks at a time at least occasionally. Among the various national-identity groups, those with a higher-than-average proportion of high-maximum drinkers included persons of Russian, Polish or Baltic stock, the Latin-American–Caribbeans, the Italians and the Canadians.

Differences Between V–V Groups

Table 110 summarizes some of the differences between persons in the various v–v groups by reversing the axes of the variables and considering the v–v groupings as independent variables for the purpose of highlighting the group differences.

Among both men and women, and in all three volume groups, those of lower-maximum intake per occasion were older, more likely to be of the highest social status, usually less likely to be members of blue-collar families, and less gregarious in terms of getting together socially fairly often with people from their own (or their husbands') places of employment.

In drinking environment and attitudes, significantly more of the low-maximum groups drank wine, as Knupfer reported (42), but generally fewer drank beer or distilled spirits. The low-maximum groups also were less likely to report that they drank more than usual when with people from work, with their neighbors, with close friends or with members of their immediate families. The high-maximum drinking groups had higher proportions reporting that someone—friends, family, spouse, employer, neighbor—had tried to get them to drink less at some time during the previous year. They were also consistently higher than the low-maximum respondents (of comparable aggregate volume) in reporting that they worried about their own drinking, more likely to say they would miss drinking if they had to give it up, more dependent upon drinking to cope with the problems of life (giving "escape" reasons for drinking), and more likely to have had hangovers or headaches or been nauseated after drinking during the preceding year.

In their outlook on life, those drinking the highest aggregate volume and a high maximum per occasion were less likely than the low-maximum group to report having a "very happy" marriage, being satisfied in attainment of their life goals, or satisfied with their (or the spouse's) occupation.

TABLE 110.—Summary of Differences Between Volume–Variability Groups, in Per Cent

	MEN						WOMEN					
	Low Vol.		Medium Vol.		High Vol.		Low Vol.		Medium Vol.		High Vol.	
	Low Max.	High Max.	Low Max.	High Max.	Low Max.	High Max.	Low Max.	High Max.	Low Max.	High Max.	Low Max.	High Max.
N	212	110	80	113	53	214	343	67	78	55	53	53
Background Characteristics												
Age 45+	46	28	45	22	69	47	39	21	43	26	70	31
Lowest group on Index of Social Position	23	22	16	15	12	21	18	21	17	27	10	15
Highest group on Index of Social Position	27	22	42	34	41	28	33	22	43	27	46	22
Chief breadwinner a blue-collar worker	48	56	31	42	27	50	44	44	34	39	38	46
Lives in central city of 50,000 or more	23	31	27	31	34	37	34	42	42	41	25	40
U.S. born, Nonwhite	10	6	9	4	9	6	7	3	8	11	19	18
Conservative Protestants[a]	47	42	34	35	27	25	36	25	22	27	17	34
Goes out often in evening for entertainment	16	15	28	22	14	29	22	22	22	34	19	24
Gets together "fairly often" with people from work	16	32	26	32	15	23	19	21	24	37		30
Drinking Environment, Attitudes												
Father approved of drinking	47	47	49	47	37	60	55	74	59	55	54	55
Mother approved of drinking	22	26	26	35	21	34	34	50	39	37	38	38
Drinks wine at least once a month	21	7	38	24	48	29	30	18	55	38	51	37
Drinks beer at least once a month	68	75	80	89	76	91	43	48	73	66	60	89
Drinks spirits or mixed drinks at least once a month	61	65	78	84	73	82	68	78	82	82	77	79
Drinks more than usual when with people from work	19	39	23	33	15	37	14	33	12	36	4	21
Drinks more when with people from neighborhood	15	15	4	15	9	18	11	22	12	23	16	16

Drinks more when with close friends	28	37	34	49	34	51	27	38	30	51	22	57
Drinks more when with members of immediate family	8	10	8	13	18	14	18	28	12	27	25	29
Someone tried to get respondent to drink less during last year	14	20	9	18	11	20	6	7	3	13	2	22
Worries at least "a little" about own drinking	5	9	4	16	11	22	4	11	8	16	18	23
Would miss drinking at least "a little" if had to give it up	25	42	44	57	66	74	19	33	47	38	57	76
At least 2 of 5 "escape" reasons important in drinking	21	29	26	40	36	50	21	39	44	48	45	69
Had hangovers, headaches, from drinking within past year	4	8	4	15	10	18	8	18	8	24	5	20
Was nauseated from drinking within past year	4	10	4	11	5	7	5	7	4	13	5	10
Had close relative with serious drinking problem	36	38	29	35	22	36	33	43	40	48	39	37

Outlook on Own Fortunes, Values

Not "very happy" marriage	43	36	20	30	23	43	36	38	45	40	23	44
Other than "very satisfied" in reaching life goals	62	73	58	65	47	67	54	60	68	66	47	53
Would prefer different occupation for self, spouse	33	40	41	30	36	39	25	26	29	39	18	30

Activities Very or Fairly Helpful to Relieve Depression or Nervousness

Having a drink	37	48	51	64	62	73	30	52	64	59	72	77
Smoking	38	50	37	45	42	51	33	64	37	47	35	72

Personality Measures

Neurotic tendencies (4–5 out of 5 symptoms)	22	26	22	23	26	25	41	47	32	45	28	49
Often get angry	11	16	8	14	12	19	18	29	29	35	17	25
High alienation score (3–4 out of 4)	11	11	12	14	10	11	11	16	10	20	11	22

a Those belonging to a denomination which officially disapproves of use of alcohol.

Among both men and women in the three volume groups, materially more of those drinking a high maximum per occasion reported reliance on drinking and smoking to relieve depression or nervousness.

In one of three personality measures (frequency of getting angry), a consistently higher percentage of the high-maximum than the low-maximum groups said they "often" got angry. But on two other personality measures—neurotic tendencies (symptoms such as frequent headaches or stomach disorders, nervousness, anxiety and depression) and tendency toward alienation or disaffection vis-à-vis society—only the high-maximum women reported a conspicuously greater prevalence of these indicators of stress and unhappiness. These are illustrations of a tendency which was found at a number of points throughout the study: if a woman flouts the norms by having as many as five or six drinks, she is more likely than the high-maximum man to show signs of other maladjustments.

Appendix II

Sampling and Data Collection

1. Sample Design

The sample was designed to give each person 21 years or older, living in a household within the United States (exclusive of Alaska and Hawaii), an equal representation in the final results. The sampling procedures conformed to established principles for probability sampling at all stages of the process: in the selection of areas for interviewing, the selection of households, and the selection of an individual to be interviewed within each selected household. The sample was designed as follows:

a. All of the counties in the contiguous United States were arrayed into 100 subzones containing approximately the same number of households, first stratified by Census regions and according to their metropolitan or nonmetropolitan character. One county or Standard Metropolitan Statistical Area (SMSA) was selected from each of the 100 subzones or strata, with the chances that any one county or SMSA would be included in the sample being directly proportional to its 1960 population.

b. Within each county or SMSA in the sample, minor civil divisions (or political units below the county level) were arrayed according to population, and a single division was selected with probabilities proportional to population.

c. Within each selected minor civil division, random selection procedures were again applied to select 1 specific subarea (ordinarily conforming to a Census enumeration district), containing about 400 households on the average; 100 such subareas or clusters thus constituted the total national sample.

d. Within each subarea, a complete listing was made of all households. These listings were returned to the home office, where every nth household was selected on a random basis.

e. Interviewer assignments thus consisted of a list of 3268 preselected households, from which 225 were later eliminated as ineligible.[1] Selection of the respondent within the remaining 3043 households was accomplished by the interviewer's enumerating, in a predesignated order on the questionnaire cover-sheet, all (nonsenile) persons 21 years or older within the household. The individual to be interviewed was randomly preselected by procedures specified on the cover sheet and not under control of the interviewer (see appended copy of questionnaire). No

[1] "Ineligible" households included 145 vacant housing units, 20 households where there was no one 21 years or over, 21 consisting only of persons too senile to be interviewed, and 39 where all eligible respondents were away for the entire interviewing period.

225

substitutions of households, or of individuals within households, were permitted.

f. As is necessary in probability samples in which only one person is interviewed in each household, the final sample results were weighted to give each selected adult a weight proportionate to the number of adults in his household. The results of any finding in this report thus are projectable to the total population of adults living in households. However, to facilitate computation of confidence intervals and significance tests, all tables in this report show as N the actual (unweighted) number of interviews in each subgroup, although all percentages shown are based on weighted figures.

2. Data Collection Procedures

a. All interviewers were personally trained and supervised by either members of the home office staff or by 1 of 20 regional supervisors. Prior experience in the California surveys and the Richmond methodological study (37), as well as the Iowa studies of Mulford and Miller (51), indicated that the interviewers should be nonabstainers. Another indication from the Richmond study was that men (who include most of the heavy drinkers) are less likely to reveal the true extent of their drinking to women interviewers. Accordingly, all initial attempts at interviews were made by men interviewers. In a few instances when a selected woman respondent refused to be interviewed upon the man interviewer's visit, interviews were later completed by women interviewers or supervisors.

b. Interviews were completed with 90% of the eligible stipulated respondents in the occupied selected households, after setting aside those ineligible because of extreme senility or illness which made an interview impossible. This rate of completion was achieved by repeated visits of interviewers and supervisors, telephone calls, and letters from the home office when repeated refusals were encountered. All interviews were completed between October 1964 and March 1965.

c. Quality controls on interviewing included personal training as well as detailed written instructions on how to conduct the interviews. An immediate check of completed interviews was made to determine whether there had been any material inconsistencies or omissions. When any were found, the interview was rechecked in most cases by return visits or telephone calls to respondents.

3. Characteristics of Sample

Table 111 summarizes the distribution of the sample according to various demographic characteristics. There was a high degree of similarity between the sample distribution and the total population on these particular characteristics. It should be noted, however, that the survey sample was not designed to represent the total adult population, but rather that portion of it living in households in the (contiguous) United States; hence certain types of places, such as flophouses, jails and other

institutions usually inhabited more by men than by women were omitted
from the sample design. These omissions are undoubtedly one reason
why there is a larger proportion of women in the sample than is found
in the general population.

TABLE 111.—*Distribution of Interviews in Survey*

	Unweighted Interviews N	Weighted Interviews[a] %
Men	1177	45
Women	1569	55
White	2511	92
Nonwhite	235	8
Men, age 21–29	216	8
30–39	243	9
40–49	264	10
50–59	197	8
60+	257	9
Women, age 21–29	256	10
30–39	345	13
40–49	333	12
50–59	265	9
60+	367	12
Age not ascertained	3	
Region		
New England	155	6
Middle Atlantic	493	18
South Atlantic	350	13
East South Central	245	9
East North Central	599	22
West South Central	246	9
West North Central	238	9
Mountain	87	3
Pacific	333	11
Urbanization SMSA		
Central City	814	30
Other urban	611	21
Rural nonfarm	297	11
Non-SMSA		
Urban	372	13
Rural nonfarm	466	17
Rural farm	186	8

[a] Each of the 2746 interviews was weighted in proportion to the total number of persons
aged 21 years and over in the household, so that the results would represent the total adult population living in households.

4. Hollingshead Index of Social Position

The system used throughout this report to supplant the more usual but less standardized indicators of socioeconomic status is derived by combining weighted scores assigned to (1) the respondent's own educational level, and (2) the occupation of his family breadwinner according to the status or power position associated with the occupation. The ISP scores (which are sequential but not continuous) range from 11 (highest) to 77 (lowest). For details on classification procedure see Kirsch, Newcomb and Cisin (37).

The following four ISP groupings, and their scores, are used in most standard tables of the present study: Highest, 11–36; Upper Middle, 37–48; Lower Middle, 49–59; Lowest, 60–77. Two-way ISP groups (Higher and Lower) combine the first two and the last two groups.

The groupings were set up, on the basis of total frequencies, for the particular analytic purposes of this report; they differ somewhat from Hollingshead's five social class groupings (28).

Appendix III

List of Detail Tables*

Headnote: The following supplementary Detail Tables, which are not published in this Monograph, may be obtained by ordering NAPS Document 00408 from ASIS National Auxiliary Publications Service, c/o CCM Information Sciences, Inc., 909 3d Ave., New York, N. Y. 10022, remitting $2 for microfiche or $6 for photocopies.

* The demographic variables in each of the tables are Sex, Age, Index of social position, Region, Urbanization, Religion, and National identity. In addition, Tables A-104(a) and (b) tabulate Family income, Occupation of chief breadwinner, Marital status, Parental rearing, Country of origin, Church attendance, and Education. And, in addition, Table A-102 tabulates Drinking of specific beverages, Social activities, Drinking habits of parents and spouse, Usual circumstances of drinking, Changes in amount of drinking, Opinions about drinking, General outlook on one's fortunes and values, Health and related issues, Activities to relieve depression, and Personality measures.

Appendix IV

The Questionnaire

The complete questionnaire used in the national survey is reproduced on the following pages.

Social Research Project
George Washington University
2400 H Street, N. W.
Washington, D. C. 20037

SERIAL NUMBER

NATIONAL SURVEY OF ATTITUDES AND INTERESTS

(Area)   (HH)

Address _____

City or Area _____   County _____

State _____   Interviewer _____

My name is _____. We are doing a nationwide survey sponsored by The George Washington University on some interesting subjects, such as what people do in their leisure time, what has been happening to families during the past year and so on. Your household is one of about 3000 in the United States that were selected by chance to be included in the survey. We interview only one person in a household. To determine which person I'm to interview here, I need some information about all adults 21 years and over.

a. Altogether, how many men 21 years of age, or over, live in your household? Include roomers only if they are considered part of the family.
Number ☐

b. What is the approximate age of the oldest? The next oldest? [ETC.] [ENTER IN TABLE A BELOW IN ORDER OF DESCENDING AGE--SKIP NO LINES--AND CIRCLE "M" FOR EACH]

c. What is the relationship of each to the head of household? (Head, son, roomer, etc.)

d. Now, how many women 21 years of age, or over, live here? Include roomers only if they are considered part of the family.
Number ☐

e. What is the approximate age of the oldest? The next oldest? [ETC.] [ENTER IN TABLE A BELOW IN ORDER OF DESCENDING AGE--SKIP NO LINES--AND CIRCLE "F" FOR EACH]

f. What is the relationship of each to the head of household?

Follow These Three Steps In Selecting Respondent:

a. Add the number of males and females, and circle this total (printed in black) on the first horizontal line of TABLE B.

b. Circle the red number immediately below the number you circled in step a.

c. Using the extreme left column of TABLE A, circle the number which is the same as the red number just circled in step b. The person who is listed on this line in TABLE A is the only one you are to interview in this household.

TABLE A   Eligible Persons

Line	Relationship to Head of Household	Age	Male	Female
1			M	F
2			M	F
3			M	F
4			M	F
5			M	F
6			M	F
7			M	F

TABLE B   Table for Random Selection of Person to be Interviewed

If the number of adults is:	1	2	3	4	5	6	7
You MUST interview the person listed in TABLE A on Line Number - - - -							

231

C A L L   R E P O R T

	DATE	TIME	RESULTS*
1st		a.m.	
Call		p.m.	
2nd		a.m.	
Call		p.m.	
3rd		a.m.	
Call		p.m.	
4th		a.m.	
Call		p.m.	

	DATE	TIME	RESULTS*
5th		a.m.	
Call		p.m.	
6th		a.m.	
Call		p.m.	
7th		a.m.	
Call		p.m.	
8th		a.m.	
Call		p.m.	

*ILLUSTRATIVE CODES FOR "RESULTS" COLUMN:

1 = No one home

2 = No adult home

3 = Refusal upon entry before screening for eligible respondent

4 = Refusal by the eligible respondent selected for interview

5 = Selected respondent terminated interview before completion

6 = No eligible respondents residing in this household

7 = Language barrier

8 = Summer residence--not presently occupied

9 = Other vacant dwelling units

10 = Person selected for interview away from his usual place of residence for entire period of survey

11 = Person selected for interview too ill or senile ever to be interviewed (Excludes persons only temporarily ill who can be interviewed on a later call)

12 = Others [PLEASE SPECIFY]

13 = Completed interview with selected respondent

[IF RESPONDENT IS NOT PERSON WHO GAVE COVER INFORMATION, REPEAT INTRODUCTION.

PLEASE RECORD THE TIME IMMEDIATELY BEFORE ASKING Q.1]

_____A.M.

_____P.M.

1. All things considered, would you say that the past year was a good or bad year
    for you?

                                        Good year 1

                                        Bad year 3

                                        [Neither good nor bad] . . 5

2. What were some of the good things that happened to you during the past year?

    _____

    _____

3. What were some of the bad things that happened to you during the past year?

    _____

    _____

    _____

4. People do different things in the evening. [HAND RESPONDENT CARD A] Which one
    of these words describes how often you <u>watch TV</u> in the evening? Which word
    describes how often you <u>read</u> in the evening?
    [ASK FOR EACH ACTIVITY.]

		Often	Sometimes	Rarely	Never
a.	Watch TV	1	3	5	7
b.	Read	1	3	5	7
c.	Spend time on a hobby	1	3	5	7
d.	Take part in church activities .	1	3	5	7
e.	Visit friends and relatives . .	1	3	5	7
f.	Have visitors in your home . . .	1	3	5	7
g.	Go out somewhere for entertainment	1	3	5	7

5. Here are a few questions on health. Would you say that your health is usually excellent, good, fair, or poor?

Excellent . . 1
Good 3
Fair 5
Poor 7

6. Compared with a year ago, would you say that your health is better, worse, or about the same?

Better now 1
Worse now 3
About the same . . 5

7a. Have you been hospitalized for any illness during the last 12 months?

No . . 1
Yes . . 3

7b. [IF "YES"] For what illness? _____

_____

8. Now I am going to read you a list of things people say they find helpful when they are depressed or nervous. [HAND RESPONDENT CARD B] Which of these choices describes how helpful you have found smoking to be when you are depressed or nervous? [ASK FOR EACH ACTIVITY. CHECK "NEVER TRIED IT" ONLY IF RESPONDENT VOLUNTEERS THIS ANSWER.]

		Very Helpful	Fairly Helpful	Not at all Helpful	Never Tried It
a.	Smoking	1	3	5	7
b.	Eating	1	3	5	7
c.	Having a drink such as a highball or cocktail or some wine or beer	1	3	5	7
d.	Working harder than usual, either around the house or on the job	1	3	5	7
e.	Taking a tranquilizer	1	3	5	7
f.	Taking some other kind of pill or medicine	1	3	5	7
g.	Going to church or saying a prayer . .	1	3	5	7
h.	Talking it over with a friend or relative	1	3	5	7
i.	Just trying to forget about it	1	3	5	7

Comments: _____

_____

9. [HAND RESPONDENT CARD A] Which one of these words best describes how often you had an upset stomach in the past year? [ASK FOR EACH ITEM]

	Of-ten	Some-times	Rare-ly	Nev-er
a. Had an upset stomach	1	3	5	7
b. Had headaches	1	3	5	7
c. Felt tense or nervous	1	3	5	7
d. Worried about things	1	3	5	7
e. Felt depressed	1	3	5	7

10. Are you married, single, divorced, or widowed?

Married 1
Single 3
Divorced or separated . . 5
Widowed 7

11a. [IF EVER MARRIED] Do you have any children living with you?

No . . 1
Yes . . 3

11b. [IF "YES"] What are their ages?

_____ _____ _____ _____

_____ _____ _____ _____

12. Please think now about the people you have met at work or through you (husband's) (wife's) work. How often do you get together socially with people you have met through work--fairly often, once in a while, or almost never?

Fairly often 1
Once in a while . . 3
*Almost never 5
*[SKIP TO Q.15 AND CROSS OUT Q.34A]

13. When you get together socially with people from work, how often are drinks containing alcohol served-- nearly every time, more than half the time, less than half the time, once in a while, or never?

Nearly every time 1
More than half the time . . 3
Less than half the time . . 5
Once in a while 7
*Never 9
*[SKIP TO Q.15 AND CROSS OUT Q.34A]

14. Among the people from work you see socially, how many would you say drink quite a bit--nearly all of them, more than half, less than half, only a few, or none?

Nearly all 1
More than half . . 3
Less than half . . 5
Only a few 7
None 9
[Don't know] . . . 0

15. The next couple of questions are about the people you have met in your neighborhood. How often do you get together with people you have met from your neighborhood--fairly often, once in a while, or almost never?

Fairly often 1
Once in a while . . 3
*Almost never 5
*[SKIP TO Q.18 AND CROSS OUT Q.34B]

16. When you get together socially with people from your neighborhood, how often, are drinks containing alcohol served--nearly every time, more than half the time, less than half the time, once in a while, or never?

Nearly every time 1
More than half the time . . 3
Less than half the time . . 5
Once in a while 7
*Never 9
*[SKIP TO Q.18 AND CROSS OUT Q.34B]

17. Among the people from your neighborhood you see socially, how many
would you say drink quite a bit--
nearly all of them, more than half,
less than half, only a few, or none?

          Nearly all 1

          More than half . . 3

          Less than half . . 5

          Only a few 7

          None 9

          [Don't know] . . . 0

18a. What is your religious preference?

    Catholic 1

    Protestant_____ 3
              (Denomination)

    Jewish 5

    Other_____ 7
              (Specify)

    None 9

18b. [IF "NONE"] What was your parents'
religion?

    Catholic 1

    Protestant_____ 3
              (Denomination)

    Jewish 5

    Other_____ 7
              (Specify)

19. About how often do you attend religious services--once a week or more,
about once or twice a month, a few
times during the year, only rarely,
or never?

    Once a week or more 1

    About once or twice a month . . 3

    A few times during the year . . 5

    *Only rarely 7

    *Never 9

    *[SKIP TO Q.22 AND CROSS OUT Q.34C]

20. How often do you get together
socially with people you have met
through your church--fairly often,
once in a while, or almost never?

        Fairly often 1

        Once in a while . . 3

        *Almost never 5

    *[SKIP TO Q.22 AND CROSS OUT Q.34C]

21. When you see people from your church
socially, how often are drinks containing alcohol served--nearly every
time, more than half the time, less
than half the time, once in a while,
or never?

        Nearly every time 1

        More than half the time . . 3

        Less than half the time . . 5

        Once in a while 7

        Never 9

22. Please think now of the people you
regard as your close friends. Are
any of your close friends:

                        Yes   No

a. People you know from
   work 1   3

b. People you know from
   your neighborhood 1   3

c. People you know from
   school 1   3

d. People you know through
   your family 1   3

e. People you met in
   other ways 1   3

f. [IF MET CLOSE FRIENDS IN SOME
   "OTHER" WAY]
   How did you get to know them?

   _____

   _____

   _____

   _____

23. When you get together socially with your close friends, how often are drinks containing alcohol served--nearly every time, more than half the time, less than half the time, once in a while, or never?

Nearly every time 1

More than half the time . 3

Less than half the time . 5

Once in a while 7

*[SKIP TO Q.25 AND CROSS OUT Q.34D] *Never 9

24. Among your close friends, how many would you say drink quite a bit--nearly all of them, more than half, less than half, only a few, or none?

Nearly all 1

More than half . . 3

Less than half . . 5

Only a few 7

None 9

[Don't know] . . . 0

- -

25. The next few questions ask you about your own use of various types of drinks. Will you please take this booklet [HAND RESPONDENT BOOKLET] and on the first page put a check-mark next to the answer that tells how often you usually have wine. Please be sure your check-mark is on the white page. *

26. Now please turn to the green page and do the same for beer. Be sure your check-mark is on the green page.

27. Now please turn to the pink page and do the same for drinks containing whiskey or liquor, including scotch, bourbon, gin, vodka, rum, etc. Be sure your check-mark is on the pink page.

28. And now turn to the yellow page and please check how often you have any kind of drink containing alcohol, whether it is wine, beer, whiskey or any other drink.

- -

[MAKE SURE THE FREQUENCY OF DRINKING REPORTED ON THE LAST (YELLOW) PAGE IS NOT LESS THAN THE FREQUENCY REPORTED ON ANY ONE OF THE OTHER PAGES. ATTACH BOOKLET TO BACK OF QUESTIONNAIRE WHEN INTERVIEW IS COMPLETED.]

[CHECK ACCORDING TO Q.28, LAST PAGE (YELLOW) OF THE BOOKLET.]

____ NEVER DRINKS OR DRINKS LESS THAN ONCE A YEAR
     [SKIP TO Q.44, PAGE 14.]

____ DRINKS LESS THAN ONCE A MONTH BUT AT LEAST ONCE A YEAR
     [SKIP TO Q.34, PAGE 11.]

____ ALL OTHER CATEGORIES
     [CONTINUE WITH Q.29 ON NEXT PAGE.]

- - - - - - - -

*The booklet has been omitted. It listed, for each beverage, the following: Three or more times a day; two times a day; once a day; Nearly every day; Three or four times a week; Once or twice a week; Two or three times a month; About once a month; Less than once a month but at least once a year; less than once a year; I have never had [beverage].

WINE

[CHECK ACCORDING TO FIRST PAGE OF BOOKLET]

29____[HAS WINE ABOUT <u>ONCE A MONTH OR MORE</u>
OFTEN, ASK THE FOLLOWING.
OTHERWISE, SKIP TO Q.30]

29a.   [GIVE RESPONDENT CARD C]
Think of all the times you have had
<u>wine</u> recently. When you drink wine,
how often do you have as many as
five or six glasses?

*[SKIP TO   *Nearly every time 1
   Q.30]   *More than half the time . 3
              Less than half the time . 5
              Once in a while 7
              Never 9

29b.   When you drink <u>wine</u>, how often do
you have three or four glasses?

*[SKIP TO   *Nearly every time 1
   Q.30]   *More than half the time . 3
              Less than half the time . 5
              Once in a while 7
              Never 9

29c.   When you drink <u>wine</u>, how often do
you have one or two glasses?

              Nearly every time 1
              More than half the time . 3
              Less than half the time . 5
              Once in a while 7
              Never 9

BEER

[CHECK ACCORDING TO GREEN PAGE OF BOOKLET]

30____[HAS BEER ABOUT <u>ONCE A MONTH OR MORE</u>
OFTEN, ASK THE FOLLOWING.
OTHERWISE, SKIP TO Q.31]

30a.   [GIVE RESPONDENT CARD C]
Think of all the times you have had
<u>beer</u> recently. When you drink beer,
how often do you have as many as
five or six glasses or cans?

*[SKIP TO   *Nearly every time 1
   Q.31]   *More than half the time . 3
              Less than half the time . 5
              Once in a while 7
              Never 9

30b.   When you drink <u>beer</u>, how often do
you have three or four glasses or
cans?

*[SKIP TO   *Nearly every time 1
   Q.31]   *More than half the time . 3
              Less than half the time . 5
              Once in a while 7
              Never 9

30c.   When you drink <u>beer</u>, how often do
you have one or two glasses or cans?

              Nearly every time 1
              More than half the time . 3
              Less than half the time . 5
              Once in a while 7
              Never 9

[CHECK ACCORDING TO Q.29 AND Q.30 ON PRECEDING PAGE.]

31____ [HAS <u>BOTH WINE AND BEER</u> ABOUT ONCE A MONTH OR MORE OFTEN, ASK Q.31a - 31j ABOUT BOTH COMBINED.

____ HAS <u>WINE ONLY</u> ABOUT ONCE A MONTH OR MORE, ASK Q.31a - 31j ABOUT <u>WINE ONLY</u>.

____ HAS <u>BEER ONLY</u> ABOUT ONCE A MONTH OR MORE OFTEN, ASK Q.31a - 31j ABOUT <u>BEER ONLY</u>.

____ HAS <u>NEITHER WINE NOR BEER</u> ONCE A MONTH OR MORE OFTEN, SKIP TO Q.32.]

31a. When you have wine or beer, where do you have them most often--at your home, at friends' homes, or at restaurants and bars?

Your home 1

Friends' homes . . 3

Restaurants/Bars . 5

31b. How often do you have wine or beer in your home--fairly often, once in a while, or almost never?

Fairly often . . . 1

Once in a while . . 3

Almost never . . . 5

31c. How often (do you have wine or beer) at friends' homes--fairly often, once in a while, or almost never?

Fairly often . . . 1

Once in a while . . 3

Almost never . . . 5

31d. How often (do you have wine or beer) at <u>restaurants and bars</u>--fairly often, once in a while, or almost never?

Fairly often . . . 1

Once in a while . . 3

Almost never . . . 5

31e. When you have wine or beer, with whom do you have them most often--with friends, with members of your family, or is it mostly when you are doing something by yourself?

With friends . . . 1

With family members . 3

By yourself 5

31f. How often do you have wine or beer with <u>friends</u>--fairly often, once in a while, or almost never?

Fairly often 1

Once in a while . . 3

Almost never 5

31g. How often (do you have wine or beer) with <u>family members</u>--fairly often, once in a while, or almost never?

Fairly often 1

Once in a while . . 3

Almost never 5

31h. How often (do you have wine or beer) <u>by yourself</u>--fairly often, once in a while, or almost never?

Fairly often 1

Once in a while . . 3

Almost never 5

31i. How often do you have wine or beer on <u>weekends</u>--that is, Friday night through Sunday night--fairly often, once in a while, or almost never?

Fairly often 1

Once in a while . . 3

Almost never 5

31j. How often (do you have wine or beer) on <u>weekdays</u>--fairly often, once in a while, or almost never?

Fairly often 1

Once in a while . . 3

Almost never 5

[CHECK ACCORDING TO PINK PAGE OF BOOKLET]

32____[HAS WHISKEY OR LIQUOR ABOUT ONCE A MONTH OR MORE OFTEN, ASK THE FOLLOWING. OTHERWISE, SKIP TO Q.34]

32a. [GIVE RESPONDENT CARD C]
Think of all the times you have had drinks containing whiskey or liquor recently. When you have them, how often do you have. as many as five or six drinks?

*[SKIP TO *Nearly every time 1
Q.33a] *More than half the time . 3
Less than half the time . 5
Once in a while 7
Never 9

32b. When you have drinks containing whiskey or liquor, how often do you have three or four drinks?

*[SKIP TO *Nearly every time 1
Q.33a] *More than half the time . 3
Less than half the time . 5
Once in a while 7
Never 9

32c. When you have drinks containing whiskey or liquor, how often do you have one or two drinks?

Nearly every time 1
More than half the time . 3
Less than half the time . 5
Once in a while 7
Never 9

33a. When you have drinks containing whiskey or liquor, where do you have them most often--at your home, at friends' homes, or at restaurants and bars?

Your home 1
Friends' homes 3
Restaurants/Bars . . . 5

33b. How often do you have drinks containing whiskey or liquor in your home--fairly often, once in a while, or almost never?

Fairly often 1
Once in a while . . 3
Almost never 5

33c. How often (do you have drinks containing whiskey or liquor) at friends' homes--fairly often, once in a while, or almost never?

Fairly often 1
Once in a while . . 3
Almost never 5

33d. How often (do you have drinks containing whiskey or liquor) at restaurants and bars--fairly often, once in a while, or almost never?

Fairly often 1
Once in a while . . 3
Almost never 5

33e. When you have drinks containing whiskey or liquor, with whom do you have them most often--with friends, with members of your family, or is it mostly when you are doing something by yourself?

With friends 1
With family members . 3
By yourself 5

33f. How often do you have drinks containing whiskey or liquor with friends--fairly often, once in a while, or almost never?

Fairly often 1
Once in a while . . 3
Almost never 5

33g. How often (do you have drinks containing whiskey or liquor) with family members--fairly often, once in a while, or almost never?

Fairly often 1
Once in a while . . 3
Almost never 5

33h. How often (do you have drinks containing whiskey or liquor) by yourself--
      fairly often, once in a while, or almost never?

                                           Fairly often . . . 1

                                           Once in a while . 3

                                           Almost never . . . 5

33i. How often do you have drinks containing whiskey or liquor on weekends--
      that is, Friday night through Sunday night--fairly often, once in a while,
      or almost never?

                                           Fairly often . . . 1

                                           Once in a while . 3

                                           Almost never . . . 5

33j. How often (do you have drinks containing whiskey or liquor) on weekdays--
      fairly often, once in a while, or almost never?

                                           Fairly often . . . 1

                                           Once in a while . 3

                                           Almost never . . . 5

- -

34.   Do you find that you generally drink more than usual or less than usual
      when you are with the following kinds of people?

		More than usual	Less than usual	[Same]	
A.	With people from work	1	3	5	34A
B.	With people from your neighborhood	1	3	5	34B
C.	With people from your church	1	3	5	34C
D.	With your close friends	1	3	5	34D
E.	With members of your immediate family	1	3	5	34E

35.   If you had to give up drinking altogether, how much do you think you would
      miss it--a lot, some, a little, or not at all?

                                           A lot 1

                                           Some 3

                                           A little . . . 5

                                           Not at all . . 7

                                           [Don't know] . 9

36.   About how old were you when you first started drinking, disregarding
      small tastes of alcoholic beverages?

                                           Age_____

37. People drink wine, beer, whiskey or liquor for different reasons. Here are some statements people have made about why they drink. How important would you say that each of the following is to you as a reason for drinking--very important, fairly important, or not at all important?
[USE CARD D]

	Very Important	Fairly Important	Not at all Important
a. I drink because it helps me to relax 1		3	5
b. I drink to be sociable 1		3	5
c. I like the taste 1		3	5
d. I drink because the people I know drink . . .1		3	5
e. I drink when I want to forget everything . .1		3	5
f. I drink to celebrate special occasions . . .1		3	5
g. A drink helps me to forget my worries 1		3	5
h. A small drink improves my appetite for food .1		3	5
i. I accept a drink because it is the polite thing to do in certain situations 1		3	5
j. A drink helps cheer me up when I'm in a bad mood 1		3	5
k. I drink because I need it when tense and nervous 1		3	5

38. Some people worry about their drinking even though they may not be really heavy drinkers. How much do you worry about your drinking--a lot, some, a little, or not at all?

A lot 1
Some 3
A little . . . 5
Not at all . . 7

39. During the past year, did any of the following people try to get you to drink either more or less than you wanted to? Did your friends try to get you to drink either more or less?
[ASK FOR EACH]

	More	Less	Both more and less	Did not try	Not applicable
a. Your friends 1		3	5	7	9
b. People in your neighborhood . . 1		3	5	7	9
c. Your (wife) (husband) 1		3	5	7	9
d. Your boss 1		3	5	7	9
e. Other people where you work . . 1		3	5	7	9

40. During the past year, what kinds of effects--if any--resulted from your
drinking? [ASK FOR EACH TYPE OF EFFECT] About how many times during the
past year did this happen?

Type of effect   No. times in year

_____   _____

_____   _____

_____   _____

_____   _____

41. Was there ever a time when you drank <u>more</u> than you do now?
                                    *[SKIP TO Q.42] *No 1

                                                       Yes . . . 3

[IF "YES", ASK a, b, AND c]
41a. How old were you at that time?   _____
                                              (Approximate age)

41b. What are the reasons you are drinking less now?

_____

_____

41c. At the time you were drinking <u>more</u> than you do now, did you consider yourself a fairly light drinker, a fairly heavy drinker, or a heavy drinker?

                                              Fairly light . . 1

                                              Fairly heavy . . 3

                                              Heavy 5

42. Since the time you were grown up, was there ever a time when you drank
<u>less</u> than you do now?
                                    *[SKIP TO Q.43] *No 1

                                                       Yes . . . 3

[IF "YES", ASK a AND b]
42a. How old were you at that time?   _____
                                              (Approximate age)

42b. What are the reasons you are drinking more now?

_____

_____

43. At the present time, do you consider yourself to be a very light drinker, a
fairly light drinker, a fairly heavy drinker, or a heavy drinker?

                                              Very light . . . 1

                                              Fairly light . . 3

                                              Fairly heavy . . 5

                                              Heavy 7

_ _ _ _ _ _ _ _ _ _ _ _ _ _ _ _ _ _ [SKIP TO Q.45a] _ _ _ _ _ _ _ _ _ _ _ _ _ _ _ _ _

44. ____ [ASK ONLY IF DRANK "NEVER" OR "LESS THAN ONCE A YEAR" ON YELLOW SHEET]

44a. What are the main reasons that you don't drink?

_____

_____

_____

_____

_____

_____

_____

_____

44b. Was there ever a time when you drank wine, beer, whiskey or liquor at least a couple of times a year?

        *[SKIP TO Q.45a] *No . . 1

                     Yes . . 3

[IF "YES", ASK c AND d]
44c. At what age did you stop drinking?

       _____

        (Approximate age)

44d. Was there ever a time when you considered yourself a fairly heavy drinker?

                   No . . 1

                 Yes . . 3

[ASK OF EVERYONE]

45a. All things considered, do you think that drinking alcoholic beverages does people more good than harm, or does it do more harm than good?

        More good than harm . . 1

        More harm than good . . 3

        [Other] 5

[IF "OTHER" IN Q.45a]
45b. What do you have in mind?

_____

_____

_____

46. What are some of the good things that can be said about drinking?

_____

_____

_____

_____

_____

47. What are some of the bad things that can be said about drinking?

_____

_____

_____

_____

48. What changes, if any, have you noticed in people's drinking in the last five years? Any other changes?

_____

_____

_____

49. Do you think people are drinking more or less now than they were five years ago?

More 1

Less 3

[About same] . . 5

[No opinion] . . 7

50. How serious a problem do you think alcoholism is compared to other public health problems in this country--not at all serious, slightly serious, fairly serious, or very serious?

Not at all serious . 1

Slightly serious . . 3

Fairly serious . . . 5

Very serious 7

[No opinion] 9

51a. Have you ever had a close relative with a serious drinking problem?

No . . . 1

Yes . . . 3

51b. [IF "YES"] How was this person related to you? _____

_____

52. Have you ever had a close friend with a serious drinking problem?

No . . . 1

Yes . . . 3

53a. [IF "YES" TO 51a OR 52] Did knowing (this person) (these persons) affect the amount of your drinking in any way?

No . . . 1

Yes . . . 3

53b. [IF "YES"] How?

_____

_____

_____

54. [HAND RESPONDENT "ATTITUDE SURVEY"] Here are some statements on a variety of subjects. Please read each statement and indicate whether you agree or disagree with it. Just give your first impression, by circling either "Agree" or "Disagree".

[MAKE SURE ALL ITEMS ON FRONT AND BACK ARE ANSWERED.

BE SURE SERIAL NUMBER ON "ATTITUDE FORM" MATCHES FRONT PAGE OF THIS QUESTIONNAIRE.

THEN ATTACH TO BACK OF QUESTIONNAIRE.]

55. Were you a cigarette smoker a year ago?

No . . . 1

Yes . . . 3

56. Do you smoke cigarettes at the present time?
*[SKIP TO Q.59a] *No . . . 1

Yes . . . 3

57. How many cigarettes do you smoke on an average day?

Just a few 1

One pack or less 3

Between 1 & 2 packs . . 5

Two or more packs . . . 7

58. Compared with a year ago, do you now smoke more, less, or about the same as you did then?

More now 1

Less now 3

About the same . . 5

59a. What is your approximate height?

_____ft. _____in.

59b. What is your approximate weight?

_____lbs.

60. Now I would like to talk with you about something a bit different. What are some of the main things you want or have wanted out of life?

_____

_____

_____

_____

61. In general, how satisfied are you with your progress in reaching these goals--very satisfied, fairly satisfied, or not very satisfied?

Very satisfied 1

Fairly satisfied . . . 3

Not very satisfied . . 5

62. [IF MARRIED, HAND RESPONDENT CARD E] With which of these statements do you agree?

Very happy 1

A little happier than average 3

Just about average 5

Less happy than average . . 7

Not very happy 9

63a. Please think back to the time before you were 16 years old. During most of this time, did you live with both your mother and father?

Yes . . . 1

No 3

63b. [IF "NO"] Please tell me with whom you did live. _____

_____

64. What was the occupation of the principal wage earner in your home before you were 16? _____

_____

65. Taking everything into consideration, would you say that you had a happy or unhappy childhood?

Mostly happy 1

Mostly unhappy 3

[About half and half] . . 5

66. [HAND RESPONDENT CARD F] What was the size of the place where you lived before you were 16?

In the country on a farm . . . 1

In the country but not on a farm 2

Town of less than 5,000 . . . 3

City of 5,000 to 25,000 . . . 4

City of 25,000 to 100,000 . . 5

City of 100,000 to 500,000 . . 6

City of more than 500,000 . . 7

67. Did your father (adult male in the household) approve or disapprove of people having drinks containing alcohol?

Approved 1

Disapproved . . 3

[Didn't care] . 5

[Don't know] . . 7

68. Which of the following comes closest to describing how often he had drinks containing alcohol at that time? [HAND RESPONDENT CARD G]

Three or more times a day 1

Two times a day 2

Once a day 3

Nearly every day 4

Three or four times a week . . . 5

Once or twice a week 6

Two or three times a month . . . 7

About once a month 8

Less than once a month but at least once a year 9

Less than once a year 0

Never had drinks with alcohol . . X

[Have no idea] . . . . Y

69. Did your mother (adult female in the household) approve or disapprove of people having drinks containing alcohol?

Approved . . . 1

Disapproved . 3

[Didn't care]. 5

[Don't know] . 7

70. Which most closely describes how often she had drinks containing alcohol at that time? [USE CARD G]

Three or more times a day 1

Two times a day 2

Once a day 3

Nearly every day 4

Three or four times a week . . . 5

Once or twice a week 6

Two or three times a month . . . 7

About once a month 8

Less than once a month but at least once a year 9

Less than once a year 0

Never had drinks with alcohol . . X

[Have no idea] . . . . Y

71. In what country was your father born?

United States . . . 1

Other [SPECIFY] . . 3

_____

72. In what country were you born?

United States . . . 1

Other [SPECIFY] . . 3

_____

73. [IF BOTH FATHER AND RESPONDENT BORN IN U. S.]
Which one nationality did most of your family come from?

_____

74. Were you the oldest, youngest, middle or only child in your family?

Oldest 1

Youngest . . . 3

Middle 5

Only child . . 7

75. [IF MARRIED] Which most closely describes how often your (wife) (husband) has drinks containing alcohol? [USE CARD G]

Three or more times a day 1

Two times a day 2

Once a day 3

Nearly every day 4

Three or four times a week . . . 5

Once or twice a week 6

Two or three times a month . . . 7

About once a month 8

Less than once a month but at least once a year 9

Less than once a year 0

Never had drinks with alcohol . . X

[Have no idea] . . . . Y

76. Who is the main wage earner in your family?

*[SKIP TO   *Respondent 1
Q.79a]   Respondent's spouse . . . 3

Other_____5
[SPECIFY RELATIONSHIP]

77. What are you doing at the present time?

Homemaker 1

Student 3

Retired 5

Employed 7

Other_____9
[SPECIFY]

78a. Do you have a full- or part-time
job for which you receive pay?

Yes, full-time job . . 1

Yes, part-time job . . 3

*[SKIP TO   *No paid job 5
Q.79a]

78b. [IF YES, EITHER FULL-TIME OR
PART-TIME]
What kind of work do you do?

_____

79a. [USE "ARE YOU..." IF RESPONDENT IS
MAIN EARNER]
Is (main earner) working full-time
or part-time?

*[SKIP TO *Yes, full-time . . 1
Q.79c]
Yes, part-time . . 3

No paid job . . . 5

79b. [IF MAIN EARNER IS NOT WORKING
FULL-TIME]
Is (main earner) working less than
full-time because retired, unemployed looking for work, prevented
by accident or illness, or for some
other reason?

Retired 1

Unemployed, looking for work. 3

Prevented by accident
or illness 5

Other_____ 7
[SPECIFY]

79c. In what type of industry does/did
(main earner) work?

_____

_____

79d. What is/was (main earner's) occupation?

_____

_____

_____

_____

[IF PARTNER OR OWNER OF A BUSINESS]
79e. Which one of these groups [HAND
RESPONDENT CARD H] covers the net
worth or value of the business?

Under $3,000 1

$3,000 - $5,999 3

$6,000 - $34,999 5

$35,000 - $99,999 . . . 7

$100,000 - $499,999 . . 9

More than $500,000 . . . 0

[IF RESPONDENT IS A MARRIED, MALE,
MAIN EARNER]
80. Does your wife work? Full-time
or part-time?

Yes, full-time . . 1

Yes, part-time . . 3

No 5

81a. If you (your husband) had it to do
over again, would you prefer to
(have your husband) go into a different occupation?

No . . . 1

Yes . . 3

81b. [IF "YES"] What occupation?

_____

_____

_____

_____

82. How much do you worry that you (or
your husband) might not be getting
ahead on the job or in business as
well as you might wish--does this
worry you a lot, some, a little, or
not at all?
A lot 1

Some 3

A little . . . 5

Not at all . . 7

83. What was the highest grade or class that your <u>father</u> completed in school?
That your <u>mother</u> completed? That <u>you</u> completed? That your (<u>wife</u>) (<u>husband</u>)
completed?

	Father	Mother	Self	Spouse
No formal schooling	0	0	0	0
Some grammar school (less than 8th grade) . . .	1	1	1	1
Completed grammar school . . .	2	2	2	2
Some high school	3	3	3	3
Completed high school	4	4	4	4
Some college	5	5	5	5
Completed college	6	6	6	6
Graduate study	7	7	7	7

84. How much do you think more education would help in reaching your goals in
life? Would more education help a lot, some, a little, or not at all?

A lot 1

Some 3

A little . . . 5

Not at all . . 7

[No opinion] . 9

85. How often do you get angry--often, sometimes, rarely, or never?

Often 1

Sometimes . . 3

Rarely . . . 5

*[SKIP TO Q.87] *Never 7

86. When you get angry, which of the following best describes what you <u>usually</u>
do: keep it to yourself, or show it but not lose your temper, or lose your
temper?

Keep it to self 1

Show it but not lose temper . . . 3

Lose temper 5

87a. I'd like to ask you now about your neighborhood. If you had the chance, do
you think you would like to move to a different neighborhood?

Yes . . 1

No . . 3

87b. [IF "YES"] In what ways would a neighborhood in which you would like to
live be different from your present neighborhood?

_____

_____

88. [HAND INCOME CARD I TO THE RESPONDENT] Into which group did your family income fall last year?

	Income
Under $2,000	1
Between $2,000 and $3,999 . .	2
Between $4,000 and $5,999 . .	3
Between $6,000 and $7,999 . .	4
Between $8,000 and $9,999 . .	5
Between $10,000 and $14,999 .	6
$15,000 and over	7

May I have your name, please? _____

And your phone number, please? _____

89. [CHECK FROM OBSERVATION]

    W 1
    N 3
    Other [SPECIFY] . 5
    _____

On what line of Table "A" on page 1 is this respondent listed? _____
                                                                  (line)

[RECORD CORRECT TIME IMMEDIATELY AFTER RECORDING ANSWER TO LAST QUESTION.]
                                    _____ a.m. _____ p.m.

Date of Interview _____

INTERVIEWER'S COMMENTS

_____
_____
_____
_____
_____   _____
_____
_____

RESPONDENT CARDS

CARD A

Often

Sometimes

Rarely

Never

CARD B

Very helpful

Fairly helpful

Not at all helpful

Never tried it

CARD C

Nearly every time

More than half the time

Less than half the time

Once in a while

Never

CARD D

Very important

Fairly important

Not at all important

CARD E

Taking all things together, which
one of the statements on this card
best describes your marriage?

1. Very happy

3. A little happier than average

5. Just about average

7. Less happy than average

9. Not very happy

CARD F

In the country on a farm

In the country but not on a farm

Town of less than 5,000

City of 5,000 to 25,000

City of 25,000 to 100,000

City of 100,000 to 500,000

City of more than 5000,000

CARD G

Three or more times a day

Two times a day

Once a day

Nearly every day

Three or four times a week

Once or twice a week

Two or three times a month

About once a month

Less than once a month but at
least once a year

Less than once a year

Never had drinks with alcohol

CARD H

1. Under $3,000
3. $3,000 - $5,999
5. $6,000 - $34,999
7. $35,000 - $99,999
9. $100,000 - $499,999
0. More than $500,000

CARD I

1. Under $2,000
2. Between $2,000 and $3,999
3. Between $4,000 and $5,999
4. Between $6,000 and $7,999
5. Between $8,000 and $9,999
6. Between $10,000 and $14,999
7. $15,000 and over

Question 54

(Area)   (HH)

ATTITUDE SURVEY

Here are some statements on a variety of subjects.
Please circle "Agree" or "Disagree" for each item.

1. I am happiest when I have a place for everything
    and everything in its place . . . . Agree   Disagree

2. When someone in my family has a misfortune, it
    upsets me as much as it does them . . . . Agree   Disagree

3. The Bible is the word of God and all of it is
    absolutely true . . . . Agree   Disagree

4. I react quickly to other people's remarks . . . . Agree   Disagree

5. This world has more pain than pleasure . . . . Agree   Disagree

6. In whatever one does, the "tried and true" ways
    are always best . . . . Agree   Disagree

7. When I go to a movie or watch TV, I live right
    along with the characters . . . . Agree   Disagree

8. There is nothing like good hard work to help
    you get ahead in life . . . . Agree   Disagree

9. I have the feeling that I am different . . . . Agree   Disagree

10. A person is always wiser to save his money for
    future needs . . . . Agree   Disagree

11. Sometimes life just isn't worth living . . . . Agree   Disagree

12. When I see an underdog win, I feel almost as
    good as if I had won . . . . Agree   Disagree

13. A person who seldom changes his mind can usually
    be depended upon to have good judgment . . . . Agree   Disagree

14. Almost everything that happens can be understood
    by studying the Bible . . . . Agree   Disagree

15. I always finish things I start, even if they
    aren't very important . . . . Agree   Disagree

16. When I hear of a man who stole because his
    family was hungry, I can easily understand how
    he felt . . . . Agree   Disagree

Please circle "Agree" or "Disagree"
for each item.

17. I often act on the spur of the moment without
stopping to think . . . . Agree   Disagree

18. Obedience to the word of God is one of the most
important virtues that children should learn . . . . . . Agree   Disagree

19. Sometimes I feel so lonesome . . . . Agree   Disagree

20. The only way to get ahead in this world is to
get a good education . . . . Agree   Disagree

21. I often change my mind rather quickly . . . . Agree   Disagree

22. There are many things in the universe that
only religion, and not science, can explain . . . . . . Agree   Disagree

23. I have more than my share of problems . . . . Agree   Disagree

24. I often spend more money than I think I should . . . . . Agree   Disagree

25. In getting ahead in the world, it is important
to mingle with the very best class of people . . . . . . Agree   Disagree

Bibliography

1. AMERICAN INSTITUTE OF PUBLIC OPINION. Gallup political index; political, social and economic trends. [Reports, 1947–1966.] Princeton, N. J.
2. BACON, S. D. Sociology and the problems of alcohol; foundations for a sociological study of drinking behavior. Quart. J. Stud. Alc. 4: 402–455, 1943.
3. BACON, S. D. Alcohol and complex society. In: PITTMAN, D. J. and SNYDER, C. R., eds. Society, culture, and drinking patterns; Ch. 5. New York; Wiley; 1962.
4. BAILEY, M. B., HABERMAN, P. W. and ALKSNE, H. The epidemiology of alcoholism in an urban residential area. Quart. J. Stud. Alc. 26: 19–40, 1965.
5. BALES, R. F. Attitudes toward drinking in the Irish culture. In: PITTMAN, D. J. and SNYDER, C. R., eds. Society, culture, and drinking patterns; Ch. 10. New York; Wiley; 1962.
6. BROWN, J. S. Gradients of approach and avoidance responses and their relation to level of motivation. J. comp. physiol. Psychol. 41: 450–465, 1948.
7. BRUNER, J. S., GOODNOW, J. J. and AUSTIN, G. A. A study of thinking. New York; Wiley; 1956.
8. CAHALAN, D., CISIN, I. H., KIRSCH, A. D. and NEWCOMB, C. H. Behavior and attitudes related to drinking in a medium-sized urban community in New England. (Social Research Project, Rep. No. 2.) Washington, D. C.; George Washington University; 1965.
9. CAHALAN, D., CISIN, I. H. and CROSSLEY, H. American drinking practices: a national survey of behavior and attitudes related to alcoholic beverages. (Social Research Group, Rep. No. 3.) Washington, D. C.; George Washington University; 1967.
10. CAHALAN, D. Correlates of change in drinking behavior in an urban community sample over a three-year period. (Social Research Group, Rep. No. 4.) Washington, D. C.; George Washington University; 1968.
11. CAHALAN, D. and CISIN, I. H. American drinking practices; summary of findings from a national probability sample. *II*. Measurement of massed versus spaced drinking. Quart. J. Stud. Alc. 29: 642–656, 1968.
12. CHAFETZ, M. E. Liquor: the servant of man. Boston; Little, Brown; 1965.
13. CISIN, I. H. Community studies of drinking behavior. Ann. N.Y. Acad. Sci. 107: 607–612, 1963.
14. CLARK, W. Operational definitions of drinking problems and associated prevalence rates. Quart. J. Stud. Alc. 27: 648–688, 1966.
15. CLOWARD, R. A. and OHLIN, L. E. Delinquency and opportunity: a theory of delinquent gangs. New York; Free Press; 1960.
16. CONGER, J. J. Reinforcement theory and the dynamics of alcoholism. Quart. J. Stud. Alc. 17: 296–305, 1956.
17. DOLLARD, J. Drinking mores of the social classes. In: Alcohol, science and society; pp. 95–101. New Haven; Journal of Studies on Alcohol; 1945.
18. FERSTER, C. B., NURNBERGER, J. I. and LEVITT, E. B. The control of eating. J. Mathetics 1: 87–109, 1962.
19. FIELD, P. B. A new cross-cultural study of drunkenness. In: PITTMAN, D. J. and SNYDER, C. R., eds. Society, culture, and drinking patterns; Ch. 4. New York; Wiley; 1962.

20. FINK, R. Factors related to alcoholic beverage choice. (California Drinking Practices Study, Rep. No. 4.) Berkeley; Division of Alcoholic Rehabilitation, California State Department of Public Health; [undated].

21. FINK, R. Parental drinking and its impact on adult drinkers. (California Drinking Practices Study, Rep. No. 5.) Berkeley; Division of Alcoholic Rehabilitation, California State Department of Public Health; 1962.

22. FINK, R. Modifications of alcoholic beverage choice in social and nonsocial situations. Quart. J. Stud. Alc. 26: 80–94, 1965.

23. FROMM, E. The sane society. New York; Rinehart; 1955.

24. GLAD, D. D. Attitudes and experiences of American-Jewish and American-Irish male youth as related to differences in adult rates of inebriety. Quart. J. Stud. Alc. 8: 406–472, 1947.

25. GURIN, G., VEROFF, J. and FELD, S. Americans view their mental health; a nationwide interview survey. New York; Basic Books; 1960.

26. GUSFIELD, J. R. Status conflicts and the changing ideologies of the American Temperance Movement. In: PITTMAN, D. J. and SNYDER, C. R., eds. Society, culture, and drinking patterns; Ch. 6. New York; Wiley; 1962.

27. HEBB, D. O. The organization of behavior; a neurophysiological theory. New York; Wiley; 1949.

28. HOLLINGSHEAD, A. B. Two factor index of social position. New Haven; 1957.

29. HOLLINGSHEAD, A. B. and REDLICH, F. C. Social class and mental illness; a community study. New York; Wiley; 1958.

30. HORTON, D. The functions of alcohol in primitive societies; a cross-cultural study. Quart. J. Stud. Alc. 4: 199–320, 1943.

31. JELLINEK, E. M. "Death from alcoholism" in the United States in 1940; a statistical analysis. Quart. J. Stud. Alc. 3: 465–494, 1942.

32. JELLINEK, E. M. Recent trends in alcoholism and in alcohol consumption. Quart. J. Stud. Alc. 8: 1–42, 1947.

33. JELLINEK, E. M. The disease concept of alcoholism. Highland Park, N. J.; Hillhouse Press; 1960.

34. JESSOR, R., GRAVES, T. D., HANSON, R. C. and JESSOR, S. L. Society, personality, and deviant behavior: a study of a tri-ethnic community. New York; Holt, Rinehart & Winston; 1968.

35. KELLER, M. The definition of alcoholism and the estimation of its prevalence. In: PITTMAN, D. J. and SNYDER, C. R., eds. Society, culture, and drinking patterns; Ch. 17. New York; Wiley; 1962.

36. KINSEY, A. C., POMEROY, W. B. and MARTIN, C. E. Sexual behavior in the human male. Philadelphia; Saunders; 1948.

37. KIRSCH, A. D., NEWCOMB, C. H. and CISIN, I. H. An experimental study of sensitivity of survey techniques in measuring drinking practices. (Social Research Project, Rep. No. 1.) Washington, D. C.; George Washington University; 1965.

38. KNUPFER, G. Characteristics of abstainers; a comparison of drinkers and nondrinkers in a large California city. (California Drinking Practices Study, Rep. No. 3, rev.) Berkeley: Division of Alcoholic Rehabilitation, California State Department of Public Health; 1961.

39. KNUPFER, G., FINK, R., CLARK, W. B. and GOFFMAN, A. S. Factors related to amount of drinking in an urban community. (California Drinking Practices Study, Rep. No. 6.) Berkeley; Division of Alcoholic Rehabilitation, California State Department of Public Health; 1963.

40. KNUPFER, G. The use of longitudinal studies in alcoholism research. [Unpub-

lished paper.] Berkeley; Drinking Practices Study, Department of Public Health, State of California; 1963.

41. KNUPFER, G. and ROOM, R. Age, sex and social class as factors in amount of drinking in a metropolitan community. Social Probl. **12**: 224–240, 1964.

42. KNUPFER, G. Some methodological problems in the epidemiology of alcoholic beverage usage: definition of amount of intake. Amer. J. publ. Hlth **2**: 237–242, 1966.

43. KNUPFER, G. Epidemiologic studies and control programs in alcoholism. V. The epidemiology of problem drinking. Amer. J. publ. Hlth **57**: 973–986, 1967.

44. LAZARUS, R. S. Psychological stress and the coping process. New York; McGraw-Hill; 1966.

45. LEVINE, S. and SCOTCH, N. A. Stress as a variable in epidemiological research. Milbank mem. Fd Quart. Bull. **45**: 163–174, 1967.

46. LOLLI, G., SERIANNI, E., GOLDER, G. M. and LUZZATO-FEGIZ, P. Alcohol in Italian culture; food and wine in relation to sobriety among Italians and Italian Americans. (Monographs of the Rutgers Center of Alcohol Studies, No. 3.) New Brunswick, N. J.; Rutgers Center of Alcohol Studies; 1958.

47. MADDOX, G. L. and McCALL, B. C. Drinking among teen-agers: a sociological interpretation of alcohol use by high-school students. (Monographs of the Rutgers Center of Alcohol Studies, No. 4.) New Brunswick, N. J.; Rutgers Center of Alcohol Studies; 1964.

48. MAXWELL, M. A. Drinking behavior in the state of Washington. Quart. J. Stud. Alc. **13**: 219–239, 1952.

49. MERTON, R. K. Social theory and social structure. Rev. ed. New York; Macmillan; 1957.

50. MOYNIHAN, D. P. The Negro family: the case for national action. In: RAINWATER, L. and YANCEY, W. L. The Moynihan report and the politics of controversy; Ch. 4. Cambridge, Mass.; Massachusetts Institute of Technology Press; 1967.

51. MULFORD, H. A. and MILLER, D. E. Drinking in Iowa. *I.* Sociocultural distribution of drinkers; with a methodological model for sampling evaluation and interpretation of findings. Quart. J. Stud. Alc. **20**: 704–726, 1959.

52. MULFORD, H. A. and MILLER, D. E. Drinking in Iowa. *II.* The extent of drinking and selected sociocultural categories. Quart. J. Stud. Alc. **21**: 26–39, 1960.

53. MULFORD, H. A. and MILLER, D. E. Drinking in Iowa. *III.* A scale of definitions of alcohol related to drinking behavior. Quart. J. Stud. Alc. **21**: 267–278, 1960.

54. MULFORD, H. A. and MILLER, D. E. Drinking in Iowa. *IV.* Preoccupation with alcohol and definitions of alcohol, heavy drinking and trouble due to drinking. Quart. J. Stud. Alc. **21**: 279–291, 1960.

55. MULFORD, H. A. and MILLER, D. E. The prevalence and extent of drinking in Iowa, 1961; a replication and an evaluation of methods. Quart. J. Stud. Alc. **24**: 39–53, 1963.

56. MULFORD, H. A. Drinking and deviant drinking, U. S. A., 1963. Quart. J. Stud. Alc. **25**: 634–650, 1964.

57. NATIONAL CENTER FOR THE PREVENTION AND CONTROL OF ALCOHOLISM. Alcohol and alcoholism. Washington, D. C.; U.S. Govt Print. Off.; 1967.

58. PARK, P. Problem drinking and role deviation: a study in incipient alcoholism. In: PITTMAN, D. J. and SNYDER, C. R., eds. Society, culture, and drinking patterns; Ch. 25. New York; Wiley; 1962.

59. PITTMAN, D. J. and SNYDER, C. R. Religion and ethnicity. In: PITTMAN, D. J.

and SNYDER, C. R., eds. Society, culture, and drinking patterns; pp. 154–156. New York; Wiley; 1962.

60. RIEGEL, K. F., RIEGEL, R. M. and MEYER, G. A study of the dropout rates in longitudinal research on aging and the prediction of death. J. personality social Psychol. 5: 342–348, 1967.

61. RILEY, J. W., JR. and MARDEN, C. F. The social pattern of alcoholic drinking. Quart. J. Stud. Alc. 8: 265–273, 1947.

62. RILEY, J. W., JR., MARDEN, C. F. and LIFSHITZ, M. The motivational pattern of drinking. Quart. J. Stud. Alc. 9: 353–362, 1948.

63. ROSENBERG, M. Test factor standardization as a method of interpretation. Social Forces 41: 53–61, 1962.

64. ROTTER, J. B. Social learning and clinical psychology. New York; Prentice-Hall; 1954.

65. SADOUN, R., LOLLI, G. and SILVERMAN, M. Drinking in French culture. (Monographs of the Rutgers Center of Alcohol Studies, No. 5.) New Brunswick, N. J.; Rutgers Center of Alcohol Studies; 1965.

66. SNYDER, C. R. Alcohol and the Jews; a cultural study of drinking and sobriety. (Monographs of the Rutgers Center of Alcohol Studies, No. 1.) New Brunswick, N. J.; Rutgers Center of Alcohol Studies; 1958.

67. SNYDER, C. R. Culture and Jewish sobriety: the ingroup–outgroup factor. In: PITTMAN, D. J. and SNYDER, C. R., eds. Society, culture, and drinking patterns; Ch. 11. New York; Wiley; 1962.

68. STRAUS, R. and BACON, S. D. Drinking in college. New Haven; Yale University Press; 1953.

69. STRONG, E. K., JR. Vocational interests 18 years after college. Minneapolis; University of Minnesota Press; 1955.

70. TRUSSELL, R. E. and ELINSON, J. Chronic illness in a rural area: the Hunterdon study. (Chronic illness in the United States, Vol. 3.) Cambridge, Mass.; Harvard University Press; 1959.

71. WHYTE, W. F. A slum sex code. Amer. J. Sociol. 49: 24–31, 1943.

72. WILLIAMS, J. J. Waxing and waning drinkers. Presented at annual meeting of the Society for the Study of Social Problems, San Francisco, 27 August 1967.

Index of Names

Index of Subjects

NOTE.—The three main variables compared throughout this monograph are *age, sex* and *socioeconomic status* (index of social position), and the several "drinking" categories: *abstainers, infrequent drinkers, light drinkers, moderate drinkers, heavy drinkers, escape drinkers* and *heavy-escape drinkers.* Hence, to avoid excess duplication, these terms, each of which could have dozens of subentries, are not featured as main entries in this Index except over a few special items. Thus, the subentry *profile* appears under, e.g., *Heavy drinkers;* but the subentry *religion* is not featured under *Heavy drinkers*—it is treated only as a main entry, *Religion, denominations.* In all cases, the "drinking" categories (including abstainers) are to be understood after the main entries. Thus, the page citations at such main entries as *Impulsivity, Marital status, Nativity, Opinions, Residence,* etc., are to be understood as referring to each or some of the several "drinking" categories.

See also *Index of Tables,* pp. x–xiii, and *List of Detail Tables* in Appendix III, pp. 229–230.